CONTENT
AND
CRAFT

CONTENT
AND
CRAFT

written expression
in the
elementary school

DOROTHY GRANT HENNINGS
Professor of Education, Newark State College

BARBARA M. GRANT
Professor of Education, The William Paterson College of New Jersey

Prentice-Hall, Inc., Englewood Cliffs, New Jersey

Library of Congress Cataloging in Publication Data

HENNINGS, DOROTHY GRANT.
  Content and craft.

  Bibliography: p.
  1. Language arts (Elementary) I. Grant, Barbara M.,
  joint author. II. Title.
LB1576.H335   372.6'044   72-3716
ISBN 0-13-171447-3
ISBN 0-13-171439-2 (pbk.)

© 1973 by Prentice-Hall, Inc.
Englewood Cliffs, New Jersey

10 9 8 7 6 5 4 3 2 1

PRINTED IN THE UNITED STATES OF AMERICA

Prentice-Hall International, Inc. *London*
Prentice-Hall of Australia, Pty. Ltd., *Sydney*
Prentice-Hall of Canada, Ltd., *Toronto*
Prentice-Hall of India Private Limited, *New Delhi*
Prentice-Hall of Japan, Inc., *Tokyo*

to George

contents

II CRAFT

III CONTENT AND CRAFT

foreword

A young American educator whose first eleven years of schooling took place in Scotland declares that his early school experience matched the integrated day in a free and open classroom characteristic of the British infant and primary schools now receiving such admiring attention on this side of the Atlantic. According to his testimony, an indispensable feature of his type of education was that all the children wrote "like crazy" from very early on. Every night they filled notebooks with reports of what they had done and what they had observed and learned from their encounters.

Anyone who has done much writing has had the experience of writing himself into a better understanding and appreciation of something. Important as pictorial, graphic, and auditory means of communication are in the modern world, lucid writing continues to give pleasure and to inform both the writer and the reader in ways no other medium can.

Authors Hennings and Grant were convinced that one of the significant contributions an elementary school teacher can make to his children is encouraging and guiding them to produce writing in which interesting and useful ideas are well-organized and expressed in words chosen with precision. Therefore, they set out to help teachers with this critical responsibility. The keynote is sounded in the chapter titles—"*Let children*" do.

This readable book explains the authors' recommendations very well. Through charming, thoroughly up-to-date, and realistic illustrations the writers also demonstrate ways of helping children select ideas to write about structure the ideas into coherent wholes, and revise their own work until it shines as every author likes his work to shine. Since the examples come from actual classrooms, they are believable and suggestive; since they range all the way from first through eighth grade, they offer help to middle and junior high school teachers, as well as to those in a typical sixth-grade elementary school.

This volume itself is an example of well-organized, interesting, and clear writing. Consuming it will be a pleasurable and rewarding experience.

ALICE MIEL
PROFESSOR EMERITUS OF EDUCATION
TEACHERS COLLEGE, COLUMBIA UNIVERSITY

preface

Every decade appears to have a series of key words employed so frequently in discussion and writing that they begin to typify the overall climate of the period. *Confrontation, demand, relevancy,* and *generation gap* give every indication of becoming key words of the seventies as youth confronts the over-thirty generation with demands for relevancy in almost every phase of living. Youth proposes that traditional patterns of existence are no longer relevant today, that values of the past are outmoded in a fast-changing world, and that most formal institutions do not relate to real life. In such a climate, it is only natural that schools are being confronted with similar demands for relevancy in the curriculum.

As youth cries out to be heard, one of the most potentially relevant areas of study in a school's program is written communication. The written word has power to change thinking, to arouse others to action, and to clarify an issue; it makes possible the exchange and the in-depth study of ideas. A lasting form of communication, the written word can affect thinking over extended periods of time. Yet a piece of writing is only relevant when it communicates clearly the intended ideas of the writer. Unless youth has the requisite writing skills, the power of the written word is diminished.

Content and Craft attempts to make writing a relevant undertaking for the youth of today by focusing both on the substance of writing—the ideas to be expressed—and on the process of writing—the medium through which ideas are communicated. In essence, the authors assume that when learning to write the child must learn to build significant idea-content to communicate: a dissatisfaction with discriminatory practices or environmental pollution, a newly found peace of mind in an undisturbed Walden, or a caring about someone special. The authors further assume that the child must learn a craft: expression or the translation of ideas into the words, lines, stanzas, sentences, and paragraphs characteristic of written material. Without this translation a significant idea can be irretrievably lost.

To develop their construct, the authors have chosen an inductive design: in the first chapter, one element basic to a writing program is considered; in successive chapters, the authors add other components, so that the construct being proposed expands with each chapter. Specifically, Part I of *Content and Craft* is an examination of the content phase of writing. In Chapter 1, the authors affirm the central position of ideas in both functional and imaginative writing; classify the idea-content of writing as reflective, conceptual, projective, expressive, and inventive; and describe the thinking processes important in the production of different kinds of content. In Chapter 2, first-hand experience is identified as a source of ideas for written expression, and talk as well as nonverbal activity is suggested as an integral part of any writing program. In Chapter 3 the authors propose that ideas for written expression can also be triggered by activities structured by the teacher and by thoughts encountered in reading and listening; the chapter contains specific suggestions for helping children search for ideas in written and visual materials and for organizing activities that will stimulate thinking. Chapter 4 is devoted to the many ways in which children may record ideas, without extensive reliance on the constructional skills of writing. The structure of Part I can be shown diagrammatically as:

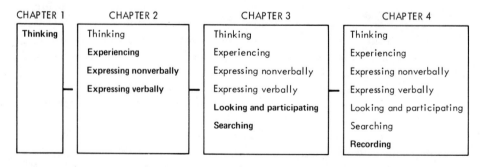

CHAPTER 1	CHAPTER 2	CHAPTER 3	CHAPTER 4
Thinking	Thinking	Thinking	Thinking
	Experiencing	Experiencing	Experiencing
	Expressing nonverbally	Expressing nonverbally	Expressing nonverbally
	Expressing verbally	Expressing verbally	Expressing verbally
		Looking and participating	Looking and participating
		Searching	Searching
			Recording

Part II considers the craft phase of writing. In Chapter 5 the authors concentrate on the organization of written composition; ways of teaching children both the necessary thinking-organizational skills and the specific aspects of paragraph development are identified. The focus of Chapter 6 is choice of words as one aspect of the writing craft; the chapter includes suggestions for helping children work more effectively with words, and it also focuses on the process of constructing sentence patterns, drawing upon linguistic concepts to propose ways of helping children work with these larger units of communication. In both Chapters 5 and 6, children's constructional problems are identified and samples of children's work are included.

Chapter 7 is based on the assumption that effective writing does not always result from the first series of words recorded on a page. Review of what has been previously written and rewriting in terms of one's knowledge of American English usage and structure are very often necessary if ideas are to be given more than perfunctory reading. In Chapter 7, the authors present the notion that revision by the elementary school writer is a process of self-editing as the child becomes his own editor; some of the detail with which a self-editor may be concerned as he analyzes material that he himself has written ·is included in the chapter. The structure of Part II can be shown diagrammatically as:

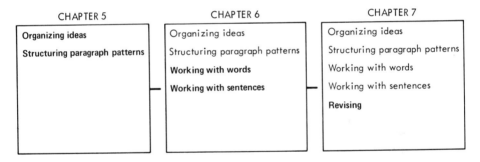

CHAPTER 5	CHAPTER 6	CHAPTER 7
Organizing ideas	Organizing ideas	Organizing ideas
Structuring paragraph patterns	Structuring paragraph patterns	Structuring paragraph patterns
	Working with words	Working with words
	Working with sentences	Working with sentences
		Revising

In Part III the authors merge consideration of content with consideration of craft. Specific aspects of writing poetry are developed in Chapter 8, and specific aspects of writing prose—story, letter, reaction, report—are developed in Chapter 9.

Although Parts I, II, and III are concerned with teaching the content and craft of writing, the other communication processes are considered as each relates to the teaching of written expression. When writing is perceived as one means of communication, then listening, speaking, picturing, dramatizing, nonverbal activity, reading, and understanding the nature of language quite naturally become integral elements within the writing program. The essential element found in *Content and Craft* is that each communication area is not considered as a discrete area of study to be taught solely for its own sake; instead, the relationships between those areas and writing are used in putting together a total writing program. In short, a major premise upon which *Content and Craft* is founded is that reading, speaking, working with linguistic concepts, listening, dramatizing, creating artistically are all important within a total writing program.

That daily encounters with writing should be a part of elementary school experiences of children is another basic premise upon which this book is founded. Too often in classrooms, the authors have seen elementary school children write only to fill in the blanks of a workbook or a dittoed exercise sheet. When children do encounter more extensive written activity, they are generally presented with a discrete lesson—a motivational activity followed by a writing period and then by a correctional-copying time. But this need not be! Written expression can be a continuing outgrowth of most ongoing classroom activity, and an open classroom can be the scene of a multitude of stimuli from which children can choose and to which they can react in oral, in dramatic, in artistic, and in written form.

It is the teacher's job in such an open classroom to provide a variety of first-hand and structured experiences that stimulate children to think and express; to encourage children to write when the "spirit moves them"; to help children record their ideas in different ways; to individualize skill building activities related to constructing sentences and paragraphs; to put together special needs groups to work on language structures being used in writing; and to build into the writing program opportunities for youngsters to revise the writing they wish to share with others. Therefore, the reader is urged not to search this book simply for an idea on which to base a lesson but rather to think of building the activities and ideas suggested in *Content and Craft* into a continuous, ongoing writing program.

In developing both a program approach to teaching written expression and a content/craft orientation, the authors have drawn heavily upon learning experiences in which they have seen children actively involved within classroom situations and upon actual samples of written work produced by children at different grade levels, kindergarten through grade eight. Because of this base in actual classroom practice, the authors owe a debt of gratitude to all the teachers and student teachers who have experimented with the ideas proposed in *Content and Craft,* who have shared with the authors their experiences in teaching writing to children, and who have given the authors the opportunity to watch children in their classrooms in the act of writing. The authors extend thanks also to the children who have allowed observers to look over their shoulders and read what they have written and rewritten.

The authors express sincere appreciation to Professor Alice Miel of Teachers College, Columbia University, for reading and reacting to preliminary drafts of the manuscript. It was Professor Miel who analyzed the authors' concept of writing and categorized the conception as a content/craft approach. In so doing Professor Miel identified the framework around which this book is constructed. The authors also appreciate the assistance of Dr. Harold Shane, University Professor at Indiana University; Dr. Shane helpfully commented on an early draft of the manuscript, giving specific suggestions as to how the final draft might be developed. Similarly the authors thank Dr. Maxine Fisher of Ohio State University for her thoughtful comments on the manuscript, Mr. William Grant for his assistance in proofreading, and Mrs. Marianne Sturman of the Prentice-Hall staff for her helpful editorial suggestions.

To Dr. George Hennings, Professor of Biology at Newark State College, the authors express appreciation for detailed reading and editing of the manuscript, for ideas offered on the nature of scientific thinking and writing, and for suggestions on the overall organization of the book.

D.G.H.

B.M.G.

CONTENT
AND
CRAFT

PART **I**   # CONTENT

Thus, great with child to speak, and helpless in my throes,
Biting my truant pen, beating myself for spite:
"Fool," said my Muse to me, "look in thy heart. and write!"

Sir Philip Sidney, Astrophel and Stella

let children
create

*Sudden a thought came like
a full-blown rose,
Flushing his brow.*

John Keats, "The Eve of St. Agnes"

A third grade child imagines how a zebra got its stripes and tells his teacher: "The zebra got his stripes by having very clean teeth and by brushing his teeth with one special toothpaste. It was called Stripe. One day he left the toothpaste lying around. He stepped on it, and it went all over him. That's how he got his stripes." A teenager, reacting to the New York City blackout, writes:

> the giant city
> roars and grinds, slowing to halt
> in total darkness.

A third student, writing a scientific paper on chemical equations, proposes that chemical equations can be solved using the mathematical technique of simultaneous equations. Each of these individuals—the third grade child, the teenager, and the science student—is able to produce an effective written piece because each has developed an idea that he wants to communicate.

The formulation of ideas is the first requisite for effective writing. An idea in its simplest form is a unique insight for a particular person as he reacts to a multitude of stimuli from the world around him and from within himself. He studies his own perceptions and restructures existing elements of knowledge and feeling to form his own product—his idea. Without such an idea to express, a writer can hardly begin to compose.

Of course, all ideas are not of equal complexity. Some ideas are relatively simple. For example, a house guest perceives that the high point of his weekend visit was a refreshing swim in the ocean. This is the thought he communicates in a thank-you note. By contrast, other ideas are more sophisticated. A book reviewer perceives that the strength of a new book lies in the author's ability to accept responsibility for a particularly odious phase in history in which the author played a significant role. This may be the theme of the reviewer's critique.

Ideas are the substance of writing. This is as true for the poet who produces an imaginative, feeling-laden communication as it is for the mathematician who produces a professional treatise and for the student who writes a term paper. The writer must create an idea before the piece can be effectively written. Let us use as examples the poem, the mathematical treatise, and the term paper to see how the formulation of ideas is an inherent aspect of written communication.

the creation of ideas

Amy Lowell has explained how ideas for poetic expression have come to her:

> An idea will come into my head for no apparent reason; 'The Bronze Horses,' for instance. I registered the horses as a good subject for a poem; and having so registered them, I consciously thought no more about the matter. But what I had really done was to drop the subject into the subconscious, much as one drops a letter into the mail-box. Six months later, the words of the poem began to come into my head, the poem—to use my private vocabulary—was "there."[1]

Samuel Coleridge, too, has given us some insight into the process of poetic inspiration. Coleridge related in the prefatory note to "Kubla Khan" that having taken a drug for a "slight indisposition," he fell asleep as he was reading the lines from "Purchas's Pilgrimage": "Here the Khan Kubla commanded a palace to be built, and a stately garden thereunto. And thus ten miles of fertile ground were inclosed with a wall." He slept for several hours,

> during which time he...could not have composed less than two to three hundred lines; if that indeed can be called composition in which all the

[1] Amy Lowell, *Poetry and Poets* (Boston: Houghton Mifflin, 1930), p. 26; copyright 1930 by Houghton Mifflin and reprinted by permission of the publisher.

images rose up before him as *things,* with a parallel production of the correspondent expressions, without any sensation or consciousness of effort. On awaking he appeared to himself to have a distinct recollection of the whole, and...wrote down the lines that are here preserved.[2]

But Coleridge was interrupted in his writing, and when he returned to it he found that—

though he still retained some...dim recollection of the general purport of the vision, yet with the exception of some eight or ten scattered lines and images, all the rest had passed away like the images on the surface of a stream into which a stone has been cast....[3]

In verse, Coleridge explained how his images reformed:

> Then all the charm
> Is broken—all that phantom-world so fair
> Vanishes, and a thousand circlets spread,
> And each mis-shape the other. Stay awhile,
> Poor youth! who scarcely dar'st lift up thine eyes—
> The stream will soon renew its smoothness, soon
> The visions will return! And lo, he stays,
> And soon the fragments dim of lovely forms
> Come trembling back, unite, and now once more
> The pool becomes a mirror.[4]

Werner W. Beyer, an authority on Coleridge, has suggested that a source of inspiration for the ideas Coleridge projected in "Kubla Khan," *The Rime of the Ancient Mariner,* "The Wanderings of Cain," and "Christabel" was C. M. Wieland's *Oberon.* Coleridge translated *Oberon,* and it is Beyer's thesis that the numerous impressions Coleridge gleaned from *Oberon* and recorded in his now famous *Notebooks* were at least as significant in the generation of ideas as were the opiate and the passage from "Purchas's Pilgrimage" of which Coleridge has written.[5] In any case, Coleridge's mind, a storehouse of impressions, was ripe for the projection of ideas.

Amazingly similar are the accounts of discovery of ideas in science and mathematics. Henri Poincaré described his work with Fuchsian functions. He deduced that—

there existed Fuchsian functions other than those from the hypergeometric series, the ones I then knew. Naturally I set myself to form all these func-

---

[2] Samuel Taylor Coleridge, *The Poetical Works of Samuel Taylor Coleridge,* ed. James D. Campbell (London: Macmillan, 1895).
[3] Ibid.
[4] Ibid.
[5] Werner W. Beyer, *The Enchanted Forest* (New York: Barnes & Noble, 1963), p. 113.

tions. I made a systematic attack upon them and carried all the outworks, one after another. There was one, however, that still held out, whose fall would involve that of the whole place. But all my efforts only served at first the better to show me the difficulty, which indeed was something. All this work was perfectly conscious.

Thereupon I left for Mont-Valérien, where I was to go through my military service; so I was very differently occupied. One day, going along the street, the solution of the difficulty which had stopped me suddenly appeared to me. I did not try to go deep into it immediately, and only after my service did I again take up the question. I had all the elements and had only to arrange them and put them together. So I wrote out my final memoir at a single stroke and without difficulty.[6]

André Ampère spoke in the same vein of the idea that was the substance of his report *Considerations of the Mathematical Theory of Games of Chance:*

I gave a shout of joy.... It was seven years ago I proposed to myself a problem which I have not been able to solve directly, but for which I had found by chance a solution, and knew that it was correct, without being able to prove it. The matter often returned to my mind and I had sought twenty times unsuccessfully for this solution. For some days I had carried the idea about with me continually.... At last, I *do not know how,* I found it.[7]

Discoveries by such scientists as Archimedes, Pasteur, and Darwin exhibit some of the same qualities described by Poincaré and Ampère: first, the preparation of the mind through considerable study and research followed by a period of incubation; then, the formulation of the idea to be later written down in some well-organized manner.

Although we cannot compare the sophistication of these ideas with the rather simplistic ideas expressed in many term papers, we can find a similar searching for ideas even in the writing of term papers. One college student has related to the authors how she produced her term paper for a course on Shakespeare, the assignment being the analysis of one of the Bard's plays. Having selected *Macbeth* as her play, she began by reading the tragedy several times and by reading everything written about *Macbeth* that she could locate; even after all this initial preparation, she did not have any idea where to begin. Then she discovered that the play was being produced in a little theater nearby. There she went, already steeped in *Macbeth,* to get more of *Macbeth* from a different perspective. Clinging to a subway strap on the way home, she saw with sudden clarity the special meaning of *Macbeth* for her. Macbeth was doomed to failure because he could not love; he had no love of man, of nature, or of God. By the time

---

6 Henri Poincaré, "Mathematical Creation," in *The Foundations of Science,* trans. George Bruce Halsted (Lancaster, Pa., 1915, reprinted 1921).

7 L. de Launay, *Le Grand Ampère* (Paris, 1925).

she reached her subway stop, she was ready to write the paper. She had found her idea.

ideas and children's writing

In contrast, a person writing without an idea to be communicated produces just a sequence of empty words. Such was the case with this letter composed by a sixth-grade student for a "friendly-letter" assignment:

> 13 Gill Street
> Exeter, New Hampshire
> September 17, 19—

Dear Martha,

I am writing this letter in school for English. My English teacher is Miss Collins. My history and homeroom teacher is Miss Wood. My geography teacher is Mrs. MacAskill, and my arithmetic teacher is Mrs. McNulty. We started school the 11th.

The weather has not been too nice.

This is all for now, but I will write again.

> Love,
> Dorothy

Obviously this child had not identified an idea that she wanted to communicate before she began to write. Her letter just filled the paper and met the basic requirements of the teacher's assignment.

Another sixth-grade student was asked by her teacher to write about her summer vacation. Again the result was a sequence of words and sentences that met the requirements of grammatical construction but really failed to communicate an idea:

My Summer Vacation

This summer I went to Canton, Maine, with my mother, father, and sister. My uncle and his family went, too.

When we got there, we played ping pong and went swimming.

We stayed there for a week, and then we came home. My cousins came home with us.

One day I went to Little Squam for three days. We had a very nice time. When we came home, we had some company.

Compare Dorothy's friendly letter and the summer vacation paragraph to a composition printed in the *Central Press,* his school newspaper, by Jack, a third-grade boy whose teacher, Miss Waldron, had encouraged him to play with ideas:

I'm Not a Girl

When I was a baby, my father took me for a ride in the cart. We met a lady who said, "What a pretty girl you have."

My Dad yelled, "Girl!" He quickly took me to a barbershop. Mom was sorry to see my curls go.

Rusty, another boy in the same class, also had an idea in mind when he wrote:

Goofy

Once there was a boy named Goofy. The reason Goofy was named Goofy was because he always goofed.

Like the day Goofy had a spelling test! Goofy spelled "ate" "aet," and he spelled "cat" "kat." Goofy marked his paper right. But the teacher didn't think so. So Goofy could never figure teachers out.

As teachers of writing in the elementary school, our first job is to help children work with ideas they want to communicate. This is necessary whether we are concerned with what has traditionally been called imaginative writing—the writing of poems, plays, short stories, jokes—or with what has been called functional writing—the writing of reports, letters, essays, reviews. Working with ideas is fundamental whether we are writing imaginatively or functionally because ideas are the essence of communication.

the content of ideas

Although ideas are the substance of all written expression, the content of ideas embodied in written expression is varied. Some written pieces are simply a reflection of the world as perceived by the observer. The observer describes his perceptions, reports on happenings, itemizes observable procedures, retells something told to him, or summarizes perceptions of events. Other pieces of writing suggest relationships existing in the world. The writer notes similar aspects found in two events; he notes differences. He identifies sequences and patterns, related positions, related evidence, or cause-and-effect relationships. In other pieces, a writer projects explanatory schemes or designs. He constructs a hypothesis or a generalization; he designs a new device, a procedure for doing something, a classification scheme, or a taxonomy.

Written content may also be an expression of feeling. The writer "pours out" on paper his personal emotional reaction to an event, a person, or an object. He expresses his happiness and his sadness, his love and his hate, his envy and his satisfaction, his anticipation and his fears, his contentment and his anxieties.

Related kinds of written content are those in which the writer expresses a preference for one item over another, an opinion or ideas concerning the value of an object, an event, an individual, or even of a written communication. He suggests why he likes one object and not another, why one event is more important than another, why a particular technique is more effective than another, why a particular course of action is more justifiable than another, why a particular communication is more consistent than another. In these cases, the writer is either making a judgment in terms of rational criteria or stating preferences or opinions.

Then too, some written communication is sheer invention. The writer builds a character, an event, and even a place. He manipulates character and action as he sees fit. He designs relationships between characters. He describes things or events that could exist in the world but have not existed exactly as he projects them, or he departs from reality, moving completely into the realm of fantasy. His raw material may be people, things, or events in the real world, but in the end he produces a unique creation.

The substance of ideas handled by writers can be classified into five major categories as shown in the following system:

Content Class A: *Reflection of the world.*   Content that purports to represent accurately objects, materials, persons, events, observable procedures, things read and heard.

1. *Description*—a factual enumeration of the attributes of an object, material, or person, including such properties as color, shape, size, smell, taste, motion, texture, quality, temperature, weight, shadow, reflection or conduction of light, and sound.
2. *Report of a happening*—a factual account of an event that tells, for example, who was involved, when it happened, where it happened, what happened, under what conditions it happened, what materials were associated with the happening, and how long it lasted.
3. *Procedures*—a systematic accounting of how to do something, how to act, how to go somewhere.
4. *Retelling of something heard or read*—a recounting in one's own words of a description, report, story, generalization, plan, or direction that has been expressed by someone else.
5. *Summary of perceptions*—a summary statement of a more complete description, report, recounting, paper.

Content Class B: *Conception of relationships existing in the world.* Content that identifies interrelationships among elements perceived.

1. *Comparison*—a statement indicating that two or more elements share a common attribute.
2. *Contrast*—a statement indicating that two or more elements differ in a particular attribute.

3. *Classification analysis*—an indication that an element belongs to a previously defined set or category.
4. *Qualitative analysis*—an indication of which elements are in a higher or lower position in an hierarchy, which elements are more complex than other elements, which are closer and which are farther away, which are bigger and which are smaller.
5. *Sequential analysis*—an indication that an element sequentially comes first, another second, another third.
6. *Explanation*—an indication of why something happened.
   a. Explanation in terms of cause-and-effect—an explanation connecting two events, one of which has a causal relationship with the other.
   b. Explanation in terms of supporting principles—an indication that certain data are supported by a known principle, that an event can be explained by reference to a known generalization.
   c. Explanation in terms of interlocking generalizations—explanation of a happening by reference to a series of known generalizations.
   d. Explanation in terms of rational intent—an indication that something was done or is being done to serve a human purpose.

Content Class C: *Projection of explanatory schema and designs.* Content that projects original ideas going beyond observable data but consonant with those data.

1. *Hypothesis*—an educated guess or prediction that is founded on the study of data, and this forms the basis for future action.
2. *Conceptual schemes*—generalizations founded on analysis of several related events that can be used to explain those events; also, a complex system of generalizations; a theory.
3. *Designs*—a scheme for classifying data, for taking action, for putting things together; a plan.
   a. Plan for action—an original procedure for doing something; a projected new way for carrying on an activity.
   b. Pattern—plans for construction of an original device.
   c. Classification scheme—a new organizational system through which elements can be categorized.
   d. Taxonomy—a new organizational system through which elements can be categorized in an hierarchy.

Content Class D: *Expression of personal view.* Content that expresses personal feelings, preferences, beliefs, or judgments.

1. *Feelings*—an outpouring of personal, emotional feelings of either a positive or negative nature; an emotional reaction to an event, person, object.
2. *Preference*—a liking or disliking for someone or something; it may be supported with reasons.
3. *Opinion*—a personal belief or point of view not necessarily in accord with fact.

4. *Judgment*—an expression of the effectiveness, justifiability, consistency, importance, overall worth of a person, thing, event, outcome, invention, or design; the judgment is supported by reference to clearly defined criteria.

Content Class E: *Invention.*   The fabrication of descriptions, speeches, persons, and/or plots that go beyond real and/or actual occurrences.

1. *Inventive description*—a description that departs from fact; description of an item that does not exist.
2. *Inventive speech*—a monologue, dialogue, or conversation that does not purport to be a record of actual oral communication that has taken place.
3. *Person*—a character devised by a writer, based not completely on an individual who exists or who has existed.
4. *Plot*—a sequence of concocted events.

writing and creating ideas

To classify the content of written expression into categories does not suggest that one piece of written communication contains content drawn from only one class; indeed, a single communication may have elements of reflection, conception, projection, expression, and invention. It does suggest, however, that the production of different kinds of written content demands different kinds and even levels of thinking—that is, *to write different kinds of content, one must be able to work with different kinds of ideas.*

To write descriptive content, for instance, one must understand the qualities that materials can have and know how to apply that understanding to the study of a new material. To write procedural content requires one to think within a logical framework that gives an orderly sequence to events. To summarize, one must identify central elements and discard less relevant elements. To write conceptual content requires the analysis of situations; one must identify key elements and relationships among those elements. To project feeling one must be able to become emotionally involved; one must allow one's most personal thoughts to surface for public perusal. To invent requires that one put elements together in new and sometimes fanciful patterns.

Pursuing this thesis to its logical conclusion, the authors propose that *to teach children to write is first to help them create ideas from the raw materials of experiences they have had and are having with the real and imaginary world.* The complexity of this instructional task is indicated by the wide range of content embodied in written expression, for this wide range of content is a reflection of the multidimensional aspects of the thinking process itself. But to help children create ideas is too general a concept to consider and too vague a goal to attack. We must break down the process into its component tasks if we are to know what we are seeking and if we are ever to reach our objectives. To do this, let us return to the classification of written content, looking at the specific thinking skills required to produce each type of content.

REFLECTION OF THE WORLD

In producing reflective content, the thinker-writer attempts to translate his impressions of objects, materials, organisms, and events into verbal pictures that are faithful representations of the real world. In so doing, of course, he is limited by his own ability to perceive accurately, which in turn is determined by his background of knowledge, his past experiences, his present interests, and the ideas he has already formulated. In the words of Goethe, "We see only what we know."

In *The Art of Scientific Investigation,* Beveridge recounts an anecdote about Darwin's failure to observe unexpected phenomena when he and a colleague were exploring a valley. Darwin stated that—

> neither of us saw a trace of the wonderful glacial phenomena all around us; we did not notice plainly scored rocks, the perched boulders, the lateral and terminal moraines.[8]

Beveridge suggests that "these things were not observed" by the great Darwin "because they were not expected or not specifically looked for."[9]

That a person observes what he expects, and sees that for which he is looking, was personally brought home to one of the authors last summer. Walking along the edge of a pond in an Audubon Society Refuge on Cape Cod, she heard a plop but thought nothing of it. A companion, a biologist, stopped in midstep, turned toward the direction of the sound, and pulled aside the undergrowth. The writer still saw nothing until the biologist pointed to the fat green bull frog well-camouflaged in the grasses of the pond. After that, she saw many other frogs. She now knew what to listen for and she knew where to look. In teaching children to write reflective content, perhaps we need first to teach them things to expect and things for which to look. ·

To begin to do this, the teacher can set up observational sites, posts from which a child can view a happening directly. Such observational sites might be a post overlooking a bird-feeding station set up just outside the classroom window, a post that looks upon a busy street outside, a stool set next to a demonstration table where experimentation is carried on in the

---

[8] W.I.B. Beveridge, *The Art of Scientific Investigation* (New York: Vintage, 1950), p. 130.
[9] Ibid.

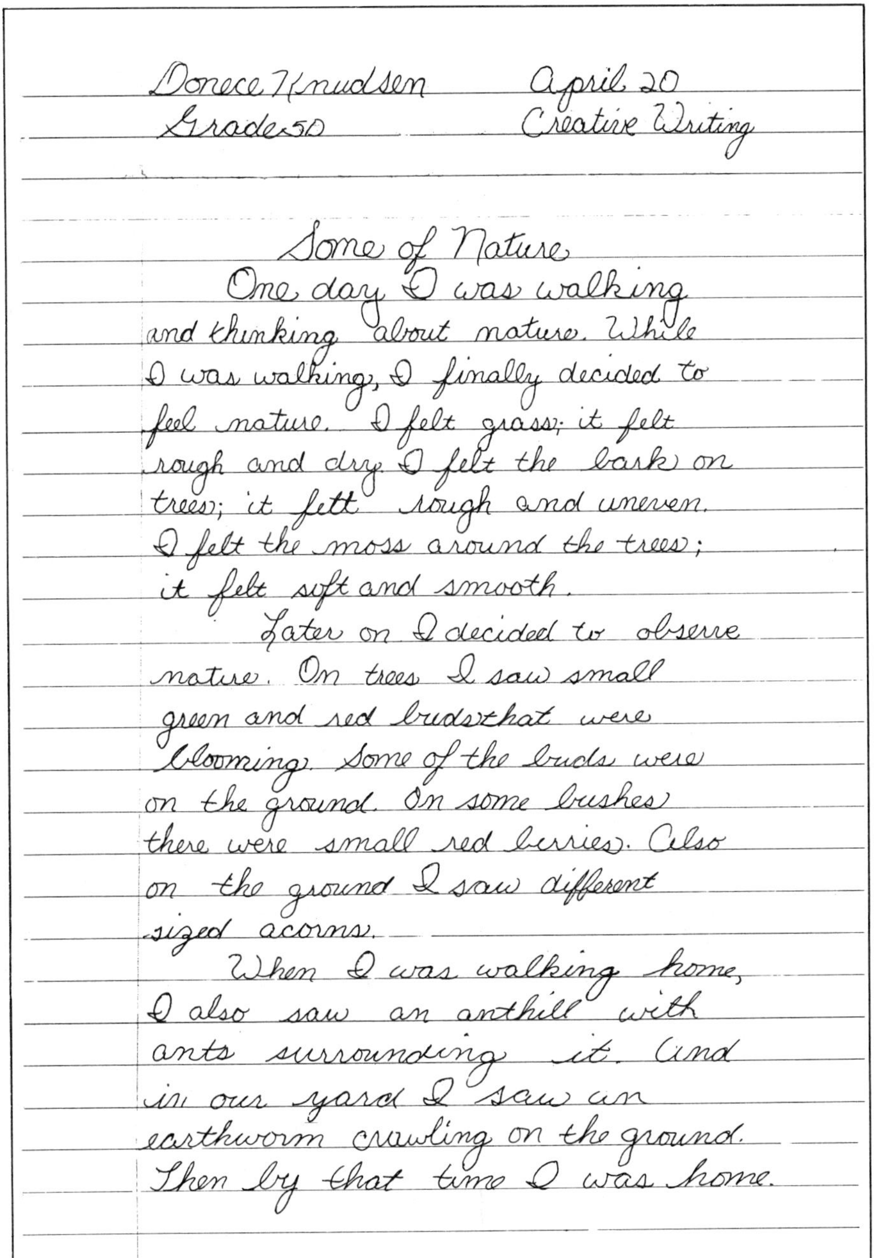

Donece Knudsen   April 20
Grade 5D   Creative Writing

Some of Nature

One day I was walking
and thinking about nature. While
I was walking, I finally decided to
feel nature. I felt grass; it felt
rough and dry. I felt the bark on
trees; it felt rough and uneven.
I felt the moss around the trees;
it felt soft and smooth.

Later on I decided to observe
nature. On trees I saw small
green and red buds that were
blooming. Some of the buds were
on the ground. On some bushes
there were small red berries. Also
on the ground I saw different
sized acorns.

When I was walking home,
I also saw an anthill with
ants surrounding it. And
in our yard I saw an
earthworm crawling on the ground.
Then by that time I was home.

Figure 1-1. *A child's composition based on her observations of nature.*

classroom. Each child can take his turn observing from the lookout post and recording what he perceives. The teacher can even tie a clipboard with a yellow pad and a pencil to the observational post. Children can note their observations on paper, to be shared later with classmates.

Description.   To describe what he sees, the thinker-writer must perceive the individual elements of the world and select the most significant elements if an accurate communication is to result. But before one is able to look at a specific situation and perceive elements about which to write, one needs some kind of framework of understanding about the attributes things generally have. This framework of understanding guides one's perception; it gives one things to expect and things for which to look. For example, knowledge that trees have girth, height, motion, bark pattern, and leaf pattern may help one identify those elements within a particular scene and write: "The towering tree swayed menacingly as each new gust of wind caught up its fragile branches and threw them higher into the air. The thick blue-green leaves appeared almost to shiver in reaction to the wind and the gray, mottled bark appeared to tighten up in protection against the cold." To write such a description requires that the observer perceive the significant elements within a situation, in this case the action of the wind against the trees. It further requires that the observer perceive more than the obvious characteristics and consider the less obvious, but often more significant aspects—blue-green leaves and the mottled texture of bark.

How can the teacher help children learn to describe? One beginning is to set up opportunities for children to describe objects in terms of an Attribute Guide—a chart that requires projection of descriptive words and phrases about objects, places, or people. The guide helps children who understand texture, relative motion, mood, and spatial arrangement to think about numbers of attributes.

An Attribute Guide for Objects might include the following items:

Object to Be Described _____

  Color:
  Shape:
  Size:
    Height, breadth:
  Weight:
  Texture:
  Temperature:
  State of motion:
    Speed of motion, evenness of motion, relationship of motion to nearby
    objects:
  Aroma:
  Taste:

An Attribute Guide for Places might include:

Place to Be Described _____

Significant living things in the place:

Objects in the place:

Spatial arrangement of objects and living things (good words to use include *by, with, above, under, opposite, away from, next to, across from*):

Relative motion of objects and living things:

Temperature of place, wetness of air:

Predominant colors:

Predominant shapes:

Predominant mood of place:

An Attribute Guide for People might include:

Person to Be Described _____

Size:
   Height, breadth:

Weight:

Facial features:
   Hair, eyes, nose, ears, complexion, glasses:

Clothing:
   Style, fit, color, amount:

Cleanliness:

Activity level:

Bodily features:
   Legs, arms, stance:

Predominant feeling one gets looking at the person:

Children on observational excursions in the out-of-doors can project descriptive words within the framework of this type of observational guide. Objects—leaves, feathers, rocks, pieces of bark, pieces of cloth—can be brought into the classroom and placed in a description grab bag; primary grade children can select an object to be described via an Attribute Guide during activity periods. Pictures, perhaps reproductions of great art of past and present, can be used in much the same way. Older children can go a step further and indicate which qualities of an object appear to be the most significant. In short, to teach children to think descriptively, teachers must encourage perceptive observations of objects, places, and people; teachers must put descriptive thinking into the everyday activity of classrooms.

Reports of happenings. The writer who reports on a happening employs similar thinking skills. He identifies the key elements of a particular happening that communicate the essence of the event. He considers who was involved, what happened, when it happened, the conditions under which it occurred, and where it happened. Working within this framework, he puts together—or, as Benjamin Bloom would say, "synthesizes"—a logical design through which to report the event.

To start children thinking as reporters of events, help them devise a Reporting Guide similar to the Attribute Guide just discussed:

> **Event** _____
>
> What action took place?
> Who was there?
> How did each participate?
> When did it happen?
> Where did it happen?
> Under what conditions did it happen?
> Why did it happen?

Children can be encouraged to report on classroom, school, community, and televised happenings they have observed by jotting down words and phrases on a guide. Completed guides can be posted on the bulletin board as a local news roundup—the news in brief.

Procedures. Procedural content requires one to think in terms of sequences and units of action. First, one must perceive the inherent sequences that occur within a happening or that are necessary to achieve a result. For example, if one is to explain how to carry out an experiment or how to bake a cake, one must be aware that there is a systematic series of steps to perform—that *a* is done first, *b* second, *c* next. If one is to explain how to go from point *x* to point *y*, one must again be aware of sequences: "*Start* out by following Main Street until it intersects with Front Street. *There* turn left on Front and *continue* . . . ; *finally* . . . ." One must also be able to perceive signficant steps in the procedure and be able to say to oneself, "Here is one significant unit of activity. This is another. That is still another unit." Procedures, after all, are composed of units of activity; the writer of procedural content must be able to distinguish these units—the unit to be done first, the unit to be done second.

A flow diagram through which a sequence of steps is schematically represented with arrows, lines, and boxes is one way of introducing youngsters to the intricacies of procedural thinking. For example, the question may be how to plant tulip bulbs. Faced with the problem of describing the process that they have just carried out, children can plot the sequence of action diagramatically as:

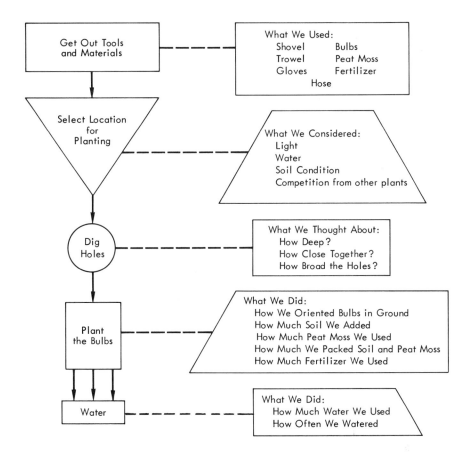

This type of diagram can be constructed as a group project in which young-sters involved in a procedure design the schematic on large sheets of brown paper and show the direction of action with colored felt pens.

Most procedures carried on in a classroom are open to analysis of this type: making papier-mâché, mixing paints, doing a science experiment, baking bread, lining up to go to the assembly hall, evacuating the building during fire drills. Although children are not writing in strict prose form as they construct flow diagrams, they are involved in sequential thinking. For that reason, we can hypothesize that there may be carryover to the writing of systematically organized content.

Retelling. In his *Taxonomy of Educational Objectives: The Classification of Educational Goals, Cognitive Domain* (New York: Longmans and Green, 1956), Benjamin Bloom has identified translation as a cognitive skill fundamental in the production of content involving retelling. To Bloom, translation is the process of paraphrasing or recounting a communication in one's own words. To be judged a successful translation, a recounting must be faithful to the details enumerated in the original communication. When we teach children to retell, therefore, we are helping them to acquire the skill of accurate reproduction of communication. Implicit in this skill is ability to understand written and oral communication, for without ability to comprehend what one has read or heard, one can hardly translate it faithfully.

There are numerous opportunities in classrooms to encourage children to build retelling skills. Children who have read a story can be asked to tell an interesting part. Children can recount something heard on television. They can listen to tapes of stories and tell the stories to friends during a story-sharing session. They can play Gossip and pass along a story just whispered by another child. They can record on tape a story they have read.

Summary. When the writer produces written summaries, he draws upon his skill to interpret. According to Benjamin Bloom in *Taxonomy of Educational Objectives* (New York: Longmans and Green, 1956), interpretation involves a rearrangement, reordering, or a new view of material, without necessarily relating it to other materials. In the case of summarization, the writer must analyze a communication to identify those elements that are pivotal if the essence of the communication is to be retained. His new view of the material is a shortened version that contains these pivotal elements with less significant elements excluded. Again the major cognitive skill is that of selecting the significant and eliminating the unimportant, while still retaining an accurate reproduction. In Chapter 5, activities for teaching summarizing skills will be considered in detail.

CONCEPTION OF RELATIONSHIPS

When the writer handles the content of reflection, he is primarily concerned with painting an accurate picture of the world; on the other hand, when he works with conceptual content, his job is to go beyond the data of perception to identify how elements within the data of experience are interconnected. The primary cognitive skill here is ability to identify connections existing in nature, in events, in nonverbal and verbal materials, between people, within ideas, and within feelings.

Comparison and contrast. To handle statements of comparison, the writer must determine how two materials, ideas, or organisms relate to a particular characteristic or attribute. He must be able to identify an attribute, such as color, within the complex context of material A and ask himself, "Can I find this same element in material B?" When his answer is yes, he writes a statement of commonality, a comparison; when he answers no, he is working with differences, a contrast.

To teach youngsters to propose similarities and differences that will later form the content of their written expression, we must give them an opportunity to recognize common features within situations of differing complexities. The young child can be given blocks to sort into piles according to a shared attribute—for example, color, size, shape, or weight. The older child can sort pictures, musical recordings, books, ideas, or events, and be asked, "Do you see anything similar in the two ideas? in the two events? in the two materials?" Through such cognitive activity carried on at higher and higher levels of sophistication, we can help children handle comparisons and contrasts.

Classification.   Reference to a classification system is very much a part of everyday living. One system is the color spectrum: red, orange, yellow, green, blue, and violet. When an individual selects a block and places it into a pile that he mentally or physically labels blue, he is classifying. Another system is the categorization of vertebrates: mammal, bird, reptile, amphibian, fish. When a person identifies an organism that has wings, has feathers, is pecking on a tree in the backyard, and lives in a nest up in the tree, as a bird, he is classifying according to properties possessed by the organism. In this respect, classification is a more sophisticated form of comparison. The thinker must identify the attributes of an organism, object, material, event, and determine whether these attributes are similar to those possessed by a whole class of related organisms, objects, materials, events.

Classificatory activity can take place in classrooms. Young children who have sorted piles of blocks according to attributes can be asked to attach a class label to the piles—for example, red and blue. Children who have recognized similarities between elements when the teacher queries, "Is there anything alike in these two materials?" can consider what other materials share this quality. They can classify books as biographies, histories, and novels; they can classify music as jazz, rock and classical.

To write a definition is also to classify. In defining, the thinker-writer first identifies the larger class to which an object, an organism, or an event belongs. For example, a definition of a horse might simply begin: "A horse is an animal—," identifying the larger group to which horses belong. Then the writer goes on to identify the attributes of the object, organism, or event that distinguish it from other members of the group. In the definition of *horse,* the writer would enumerate the specific, identifying attributes: "A horse is an animal that has x, y, and z."

That many children have trouble handling this type of thinking is indicated by the typical way in which they attempt to define: "A horse is *when*——" To help children overcome this problem, the teacher can have children complete statements in which a determiner is included: "An elephant is *an*——" or "King George III was *the*——." In this way children may come to know and use the linguistic pattern in which this type of thinking is expressed.

Qualitative analysis.   When a thinker begins to handle qualitative analysis, he is working with another form of difference and similarity. He must identify qualitative differences in the amount of an attribute possessed by related items. For example, he identifies a similarity, that two items are big, but he interjects the notion that one is bigger than the other. Working with two organisms, he recognizes the inherent complexities of the two organisms, but then indicates that one has elements of greater complexity. Based on analysis of qualitative difference, a thinker can place numerous items in a *hierarchical* scheme according to a fundamental attribute, such as speed, size, complexity, distance, or height.

Children can be asked to do much the same thing in simplified contexts to develop this thinking skill. We can ask them in many different settings to determine—

- which is bigger
- which is farther away
- which is higher
- which is greater
- which is longer
- which has more feet
- which has more antennae
- which is louder
- which is harder
- which is colder
- which is greener
- which is darker

Sequential analysis.   In producing some kinds of written content, the writer cognitively analyzes the elements within an event or within a communication to determine the sequential order in which the elements occur. Basically what the thinker-writer determines is how something happened or how something is organized. To do this he must identify discrete subunits of an event or of a communication and perceive the chronological ordering of an event or the organizational ordering within a communication.

These skills are similar to the skills necessary to produce procedural content, for after all, the concern in both kinds of content is with breaking an event into subunits and assigning a sequential order to the subunits. In the case of sequential analytical content, however, the objective is not to indicate how to do something, as in the case of procedural content; rather, the purpose is to indicate either how a communication is organized or how an event occurred.

An elementary school teacher can help children acquire sequential analytical skills. After children have read a story or seen a film, a teacher can ask, "What was the first thing that happened? What happened then? How did the story or film end?" After a talk by a guest, she can ask, "What was the first point Mr. Janick made? What did he say next?" After an accident has occurred in the classroom, after the children have returned from an excursion, or after the children have carried out an art, science, or crafts project, she can ask, "What happened first? What did we do next?" Activities involving new content—reading, seeing a film, hearing a speaker, participating in a project, going on a trip—may have value in and of themselves. Yet these activities can also be used as a springboard to develop cognitive skills.

Explanation in terms of cause and effect. To explain why an event occurred, a thinker-writer sometimes identifies another event or a series of other events that has a causal relationship with the first. He must go on to identify connecting elements that tie the two events together and explain why one of the events occurred. To do this, the analyzer must be able to distinguish between an occurrence that happens to take place before or concurrent with another event, and an occurrence that actually has a causal relationship with the event.

The young child has difficulty making this association, for he is still operating within the confines of his rudimentary perceptual system. Piaget's studies show how a young child perceives that pouring a volume of liquid from a cylinder to another of different shape changes the volume of liquid, and that stretching or flattening a piece of clay changes the volume of the clay. The child perceives that a volume change has occurred and even identifies a cause—the pouring, the flattening, the stretching. In actuality, no volume change has taken place.

As a preliminary step in helping children handle cause-and-effect relationships, the teacher can give children experiences involving manipulation of concrete materials so that the children can begin to perceive the effect that manipulation has on the materials. Play activity with water, with clay, with solids that can be broken up into segments, and with sand that can be poured into piles, is background for thinking about relationships. With older, more perceptually mature children, a teacher can trigger causal thinking by asking the "why" question: "Why did the accident occur?" "Why did the snow melt so quickly?" "Why did the plants die?"

Explanation in terms of supporting principles. Another way of explaining an occurrence is through reference to known generalizations that explain a class of phenomena. For instance, fill a glass with water so that the surface of the water is level with the rim of the glass. Is it full? Some will say yes. Add more water, drop by drop. What happens? The water does not cascade over the sides of the glass; it "stands up," taking on a lenslike shape. Why? Molecules of a material tend to cohere. When we make this last statement, we are resorting to a commonly known generalization to explain a particular occurrence; we are relating occurrence to generalization.

Of course, a child, writing an explanation of why the water does not overflow, need not employ the sophisticated terminology used in the generalization, but he can be given the opportunity to make this type of association through classroom activity. Fifth-grade students can look at mercury bowing upward in a narrow glass tube and talk about how the particles or molecules of mercury stick together. The students can pour water on an oily surface and talk about how the water molecules also stick together. They can pour cooking oil on a surface and talk again about how the oil molecules stick together. During this type of activity the children begin to formulate a concept that they can apply to similar kinds of situations. Faced with explaining why water, added drop by drop to a glass filled to the top with water, does not overflow, they may be able to relate that instance to their newly acquired generalization: that molecules of a material tend to stick together. This relationship that they have discovered can be the idea contained within a paragraph of explanation.

Explanation in terms of interlocking generalizations. In the preceding example, an explanation was given in terms of a single generalization: molecules of a material cohere. In more complex problems, however, an adequate explanation requires drawing upon a number of interrelated generalizations. This, of course, means that the thinker-writer must have a rather thorough understanding of the generalizations, must identify numerous elements in a particular situation, and must perceive relationships among the generalizations and between the situation and the generalizations. To say the least, this is sophisticated relational thinking.

If one conceives of learning how to think as a developmental process, he may well place explanation in terms of interlocking generalizations as a developmental step that follows explanation based on a single generalization. This seems to be a plausible hypothesis and suggests that after a teacher has given youngsters in the upper elementary grades activities like those related to molecular cohesion, he may attempt more sophisticated problems that involve several interlocking generalizations.

Explanation in terms of rational intent. A fourth way of answering the "why" question is through an explanation based on purposes, motives, or intentions. The thinker-writer attempts to identify the logical or illogical reasons why an action was taken by a thinking human being. This involves an analysis of human motivation and the objectives sought through the action.

For example, the question "Why did the little boy climb upon the counter?" is answered by suggesting that he *wanted* a cookie that was there.

The more sophisticated question "Why did the American colonies revolt against England?" again is answered by indicating what the country *wanted* to achieve.

Since the young child's world centers on himself, a good beginning in teaching explanation based on intent is to focus on the child's actions and his purposes for the actions. The teacher can ask questions to which the child can respond, "I did it because———." She can encourage a discussion of the reasons for carrying out certain classroom procedures and activities. "Why do we do that?" she may query. "We do it to———."

As the child matures, the same kind of thinking activity can be transferred to explanations outside the child's environment. In the upper elementary grades the teacher may ask:

- Why is the United States trying to establish a new relationship with China?
- Why do the Amish prefer to live the way they do?
- Why are astronauts willing to risk their lives to go to the moon?
- Why are some industries making efforts to manufacture safer products?

PROJECTION OF EXPLANATORY SCHEMES AND DESIGNS

Written content not only reflects aspects of the world and identifies relationships; it also jumps beyond observable data to project original ways of realistically interpreting, looking at, and organizing the world. To project, the thinker-writer is fundamentally involved in what Benjamin Bloom has called synthesizing—putting together elements and parts to form a whole. He reorders parts, combines them in ways that result in patterns and structures not clearly visible before, eliminates elements, adds pieces, and ends with a product consonant with his data but extending far beyond it. In brief, he concocts.

Much of what has been written on creativity applies to the cognitive processes inherent in projective thinking. The thinker-writer must have the intellectual flexibility and curiosity to play with ideas, to try different approaches, to attempt the outrageous, to conform not to established patterns but to construct new ones, to diverge from expected modes of performance and from traditional ways of viewing things. In so doing, he is able to put together innovative hypotheses, generalizations, theories, and designs.

Hypothesis. When a man proposes a hypothesis, he is projecting a guess or a prediction founded on certain basic conditions he has observed in the world. His guess or prediction goes beyond the data of direct observation but still is in accord with those data. The hypothesizer reasons, "*If m* is true, *if n* is true, and *if o* is true, *then g* must logically follow."

One of the best reasoned hypotheses recorded in the annals of science is Mendel's belief that organisms carry two factors for each inherited characteristic. Although Mendel had not looked inside the cell to see or touch the two factors, it appeared to him that all his evidence pointed toward this explanation. He had crossed tall plants with short plants, and all the offspring of the first filial generation were tall. He then crossed these tall plants with tall plants of the same generation and obtained 3/4 tall and 1/4 short. He reasoned that if shortness shows up in the second filial generation, then the first filial generation must carry a factor for shortness. If it carries a factor for shortness, and obviously one for tallness since it is tall, then perhaps organisms carry within a cell two factors for each characteristic. This hypothesis was the basis for his further research.

We do not expect children to make such large-scale hypotheses as Mendel's, but we can give them the opportunity to make intellectual jumps so that they will learn to hypothesize. Alexander Osborn's thoughts on brainstorming are relevant here. In *Applied Imagination* (New York: Scribner's, 1957), Osborn suggests that one way to get thinkers to go beyond observable fact is to raise wild possibilities for which there are no factual answers:

- What would happen to an elephant if it had a longer trunk?
- What would happen if the elephant had an extra foot instead of a trunk?
- What would happen to object B if we made it heavier, longer; if we changed its color, its shape, its texture; if we added a block to it; if we took a segment away?
- What would be the result of moving all the cars in our town onto the roads at one time?
- What would happen if the population of the world were to double tomorrow?
- How would the world change if there were no TV?

Then, too, experiments can be set up so that children must guess the outcome before the outcome becomes obvious. For example, after children have experienced the previously described observations of mercury, oil, and water beading, the teacher can ask, "What will happen if I add a little more water to this beaker, which is already filled to the top with water?" Children can make educated guesses based on their previous knowledge of molecular cohesion and then try the experiment to determine whether their hypotheses can be validated. Scientific study carried on in an experimental way can prove to be an excellent means for teaching the skills of hypothesis.

Conceptual schemes. In *The Art of Scientific Investigation,* Beveridge writes that—

> facts obtained by observation or experiment usually only gain significance when we use reason to build them into the general body of knowledge.

Darwin said: "Science consists in grouping facts so that general laws or conclusions may be drawn from them."[10]

These general laws and conclusions are what James Conant has termed
conceptual schemes.[11]

To project conceptual schemes is basically to think inductively: first,
to select and group together factual data that appear to be related; second,
to study rather systematically a series of related phenomena; third, to attempt rearrangements and reorderings of the data; fourth, to jump beyond
the data to identify underlying connecting principles. Inductive thinking
obviously has shades of both analysis and synthesis. As one studies each
phenomenon, attempting to perceive essential elements, one is analyzing.
As one jumps the gap from fact to generalization, one is synthesizing—
putting the individual pieces together in a unique whole.

To teach children to think inductively is often to teach inductively.
Start with several instances of a known generalization: for instance, use
our previous examples of mercury bulging upward in a narrow glass tube
and water beading on an oiled surface. Have children describe and analyze
these phenomena. Then add a related phenomenon—the beading of oil.
Create still another example by dropping coins into a glass of water that
is filled exactly level with the top. Describe the result and analyze. Somewhere in the sequence children may jump the gap between specific and
general to discover for themselves a generalization that can be used to
explain those and other instances of a similar type.

In discussing the projection of conceptual schemes, Conant proposes
that generalizations can be produced through the use of deductive reasoning
by deriving more generalizations from the "speculative ideas of an earlier
time."[12] Although children should have opportunity at some point in their
schooling to carry on this type of highly sophisticated reasoning as a base
for writing complex deductive content, it hardly seems possible to expect
children in the elementary grades, who are functioning in what Piaget has
called the concrete operational stage, to manipulate ideas that are completely in the realm of the abstract, completely removed from the concrete.

Design: Plan of action. One kind of written content incorporates a
plan for carrying on an activity. To design a procedure, one must devise
units of activity—in other words, the steps required. In addition, one must
place the units or steps into some logical order. This may require some
knowledge of other plans of action and how they have functioned under
differing conditions. The result may be a recipe, the procedure for carrying

10 Ibid., p. 123.
11 James Conant, *Science and Common Sense* (New Haven, Conn.: Yale University Press, 1951), p. 25.
12 Ibid., p. 46.

on a research project, a plan for carrying on an operation more efficiently, or a number of other possibilities.

To help children gain the skills required to project procedures, the teacher can apply brainstorming techniques. She can suggest rather wild situations and have children propose plans of action.

- What would you do if an elephant came charging at you at fifty miles per hour?
- What would you do if you won the New York State million-dollar lottery?
- What would you do if the brakes on your bike gave way as you were coasting downhill?
- What would you do if the water in your house were turned off for twenty-four hours?

Design: Pattern. Designing may also involve concocting a pattern to be used in the construction of an appliance, a contraption, a tool, or a piece of clothing. Basically the written communication is a description, but it is one not founded on something known to exist; rather, it projects something that has some original quality. It may include a graphic representation of the item to be constructed.

To handle patterned content one must organize known materials in new ways, form mental images of the proposed construction scheme, represent ideas graphically, and translate visual images into a verbal description. The brainstorming question, "Let's visualize how *this* would look if we cut it in half, changed its color, shape, texture, gave it an odor, added a mirror image, made it longer, taller, shorter, heavier, or added a square block on top," is one way to have children begin to design original patterns. A follow-up step is to have them describe the resultant. Work with concrete materials —clay, wood, paper, plaster of Paris—is a natural in this context.

Design: Classification schemes and taxonomies. Discovery of discrete units into which items can be grouped according to their attributes is one aspect of designing classification schemes and taxonomies. In the case of the development of taxonomies, an additional task is the hierarchical ordering of the classification units. Since the projected units and ordering are not phenomena existing in nature, but are inventions of the mind, to devise taxonomies and classificatory schemata requires the thinker-writer to analyze the factual data and to design new patterns for organizing the data.

Teaching children to discover methods of classifying is a natural outgrowth of experiences used to teach children how to classify in predetermined sets. More specifically, classificatory exercises in which children sort piles of blocks that differ only in one attribute, such as color, size, or shape, can be followed by exercises in which children sort piles of blocks that differ in several attributes. In the latter instance the question to be answered is, "What are the many different ways in which we can classify our blocks?"

Later in the developmental sequence, children can handle highly heterogeneous materials—a walnut, a plastic comb, an olive, a piece of paper, a ball point pen, a piece of chalk, a bobby pin, an onion—and the question can be raised, "What categories can we invent into which we can class these items?" Answers are almost endless: use, whether manufactured, organic or inorganic, size, reaction to light, reaction to heat or flame. Again, in a sense this is a brainstorming activity; so the more heterogeneous the materials the better, and the wilder the suggested categories, the more the imagination is stretched.

EXPRESSION OF PERSONAL VIEW

Written content, as we have seen, can reflect the world, suggest abstract relationships existing in the world, and propose new relationships and designs. It can also express personal emotions elicited by the world and individual reactions to it. Perhaps differing more in the degree of logic upon which they are founded than in any other characteristic, personal emotions and reactions appear to be of four kinds: feelings, preferences, opinions, and judgments.

Feelings.

> In the morning the city
> Spreads its wings
> Making a song
> In stone that sings.
>
> In the evening the city
> Goes to bed
> Hanging lights
> About its head.[13]

In "City," Langston Hughes embeds his feeling about the city in descriptive songlike lines of lyric poetry. Much of what has been called lyric poetry has the form and musical quality of a song and embodies feelings or emotional reactions toward all manner of things: events, persons, objects. In the work of Robert Frost there is an outpouring of feeling about the beauty of nature. In the poems of Elizabeth Barrett Browning there is an expression of love. Feelings about discrimination and poverty spill over in other poems by Langston Hughes.

To write in this vein, one must be able to react with a full range of emotions and feel free to share innermost feelings with others. To do this, of course, the thinker-writer must distinguish as he reflects upon the object

[13] Langston Hughes, "City," in *Langston Hughes Reader* (New York: George Braziller, 1958). Copyright 1958 by Langston Hughes; reprinted by permission of Harold Ober Associates Incorporated.

of his feelings the attributes contained within that object; only by doing this can he write the passages of description in which his feelings are laid bare. On the other hand, since expressions of feeling are not logical treatises, the writer need not produce a reasoned argument to support his emotions.

How do we prepare children to write about their feelings? If one must be capable of reacting with a full range of emotion and must feel secure in the expression of that emotion in order to write emotion-laden content, then it seems logical to propose that most essential is the acceptance of emotion by the teacher. She must communicate to her children that emotions are a quality of humanness, not something of which to be ashamed.

This can be done in many contexts. When reading a story with her children, she can ask, "How do you think the little boy in *Where the Wild Things Are,* by Maurice Sendak (New York: Harper & Row, 1963), felt when he was sent to bed without supper? When have you felt this way?" She can take the experience a step further and suggest, "Let's draw a picture of our feelings. What colors can we use to express being happy, being mad at somebody, caring about someone?" When children have had arguments or even fights, she can encourage them afterward to talk about how they felt. When children are taking pleasure in doing something, she can similarly encourage them to talk about their feelings of delight. And when children have actively enjoyed an experience together, such as building a snowman, she can suggest, "Let's draw our feelings into a picture and add words to show how we feel about our snowman." (See Figure 1-2.) Eventually children may write their feelings, encouraged perhaps by the writings of Robert Frost and Langston Hughes.

Figure 1-2. *"The Snowman"—a concrete poem by a fourth grader.*

Preferences. A less emotional reaction is the expression of preference: The thinker-writer states, "I prefer x to y." The x may refer to almost anything—a person, a color, a piece of clothing, a restaurant, a type of food, a book, or a type of activity. It may be chosen because it is really liked, because y is really disliked, or even because x is the lesser of two evils.

In choosing among options, the thinker-writer is involved to some extent in comparison; he identifies the attributes of the options. Then he goes a step further and interjects his personal view, jumping the gap between factual analysis and subjective determination. To do this, he must know his own mind and feel free to express it.

To teach children to make choices among options, the teacher must give children genuine opportunity for choice within the classroom and abide by their choices. Which book would you prefer reading? Which seat do you choose? Which colored chalk do you want? Here are three ways we can carry out this task—which way do you prefer? In making a selection, children can be encouraged to examine the bases of their preferences by being asked why and being urged to reply, "I prefer this because——." The statement of preferences does not require a lengthy rationale or validation by reference to a series of criteria. A simple enumeration of reasons is all that is necessary.

Opinions. Another kind of idea expressed in written content is an opinion or belief about the rightness-wrongness, propriety-impropriety, or goodness-badness of a course of action, a happening, or even a person. Such a belief is founded on an analysis of elements within the course of action, the happening, or the person; hopefully the thinker-writer studies the related attributes before expressing an opinion. When he states his opinion, he may support it with a simple statement of reason: "I believe we should do x because——." Of course, there are no physical connections existing between a situation and one's opinion of that situation; that a particular course of action is the proper one is a subjective determination. In stating an opinion, one goes beyond fact.

To state an opinion, the thinker-writer must know that to look at a situation and come up with an opinion of it is a valid mental activity. He must feel that his beliefs are worthy of public perusal. He must have the skill to analyze situations as a basis for the expression of belief, and he must be able to identify reasons that he can employ to support his belief. Teachers can encourage the development of these skills, knowledges, and attitudes by simply giving children the opportunity to express their opinions about problems that concern them. What do you think about the new school regulations on dress? What do you think about women being trained as astronauts? What do you think about the way black children may be discriminated against? What is your opinion of smoking, taking drugs, shoplifting, looting? The follow-up question is "Why?"

Judgment. A judgment, as used here, is an evaluation or assessment of an item, person, event, or quality in terms of carefully stated criteria. Obviously, a statement of judgment is a more reasoned kind of written communication than the outpouring of feeling embodied in lyric poetry.

The initial step in judging is to develop an external measuring stick. Since concern in assessing is with such value designations as effective-ineffective, efficient-inefficient, and consistent-inconsistent, there is no way in which a quantitative measure can be made. The external measuring stick has to be a series of criteria developed outside the context of a particular item being evaluated. These criteria become the standard of effectiveness, efficiency, or consistency, against which each item to be evaluated is tested.

The next step in judging is to determine the attributes of the item under evaluation and to compare these attributes to those identified in the criteria as being effective, efficient, or consistent. If the item possesses qualities identified as effective or efficient, the judgment is positive; if not, the judgment is negative. If some qualities exist but others are found lacking, the judgment has both positive and negative elements.

At first glance, the formulation of a statement of judgment appears to be a rather objective one, but this is not so. First, the selection or projection of criteria is a subjective process, based on a person's own value system. Try to get a group of individuals to agree on a set of criteria by which to evaluate. It will quickly become obvious that to achieve complete agreement is almost an impossible task. Second, even if complete agreement on criteria could be achieved, individuals would apply the criteria in ways that lead to different evaluations. The reason for the divergency becomes evident when one considers how the criteria, the object being evaluated, and the judgment are connected. There is no physical connection; the human mind must bridge the gap between criteria and object, between object and judgment. In this respect, evaluating is a creative process in which elements are reorganized into a new whole—the judgment.

With older elementary school children, the teacher may want to attempt judgmental thinking and writing. Initially, teacher and children can propose a list of criteria by which something can be judged. A good beginning is the children's own work. Faced with several samples of handwriting, children can suggest qualities that good handwriting exhibits. They then can apply these criteria to the evaluation of their own work samples, coming up with a judgment about which are their better productions and which are their poorer productions. A fringe benefit is that the children are not only introduced to the process of formal judgment, but also they are started down the road of self-analysis, a process extremely important in writing, as we shall see in later chapters of this book.

INVENTION

Some writing is pure invention. The thinker-writer is working in the realm of imagination. He develops characters who have never existed, though they may, of course, resemble in certain respects people who have existed. He verbally paints pictures of scenes with colors, shapes, shades, and masses that he himself may never have seen nature put together in such an arrangement. He invents relationships among his characters as they interact within his painted landscape. These relationships may bear some resemblance to relationships in real life, but they do not exactly follow events as they have occurred at a precise point in time.

The products of invention are the characters, descriptions, events, and interrelationships that are found in narrative poetry, plays, short stories, and novels. To create this type of written communication requires one to synthesize: to formulate the new, to re-view what has been perceived with the senses, and to let the imagination fly loose.

A teacher can encourage children to let their imaginations fly by allowing time for the "let's pretend" type of activity. Very young children can role play Mother Goose characters; they can pretend to be Big Bird from Sesame Street or a character from their favorite TV cartoon. Youngsters can be asked to speak as if they were animals. The teacher suggests, "Pretend you are—

a fly sitting on the end of my nose,
a poodle on a leash,
a mosquito about to bite,
a turtle trying to cross a busy highway,
a crocodile who lives in a bathtub.

What would you be thinking? What would you say?" The teacher can record youngsters' animal-talk for them.

Similarly, art activity can carry very young children into inventive thinking. Instead of centering art experiences solely on real and observed events, the teacher can suggest that youngsters paint (or perhaps finger-paint)—

an enchanted forest,
a magical apple orchard,
a wizard who lives in an enchanted cave,
a house where magical things happen,
a horse who lives on the moon,
an elephant who can fly.

Song and story are other media that stimulate inventive thinking. A little song about "Puff, the Magic Dragon" (Peter Pan Records) can encourage children to enter the world of "let's pretend." As children sing about the magic dragon who lives by the sea, they are toying with make-believe and can be encouraged to talk about other things that the dragon might do and say. The same holds true with stories. Leo Lionni's delightful story of *Swimmy* (New York: Pantheon, 1963), the little fish in search of companions, tickles children's imaginations to think about other adventures Swimmy might have. Barbara Emberley's *One Wide River to Cross* (Englewood Cliffs, N.J.: Prentice-Hall, 1966) encourages children to concoct what would happen when "the animals came in" eleven by eleven, twelve by twelve. Maurice Sendak's *In the Night Kitchen* (New York: Harper & Row, 1970) leads children to think about other things that could happen in the kitchen at night, or in the attic at night, or on the apartment house rooftops at night. In so doing, youngsters become involved in the kind of thinking and talking that can result in inventive description, plot, character, and dialogue.

a summary assumption

A basic assumption upon which this book is founded is that a prime requisite for the production of written content is the ability to create ideas. The authors propose that this assumption is true regardless of the kind of content with which one is dealing.

If this assumption is true, then to teach children to write is, in the first place, to help them work with ideas, which means they must invent, feel, project, and reflect on what the world is all about. To achieve this objective, experiences with ideas cannot be centered solely in the third grade, the fifth grade, or the junior high school grades. We need to look at teaching for idea formation as a developmental sequence in which children at each level encounter activities that build on previous ideas and are more sophisticated than those they have experienced at an earlier stage. Classroom activity in idea formation cannot be a narrow endeavor, for creating ideas involves highly divergent processes that are nonetheless fundamental if our children are to produce relevant content in which they reflect the world, conceive of relationships about the world, project conceptual schemes and designs, express personal views, and invent imaginative views of the world.

let children
experience
and express

> All experience is an
> arch to build upon.
> *Henry Adams,* The Education of Henry Adams

How does the teacher begin to help children create meaningful, relevant idea-content for expression in their writing? The answer to this question has three dimensions:

- children need first-hand experiences as a base from which to develop ideas;
- children need to express their ideas through nonverbal and dramatic activity;
- most essential—children need to have endless opportunities to talk about their ideas.

first-hand experiences

Ideas cannot sprout in a vacuum. Ideas are relational products based on impressions, sensations, feelings, facts, or understandings that the writer puts together in his own way. The best ideas come when the writer knows intimately that about which he writes.

Consider Wordsworth. Wordsworth wandered for miles in the peaceful Lake District of England feeling the power of nature all around him. From his intimate association with the stillness and beauty of the English countryside came his nature poems and sonnets, his youthful "Prelude," "Tintern Abbey," and "My Heart Leaps Up." The content of his poetry was the content of his experience in the Lake District. A London-bound Wordsworth could never have written as the real Wordsworth did.

In like manner, the environment that provided the first-hand experiences for Washington Irving's *Tales of Alhambra* was the Alhambra. Irving wrote *Tales of Alhambra* in a little room high in the palace at Granada. For Elizabeth Barrett the experience of love for Robert Browning was the source of impressions and feelings expressed in her poems.

Young writers also need the raw material of real experiences to create ideas. How can a third-grade child perceive a relationship between the stripes on a zebra and toothpaste unless he knows of a particular brand of toothpaste? How can a teenager write about darkness unless he has experienced a complete blackout? How can a third-grade boy suggest that it is goofy to spell *ate* as *aet* unless he has experienced the difficulties of spelling in our mixed-up language?

Experiences of all kinds can be provided for children in the elementary school. Children can go to zoos, farms, and aquaria to discover the wide variety of living things. Children can take nature walks and walks on city streets. They can tramp through newly fallen snow and leave angel prints behind them. They can stand and watch water trickle in rivulets down a windowpane. They can dig into the earth and find all sorts of things. They can run as fast as they can against the wind. They can walk in soft sand on a beach and feel themselves sink in deeply. They can play tag and ghost and hopscotch. They can peer at the stars and the moon through the lens of a telescope, and they can look at skin and blood, algae and paramecia, under the lens of a microscope. They can experience the difficulty of understanding fractions, equations, spelling inconsistencies, and even people. They can watch spontaneous combustion, melting and freezing, and chemical combination occur on the laboratory table. They can watch a colony of ants make an anthill, a hermit crab navigate in its borrowed house, and a spider spin its web.

They can bake a marble cake and swirl chocolate through the batter. They can stand aghast and watch the swirls of air pollution spiral from a smokestack. They can grow plants from seeds and follow each day's growth. They can rub fat on the bark of trees and watch the woodpecker feed on it. They can just lie in the grass and watch the clouds make pictures overhead. They can get excited over the inequities in life and can try to do something constructive. They can chop wood and build a fire. They can look into someone's eyes. They can play with their own reflection in concave, convex, and flat mirrors. They can shout as loud as they can shout, throw as far as they can throw, and jump as high as they can jump. They can hammer nails and turn screws. They can watch 747s climb into the sky at a nearby airport. They can eat apple butter, comb honey, and bagels. The experiences we can provide for children are limited only by our own imagination and the resources of our surrounding environment.

experiencing with all the senses

The person who can get the most from an experience is the person who is primed to receive impressions through all his senses. Impressions come to us through smell. We smell the rain, the good odor of fresh-baked cake, and the heavy odor of stale cigarette smoke. Impressions come through sound. We hear the crashing of breaking glass, the chirruping of crickets on a hot evening, and the even roar of an airplane engine. Our sense of sight brings us perceptions of lightness and darkness, of reds and roses, of greens and blue-greens. Sight allows us to judge distance, the size and shape of objects, motion, and relative motion. Other impressions are tactile: we feel heat and cold, we react to pressure, we receive sensations of pain and pleasure. Still other impressions bombard us via our taste buds. The taste of salted, buttered new corn brings a smile to our faces, whereas the taste of bitter orange rind brings a frown.

The teacher's job is getting children to react with all their senses—sound, sight, taste, smell, and touch. She must help children see and feel the concrete; she must help them become more keenly aware of odors; she must help them listen for unusual sounds. In the following section, experiences to awaken the senses are suggested.

SOUND

1. Ask children to close their eyes and listen. Do this in different situations—in a quiet woods, on a busy city street corner, at the airport, on the bank of a stream, on a windy day.
2. Ask children to listen to a record with the volume turned down and then with the volume turned way up, with the speaker placed at a distance and placed near by.
3. Take children for a walk in the woods on a fall day. Encourage them to listen to the leaves crackling beneath their feet. Have them listen to distinguish the sounds of birds.
4. Listen to musical compositions and try to distinguish instruments. As a preliminary exercise, have children listen for the precise sound of rhythm band instruments. Students can close their eyes while the teacher plays each instrument.
5. Listen to the imaginative sounds on records like *Sounds and Images* by Bert Cunningham and E. Paul Torrance (Boston, Mass.: Ginn and Company).
6. Take a walk on a city street, note pad in hand. Record the different sounds heard.

7. Make a tape with the children entitled "Sounds Around Us." Take the tape recorder outside and tape sounds of lawn mowers, garbage trucks, fire engines, running water, pneumatic drills, fog horns, and insects singing— whatever sounds make up the local environment.

8. On a city walk, run a stick along a metal fence; try it in different ways to see if sounds of different pitch and amplitude can be produced.

9. Have children vibrate rulers over the edges of their desks. Experiment to determine how the sounds can be changed.

10. Listen to and contrast the sounds of motorized vehicles—cars, motorcycles, trucks. Think about differences both in pitch and amplitude.

SIGHT

Color

1. Play with watercolors. One child has only red, orange, and yellow with which to work; another only yellow, blue, and green; another only orange, blue, and violet; another only blue, green, and violet. Afterward, compare the effects achieved.

2. On a nature walk, collect "greens" and compare the different shades of green produced by nature.

3. Have a "red" day. All children should try to wear something red to school. Compare shades.

4. Observe eye colors of children in the class and describe.

5. Study the colors of rock samples and describe the pinks, grays, greens, golds that are found in nature.

6. Play with a prism or a crystal. Make dancing rainbows on the ceiling and distinguish the colors produced.

Motion

1. Watch cars moving along the street. Describe how fast they are going.

2. Watch people walking along the street and describe their gait.

3. Observe the relative speeds and kinds of locomotion of different animals: the hermit crab, the grasshopper, the toad, the turtle, the bird. (A follow-through on this might be a reading of the well-known Aesop fable, "The Tortoise and the Hare.")

Size and shape

1. At an airport, study the relative sizes and shapes of airplanes.

2. On a street, study the relative sizes and shapes of cars.

3. Study the clouds and imagine what pictures can be "seen" in the clouds.

4. Look at buildings. Find rectangles, squares, circles, parallelograms, and other geometric shapes in their structures.

5. Study a seashell and then sketch its shape. Make sketches that show the shell half its size, double its size, giant size.

6. On a large sheet of brown paper have children trace the outline of their hands and feet. Then describe the shapes produced and compare sizes.

7. Bring in a collection of work tools, kitchen gadgets, fruit, or bottles. Look at them and describe the shapes.

8. Study the shape of smoke as it comes from smokestacks.

SMELL

1. Smell sliced lemon, chocolate, mint, onion, and ammonia.

2. Go down to the cafeteria or the nurse's office and notice the odors that are there.

3. When out on a nature walk, break leaves of wintergreen, mint, bayberry, sassafras, skunk cabbage, and spice bush. Catch the aroma.

4. Take an "air-pollution excursion." Stand on a crowded street corner and distinguish the smells. Go into an industrial area and sniff odors of cookies, perfume, or burning fuels.

5. Burn things like bread, paper, sulfur, and tobacco. Distinguish the odors produced.

6. In farm areas, stand near a barn and distinguish the farm smells—cows, chickens, hay.

7. Distinguish the odors on a trip to the zoo.

8. Smell different spices like thyme, oregano, bay leaf, nutmeg, cinnamon, and distinguish the odors.

9. Read to primary children Katherine Howard's *Little Bunny Follows His Nose* (New York: Golden Press, 1971, available through the National Audubon Society). Children scratch and sniff the fragrance strips to discover roses, peaches, dill pickle.

TASTE

1. Taste different spices and condiments—salt, pepper, thyme, nutmeg, chocolate. Distinguish their tastes.

2. Conduct tasting tests of a common product such as chocolate. Taste different brands and see if differences are apparent.

3. Conduct tasting tests between butter and different margarines. See if differences can be noted.

4. Conduct tasting tests with a canned, a frozen, and a fresh sample of a commodity: orange, pineapple, or grapefruit juices. See if differences can be noted.

5. Taste a strip of PTC test paper. See who can taste it and who cannot. (PTC paper tastes bitter to some and is tasteless to others. Ability to taste is an inherited characteristic. Paper can be purchased from Carolina Biological Supply, Burlington, N.C.)

6. Compare the tastes of natural products—orange rind (bitter), lemon (sour), sugar (sweet), salt (salty).

TOUCH

1. Feel sandpaper, cotton, wood, a mirror, fur, a piece of carpet, a piece of textured wallpaper with eyes closed. Give adjectives to describe the impressions.

2. Put the left hand into water of one temperature. Have dishes with water at different temperatures. Put the right hand in these dishes, and judge the relative temperatures of each. This could be carried out as an "impressions lab." The teacher has large buckets of water at different temperatures on a counter. Children ladle samples into small containers (plastic ice-cream containers) to analyze back at their desks. They set up categories labeled with adjectives to describe the different temperatures.

3. Have children "feel" a cloud by taking them for a walk on a foggy day and having them feel mist brushing their faces.

4. Have children "feel" sunshine by taking them for a walk on a bright, hot, sunny day and having them stand still to let the sun warm their skin. Have them "feel" cold by taking them for a brisk walk on a very cold day.

5. Have children "feel" snow by picking up a handful of newly fallen snow, of closely packed snow, and of dirty, melting snow.

6. Have children "feel" wind. Go outside and stand facing the wind as it blows all around.

7. Have children feel grass, feathers, tree bark, leaves.

8. Have children walk on different surfaces—sand, grass, concrete, and wood—and feel the differences.

9. Have children feel the textures of such fabrics as woolen tweeds, silk, cotton, wash-and-wear, linen, and knits. Have them feel the differences.

10. Conduct consumer tests of products, for example, blankets, sandpaper, and pillows. Which feels the best for the job each has to do?

action as a means of expressing experience

Heinz Werner suggests in *Comparative Psychology of Mental Development* that the younger the child, the more likely he is to organize his world in terms of *activity* and in terms of *himself*. In an overall situation, the younger child perceives action, rather than specific elements within the situation; the child creates and fashions his world through a blending of motor-emotional activity and object stimuli.[1] Then too, the young child's organization of time and space is active and egocentric. Time to him is based on the great events in his own life: waking-up time, breakfast time, snack time, nap time, father's coming-home time. His concept of space is similarly organized around himself. The child uses his own body to determine possible relationships in space; he physically interacts with a situation in order to gain understanding of it. This is seen in the action of a young

[1] Heinz Werner, *Comparative Psychology of Mental Development* (New York: Science Editions, 1948).

child who enters an unfamiliar house: he runs from room to room, physically sensing the size and exploring the shape of his environment. Piaget calls this period of intellectual development the "pre-operational stage"—a stage in which the child establishes "relationships between experience and action"[2] by manipulating the world.

As the young child enters school in his fifth or sixth year, he is very likely entering the successive stage, the "concrete operational stage" in which he learns to manipulate symbols and to represent his external world symbolically. At this stage he depends on a concrete referent in order to gain symbolic understanding. Only as the child moves into junior high school at approximately twelve years of age is he able to handle abstract relationships without concrete referents.[3]

Vygotsky, too, considers the manipulation of environment important for the young child. In making the transition from vocal to inner speech, the child uses egocentric speech accompanied by the manipulation of the concrete; he manipulates objects and materials in his environment as he talks to himself.[4] This type of activity helps the child make the transition from perceiving his world in terms of action to perceiving it in terms of symbols and abstractions.

The studies of Werner, Piaget, and Vygotsky suggest that the young child may more readily translate his impressions of the world into physical activity than into the verbal patterns characteristic of written expression; he is able to act out his feelings and ideas with greater facility than he can tell about them. This conclusion further suggests that as a teacher works with a young child in composition, she must broaden her conception of writing to include experiences in which the child translates his experiences into physical motion. Even with the older elementary school child who still needs concrete references, the teacher may be wise in having a child employ nonverbal activity as a base for verbal expression.

TRANSLATE IMPRESSIONS INTO NONVERBAL ACTIVITY

A child can interpret a musical selection through his physical motions. The young child who enjoys the "let's pretend" kind of activity can be a rabbit, involving his whole body in rabbit action. He can be an elephant, a camel, a lion, a fish, or any other animal that seems to intrigue him at this stage of development. The primary school teacher who is skilled at the piano, with the guitar, or even with an instrument like the cello, has an

---

2 Jean Piaget, *The Psychology of Intelligence* (London: Routledge & Kegan Paul, 1964), p. 123–55.
3 Ibid.
4 L.S. Vygotsky, *Thought and Language* (Cambridge, Mass.: M.I.T. Press, 1962).

advantage at this point. She can quickly produce one kind of tune, change to another, and then change to still another as children react physically with a nonverbal, interpretive impression of an animal. The teacher who is unskilled in music should not give up, for recordings can be used in similar fashion. Rather than making the bass notes on a piano growl like a bear or the treble notes sing like a bird, the teacher can use recordings such as Prokofiev's *Peter and the Wolf* in which a flute trills like the Bird, an oboe clacks like the Duck, a clarinet slinks like the Cat, the horns play the Wolf, the strings sing Peter's sound, a bassoon is Grandfather, and the full orchestra plays the role of the Hunters. Children can be cast in each of these roles, and as they recognize their themes, they can do their own impressions.

Other kinds of pantomiming activities that involve action and therefore may be useful with the younger child include "let's pretend" we are—

- jumping jacks
- floating bubbles in the air
- riding on a subway
- driving a motorcycle
- bobbing up and down on the waves
- riding a horse
- walking in the mud, splashing in puddles, slipping and falling—all on a rainy day

Again, musical accompaniment may provide an environment that will be conducive to freedom of expression and individual interpretation. On the other hand, children themselves may provide not only the physical interpretation but also the noises—the screeches, the squeals, the whinnies, the roars, the splashes, the crashes, the plops—that accompany the action.

Still another device for translating this type of impression is shadow play. Employing a slide projector as a source of light, the teacher can project the beam of light onto a screen. Children in the primary grades are fascinated with the process of casting their shadows on the screen, and they will move creatively to produce original effects. They will dance, slink, hop, bob, gesture, and gyrate with little or no inhibition as they watch their shadows carry on the same activity.

Story and poem can also be used as the frameworks for creative nonverbal expression. Having heard the story *The Camel Who Took a Walk* (Jack Tworkov, New York: Dutton, 1951, K–3), children can become the camel, the lion, the squirrel, the monkey, and the bird, and act out the story in pantomime. Other picture-story books that involve a sequence of actions and are particularly adaptable to nonverbal interpretation are—

Bishop, Claire. *The Five Chinese Brothers.* New York: Coward, 1938 (1–4).
Chaconas, Doris. *The Way the Tiger Walked.* New York: Simon & Schuster, 1969 (K–3).

Ets, Marie H. *In the Forest*. New York: Viking Press, 1944 (K–1).

Haley, Gail. *A Story, A Story*. New York: Atheneum, 1970 (K–3).

Hogrogian, Nonny. *One Fine Day*. New York: Macmillan, 1971 (K-3).

Langstaff, John, and Rojankovsky, Feddor. *Frog Went A-Courtin'*. New York: Harcourt Brace Jovanovich, 1955 (K–3).

Sendak, Maurice. *Where the Wild Things Are*. New York: Harper & Row, 1963 (K–3).

The Three Billy Goats Gruff, available in many anthologies of children's fairy tales (K–2).

Since nursery rhymes very often embody action, they too can be interpreted physically. As children recite in chorus a rhyme such as "Ride a Cockhorse to Banbury Cross," they can move their bodies to emulate the motion of the horse. With "Jack be nimble, Jack be quick" they can jump over the candlestick at the appropriate moment. Very young children can pretend to be Humpty Dumpty falling off the wall, Little Miss Muffet sitting on her tuffet, or Little Jack Horner putting his thumb into the pie. In so doing, they are translating their impressions of the piece into action.

Upper elementary school children can participate in more sophisticated pantomiming experiences that may encourage them to be more perceptive of events and people. These experiences may be a prelude to talk activity and to the actual writing of descriptive paragraphs. For instance, a perceptive youngster may mimic the actions of—

- a young lady trying to sit down while wearing a miniskirt
- a boy trying to sneak something past his mother
- a boy who overslept and must rush to get to school on time
- a man fighting off a mosquito
- a man trying to unlock a door when both his hands are loaded with packages
- a girl who just realized her slip is showing

In acting out the ramifications of the situation, the child has a concrete referent and thereby may identify elements that would have gone unnoticed if he had begun by talking or taking pen in hand.

In *The Composite Art of Acting*, Jerry Blunt gives a description of the intricacies of pantomime that may be of value to the elementary school teacher interested in encouraging expression through pantomime. According to Blunt, the skilled pantomimist is one who perceives in a situation all the contingencies that could occur because he has studied the situation in depth and has become part of the situation himself.[5] For instance, the pantomimist who mimics the actions of a girl in a miniskirt may include the following sequence: easing into the chair; pulling down the skirt; looking around with a satisfied air; looking down; seeing the slip showing; surreptitiously

[5] Jerry Blunt, *The Composite Art of Acting* (New York: Macmillan, 1966).

tucking it under; looking up; noticing she has dropped her handkerchief; bending down with a stiff body to retrieve it; sitting up quickly as the skirt rides up; holding the skirt down; moving with a determined, deliberate motion to pick up the handkerchief.

Not all children are equally successful in pantomiming. In this activity, as well as in others, individual differences are to be expected. Yet children who become masters of the art of nonverbal communication can supply a concrete referent for the other children and can help them see the complexities of situations that appear deceptively simple when only a superficial examination is made.

TRANSLATE IMPRESSIONS INTO DRAMATIZATIONS

Nonverbal interpretations of impressions very naturally lead to interpretations having both nonverbal and verbal components; the child simply adds words to his physical actions. In essence, this is an outgrowth of the child's normal creative-play activity. The young child simulates aspects of the world around him in his play activity. He plays house, school, and subway, and as he does, he melds actions with words. The teacher can engineer similar situations that encourage children to express their feelings and ideas dramatically as a base for eventual or parallel expression in written form.

Since the purpose is for children to express themselves freely and to experience the varied dimensions of a situation, no written script for this type of dramatization is required. Rather, each child improvises, moving from some notion of the character he is assuming to a portrayal of how that character would act in a particular situation. The result might be an action-conversation skit that is based on actual experiences encountered by the child in everyday living.

For instance, working with fifth-grade inner-city children who tended to define misery in terms of discrimination, a teacher divided his class into subgroups of four. The subgroups met briefly to decide what characters they would be in their action-conversation skits; they identified the Boy, the Shopkeeper, the Cop, and the Passerby. They talked about what could happen to these characters. Then each group created a story not in written but in on-the-spot dramatic form.

Humorous action-conversation skits on topics of current interest may be improvised in the same way by upper elementary school children. For example, working with ideas related to the preservation of the environment, children can project the action-conversation—

- between the lungs of a man who is smoking a cigarette and the man himself;
- among three fish and a turtle that live in a polluted river;

- among a garbage can, a man who has just littered, and a metal soda can;
- between Smoky the Bear and two boys who are building a campfire;
- among three pelicans watching an oil slick come toward them;
- among three birds sitting on a roof as they smell the foul gasses from a nearby chimney.

Dramatizations related to the social-science content of the curriculum can also be used to encourage free expression of ideas as a step toward eventual or parallel expression of ideas in written form. Broad topics that can be opened to dramatic improvisations include life (1) with the Indians, Eskimos, Egyptians, (2) in the Middle Ages, (3) at Valley Forge with Washington, (4) on a slave plantation, (5) in Plymouth, and (6) on the frontier.

Children can approach a broad topic by associating it with the problems inherent in survival within communities—problems of—

- securing food, water, and shelter
- determining governmental structure
- achieving freedom
- replacing war with peace
- overcoming threats from outside the community
- providing transportation
- maintaining good health.

Within the context of the specific situation dramatized, such concepts as freedom, peace, and government have a concrete base. Therefore, a child can work with the concepts in a more meaningful way, expressing ideas that he might not have been able to perceive if he had begun on the abstract level.

INVOLVE CHILDREN WITH PUPPETS

A device commonly used to encourage children to express themselves freely in dramatic contexts is puppetry. The child who may be a tongue-tied performer can lose his inhibitions when he is hidden behind a box, screen, or mask; it is the puppet who is talking, not he, so the verbal and nonverbal expression takes on new dimensions of creativity.

Generally speaking, puppets need not be overly complicated to be effective. Sometimes the most effective puppet is the one that can be made rather quickly to supplement ideas that begin to develop and need to be expressed in the immediate context. Styrofoam balls about an inch and a half to two inches in diameter can serve as a basic material from which to construct simple finger puppets. With colored felt pens the child can add ears, nose, eyes, mouth, and facial expressions. A bow tie made of string, a ribbon, yarn pigtails, shaggy ears, a mustache, and a paper hat can all be affixed with straight pins. On one's finger, the puppet can become anything or anyone the child imagines. Manipulated from behind a desk, one or more puppets can be used to tell a story.

Stick puppets are similarly adaptable. Faces, animals, people, and objects can be cut from heavy construction paper and colored with crayon or felt pen. Pictures can also be cut from magazines and mounted on construction paper. These materials are stapled on sticks to form the characters and scenery required in telling the story. The sticks can simply be discards from ice-cream bars, tongue depressors, or even plastic soda straws. Again the puppet can be manipulated from below the level of a desk, or a simple puppet stage can be constructed from a shoe box by cutting a slit along one side of the box and moving the puppets along the slit. (See Figure 2-1.)

Very much like stick puppets are head puppets. The child makes a mask and holds that mask over his own face during the dramatization, which gives him the feeling of actually being that character. He can begin by cutting a circle from lightweight cardboard, perhaps using the bottom of the wastebasket as a pattern. With scissors he cuts out ears, eyes, nose, and mouth. With felt pen he adds color. Little time is consumed in the construction process; the child rather rapidly has a puppet through which he can more freely translate his impressions into both words and actions.

Slightly more time-consuming to construct is the body puppet. The child stretches out on a very large piece of construction paper while another child sketches his outline on the paper, leaving approximately two inches of additional paper beyond the perimeters of the body. The child then colors in features and clothing that will be required for the dramatization, and he staples strips of heavy-grade cardboard to the back of the arms, legs, and head for support. He holds his puppet by the central support, using it to cover his entire body. Another way to achieve a similar result is to use large cartons. A hole can be cut in the top, out of which the child sticks his head. Holes can be cut on both sides, out of which the child's hands can be extended. There is no bottom in the box. The child again colors his puppet to meet the needs of the dramatization.

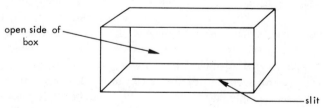

open side of box

slit

Figure 2-1. *Shoe box puppet stage.*

One of the simplest kinds of puppets to use in dramatizations is the type made from a small-sized paper bag. Pieces of construction paper can be affixed to the flap of the bag to simulate hair and to the sides to simulate ears. Features can be drawn using crayon or felt pen. The child then slips the puppet over his hand and is ready to take his part.

The expression of impressions with puppets is often more meaningful to the youngster than the translation of impressions into a form of written communication. The child is involved in action at a time in his development when action is a most significant aspect of experience. He is placed *within* the situation, which is important to the egocentric child whose center of the world is himself.

talk as a means of expressing experience

On the facade of the Royal Oak Hotel in Keswick in the Lake District of England is a plaque bearing this inscription:

> This ancient hostelry, formerly the Oak Inn, has been from the days of Queen Elizabeth the centre of the commercial activities and social life of Keswick. The headquarters in the 18th century of a thriving packhorse trade, this inn became subsequently, no less renowned as a posting establishment and halting place for stage coaches. No less celebrated are the literary associations of this house, for it was frequented by Robert Southey, Samuel Taylor, Hartley Coleridge, the Wordsworths, Shelley, Thomas De Quincey, Christopher North, and other Lake Land poets and writers. Here Sir Walter Scott wrote part of his "Bridal of Triermain" and here too Lord Tennyson and Robert Louis Stevenson were visitors, while the "Skiddaw Hermit" and John Peel of hunting fame were frequently to be seen within its walls.

The Coleridges, Wordsworths, and Shelleys came to inns such as the Royal Oak because there they could talk about their experiences and their impressions. After solitary walks amid the lakes and hills, a writer could share his ideas with others who were similarly attuned to the beauty of the countryside. Warmed by a crackling fire and encouraged by companionship with friends, a man could mentally play with his impressions as he expressed them. His embryonic ideas could snowball and gather substance.

Children can gain even more from talking about their experiences than did the Coleridges and Wordsworths. For them the oral sharing of impressions is an important first step in the process of translating ideas into the verbal patterns of written expression. This is essential for the young child. At a stage in his development in which he is more concerned with actions than he is with words, he needs considerable experience in handling his ideas expressed in verbal form. To ask a child to put thoughts on paper before having the opportunity just to talk about them is almost asking more of a child than he can deliver. For this reason, talking experiences are a vital part of any writing program; talk lessons are essentially preliminary writing lessons.

CONVERSATION

Talk with a child, as a means of encouraging the expression of impressions, need not be a formal activity; just the opposite can be true. The teacher meets a child with conversation as he comes into the class in the morning, she chats with him in the playground, and she talks with him as she circulates during seatwork periods. Topics of conversation are those that are part of the experiences of the child and that have meaning for him at his stage of development. How is your new baby sister? What did you like most about your trip to the beach? Is your mother feeling better? Did you like running through the snow on your way to school this morning? When is the new baby coming? How did you feel when the lights blacked out last night? Is there still no heat in your apartment building? What did you do over the weekend? Is your cold getting better? Did you like the puppet program on TV last night? Did you see *The Grinch Who Stole Christmas* last night on television? What do you think about it? How is your dog Wilbur?

Conversation with the teacher is significant too for the older elementary school child, although the topics become broader and less focused on the child himself. What do you think of the latest moon landing? Who do you think will win the World Series? Why? Have you been following the election for——? Whom do you support? How did you enjoy the camping overnight? Did you like that biography of Martin Luther King that you just finished? Would you like to read another book by Konigsburg?

A child who does not have the advantage of conversation with adults within his home environment has a special need for conversation in school. When parents do not have time to listen, when they do not realize the importance of talking with their child, or when a child has little contact with a parent figure, the child may have almost no ability to create ideas to communicate verbally. This child is idea-disadvantaged and can benefit from informal conversation with the teacher.

Conversation with fellow students can also aid in the exploration of an idea. Dividing the students into conversation-pairs is one approach to encourage talk. Each child has his own conversation-mate, and time is set aside during the day for the mates to talk about some feeling or impression they have had. The teacher can suggest talk-topics with which the conversation can begin:

- One thing I didn't like in school today
- What I'm going to do after school
- An argument that I had with someone

- What happened to me on the way to school
- What my brother (sister, mother, father, dog, cat) did
- The coming election, ballgame, or moon landing
- A program I saw on TV
- A book I read
- A place where I'm going
- What it's like in my apartment house
- My favorite person; or
- Something I saw that I didn't like.

If children deviate from the suggested topic, the teacher should not consider her talk-time unsuccessful. The children have identified areas in which they have thoughts to express, and that, after all, is the ultimate goal.

Conversation among children on a less formal basis can also produce ideas. We observed a student teacher who had children make "Rorschach" ink blots from yellow and blue paint blobs pressed against the folds of a piece of paper. The children were asked to study their blobs and write about what they perceived. Almost automatically, children at adjacent tables began to share ideas, and the exchange encouraged some children to think more deeply and more creatively. To have required silence in the room at this stage of writing would have been less productive.

INFORMAL DISCUSSION

Informal discussions with the whole class can also stimulate children to express their impressions of a common experience. For instance, upon returning from a nature walk through the park in the fall, one teacher encouraged oral consideration of the experience with the following questions:

Auditory Sense
What sounds did you hear when you kicked the leaves?
What sounds did the leaves make as they fell to the ground?
What sounds did you hear when you picked up a large pile of leaves and threw them high up into the air
How did these two sounds differ?
What kinds of things make similar sounds?
When we stood perfectly still, what other sounds did you hear?

Visual Sense
How did the trees look in the woods?
What colors were the leaves?
Did some kinds of leaves look different from others?
What other things on our walk looked about the same?

Sense of Touch
  How did the leaves feel when you touched them?
  How did they feel along the edges and surface areas?
  How did they feel different?
  What other things did you feel in the woods?
  How did these things feel in comparison to what you felt when you picked
    up a leaf?

Sense of Smell
  What odors did you smell in the woods?
  How did the odor of the leaves compare to the odors of wild flowers?
  How do odors you smell in your kitchen compare to those you smell in the
    woods?

Through this type of questioning the teacher helped the boys and girls
sharpen their perceptions and encouraged them to translate into words their
impressions of the world around them.

Another teacher used her discussion period as a prelude to actual
written expression. She took her fifth-grade class for a "wind walk" to feel
the wind that was blowing rather fiercely that day. When they returned, the
children talked in detail about how the wind made them feel, what they saw
the wind doing, and how the wind sounded. Then they paired off in groups
of two to write just one line that began "Wind blows——." The lines were
put together to form a cooperative poem:

  Wind blows big gusts against our faces.
  Wind blows our skirts in whirls around our legs.
  Wind blows into our jackets and turns them into balloons.
  Wind blows so hard it lifts us off our feet and carries us running down the
    street.
  Wind blows into the trees and turns the branches into dancing arms.
  Wind blows around corners to make whistle sounds.
  Wind blows big slaps of air all around.
  Wind blows.
  Wind blows.

Two groups of children produced only the words that the teacher had given.
Their lines became a simple refrain.

John Neill, a student-teacher working in an urban school, tried a
similar technique. Fifth-grade students talked about times "when they felt
absolutely miserable." They orally shared experiences, and then each child
wrote a line that began "Misery is——." Later the class put the lines together
to build a poem.

  Misery is being sick.   *Darren*
  Misery is when a girl is sitting next to you and smacking gum.   *Vance*
  Misery is when your big brother picks on you for something you
    didn't do.   *Deborah*

Misery is when your money to get an ice cream drops down a
crack.   *Rene*

Misery is when you can't have your own way.   *Judy*

Misery is when you go to school in slippers.   *Bobbi*

Misery is when you take a bath and still come out dirty.   *Michael*

Misery is being bossed around.   *Sandra*

Misery is when a white boy calls your dog "Blackie" and you
don't have a dog.   *David*

Misery is when you have to do homework.   *Kevin*

Misery is someone always talking in the classroom.   *Kim*

Misery is when my baby brother kicks me in the eye.   *Erwin*

Misery is when I do something wrong and get a spanking.   *Alzera*

Misery is when a car splashes water on you.   *Timothy*

Misery is when you get a new bike and someone takes it.   *William*

Misery is when you can't have a new bike.   *Marvell*

Misery is when my mother has another baby and it's a boy.   *Donna*

Misery is when the ponytail in your hair won't stay.   *Pat*

Misery is when someone is prejudiced.   *Robin*

In the upper elementary grades, youngsters can talk about impressions in groups of three, four, or five. These group-talk experiences can be structured simply by the teacher, who can supply a talk-guide for groups that have not operated independently before. After a walk on city streets, for instance, the talk-guide might include the following:

1. List all the noises you heard.
2. Next to each noise list three words or three phrases you could use to describe the noise.
3. Decide whether the noises were pleasant or unpleasant.
4. Noise pollution means that the environment is being spoiled by too many extremely unpleasant noises. What steps can be taken to overcome noise pollution?

This type of small group discussion can be used as a prelude to writing activity. After students talk for five to ten minutes about the problem of noise pollution, they can write a piece describing the kinds of noises that spoil the environment, what can be done to cut down on noise pollution, or their personal reactions to noise in the environment.

Book-sharing sessions with small groups can be conducted in a similar manner. If all the youngsters in the group have read the same book or seen the same movie or TV show, they can share impressions and try cooperatively to develop a general reaction to the book, film, or TV show. Again, for groups that have had little experience in independent discussion, the teacher can supply a discussion format for a book and/or show that might include the following items:

1. Have each group member describe an incident in the book or TV show that he either liked or disliked.
2. Talk about whether there were more incidents that most of the group members liked or more incidents that they disliked.
3. Decide whether you would recommend to a friend that he read the book or see the show.

Informal discussion with individual children involved in an actual writing activity can also have positive results. Discussion may cause a child to go beyond superficial consideration to look for the more unusual impression. A boy in the fourth grade made a creative drawing with string dipped in green ink and swirled across the page. As he looked at his art work, trying to find an idea about which to write, the teacher walked by and asked, "What do you see?"

He responded, "Don't you see the frog sitting on the leaf?"

She replied, "Could he be sitting on something other than a leaf?"

The result was an imaginative story about a frog that jumped on a feather and blew away.

The sixth-grade girl who had vacationed at a camp in Maine and could write only that she had gone with her family and that she had played ping pong and had swum needed this type of individualized, informal discussion of ideas. She needed to explore her experience and to perceive with greater insight the details of her vacation. With this child, talk could have included:

- Tell me about the place where you went swimming.
- How did you feel when you went into the water?
- What was the water like? Cold? Deep?
- Did anything happen while you were playing in the water?
- Tell me about the people with whom you went swimming.

Any one of these questions might have stimulated a discussion that could have elicited ideas for writing and perhaps for sharing with classmates.

INFORMAL ORAL PRESENTATIONS

Mark comes into the classroom bubbling with excitement. He tells his teacher, "We have a new baby at home," or "We're going to move," or "Did you see the astronauts on television?," or "I went fishing and caught a fish this long," and he begins to elaborate. A teacher who perceives oral expression of ideas as important in its own right and as a preliminary step to expressing ideas in written form can build classroom oral activity on this child's enthusiasm for talking about events that are meaningful to him.

"Come and tell us all about it," she responds, and she gathers the other youngsters into a group to hear Mark talk about the big event in his life. The teacher interjects questions as Mark's story begins to wind down. The other children are encouraged to ask questions. In this context the oral expression of experiences is a natural component of classroom living.

Important characteristics of individual oral presentation in the elementary school are informality, naturalness, and child interest. The child with interesting ideas to share should not be required to stand up straight in front of the class; such a procedure is more likely to discourage rather than encourage the production of ideas and their verbal expression. Instead, the teacher should select and organize the props of her classroom to allow for informality in oral presentation.

With young children, she can establish a listening corner in her room, a piece of rug on which children can sit while sharing the thoughts of Mark. Perhaps Mark can be supplied with a hassock or a piano stool on which to perch as he relates his impressions. With older children, the swivel armchair made famous on television talk shows can serve the same purpose. The child with the event to share can relax in the "David Frost chair" as he talks to his classmates. For junior high school youngsters a "Perry Como" high stool is a relaxing perch from which to share ideas with fellow students.

As children move up in the elementary grades, individual oral sharing of ideas may become slightly more complex, though not necessarily more formal, because of the greater complexity of ideas to be expressed. The youngster may want to think through his ideas before expressing them and have some preliminary notion of the way in which he wants to present his thoughts to his classmates. The clipboard technique is a possible aid in such a situation. The child jots down his ideas on paper, clips them to the clipboard, and refers to them as he talks from the swivel chair. Notes used for this purpose should not be detailed, but merely a skeleton of the thoughts to be expressed.

As thoughts to be expressed become more complex and children begin to want to share their ideas on environmental survival, the drug culture, discrimination, elections, or war policy, a group sharing of ideas is profitable. Children who have read rather extensively on a problem become a panel of experts on that topic. As a panel, one at a time they present their ideas, often conflicting, and respond to questions from classmates. This type of activity can serve as a prelude to actual written expression of ideas. Faced with points of view proposed by a panel of experts, youngsters can respond with a written paragraph or two on their personal points of view or on a related topic.

experiences, action, and talk

In summary, a writing program has three foundational dimensions. First, children need experiences on which to base their ideas, which in turn

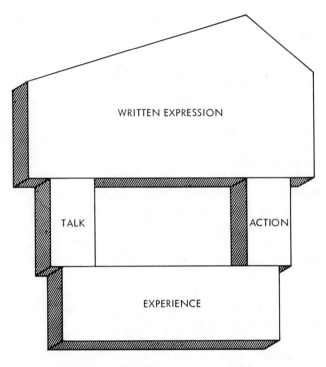

will be the content of their written expression. A writing program has as its underlying framework activities that supply children with experiences that encourage them to react to their environment with all their senses. Second, children need help in expressing their impressions of first-hand experience. For the young child who perceives things of action as a significant aspect of the environment, this means that a writing program begins with a translation of impressions into the action of nonverbal and dramatic experience. Third, since the child needs help in verbalizing ideas, a major dimension of a complete writing program is oral expression of thought in conversation, discussion, and informal presentations. Above is a schematic depicting the three building blocks of a writing program.

let children
look for
ideas

First-hand experience can be the spark that ignites an idea. In addition, meaningful activities structured by the teacher and thoughts encountered in reading and listening can serve as the spark. Chapter 3 proposes ways that teachers can organize motivating activities and can encourage children to search for ideas.

structured activities

We can all recall an occasion when a specific suggestion offered by someone else proved to be the inspiration for an idea. The suggestion seemed to trigger a train of thought that otherwise would not have occurred. As teachers, we can use many types of suggestion to help children formulate ideas for writing. We can structure idea-stimulating activities through use of pictures, music, literature, characters, objects, titles, words, trips, news-worthy events, world and school issues, and the content of the sciences and social sciences.

PICTURES

For the cover of one Sunday's magazine section, the former *New York Herald Tribune* printed pictures of the eyes of different animals. One picture was easily identifiable as the eyes of a fish; the others could be perceived by children as the eyes of almost any animal. A fourth-grade teacher suggested that the children study the pictures and pretend to see the world through the eyes of one of the animals. She motivated some exceptionally good written work in this way. Another teacher found that reproductions of modern abstract art achieved a similar result. A third teacher, adept at photography, took some rather unusual 35mm slides of pebbles, water trickling down a windowpane, puddles, railroad tracks, jet trails in the sky, froth on beer, footprints in the sand, and ripple marks on a beach, and she used them to test the power of suggestion. These examples seem to indicate that the unusual picture is especially effective as a structured situation to trigger ideas for writing. Individuals can bring their unique backgrounds into the situation, producing different ideas.

Children's own abstract art work can be used in much the same way. Children's finger painting, collages, ink blobs smeared across a page, or creative sculpture in metal or glass can inspire written ideas.

Film, too, can stimulate writing. The National Film Board of Canada has produced a film entitled *The Loon's Necklace* that relates an imaginative folk explanation of how the loon acquired the beautiful spotted collar around its neck. Children who have viewed that film have gone on to volunteer creative explanations (see Figure 3-1, for example) about how the red-headed woodpecker got its cap, how the crow got its caw, how the shunk got its stripe, how the turtle found its home, how the elephant earned his trunk, and how the toad learned to hop. Reacting to the film, Michael Liss, a third-grade boy, wrote:

How the Octopus Got Long Arms

One day an octopus was looking around. He found a whirl pool and before he knew it, he was stuck in it. A boat was over him so he put his arms on the boat and the boat pulled one way and the whirl pool pulled the other way. His arms stretched so much he could never pull them in again. That's how the octopus got such long arms.

Paddle-to-the-Sea, a book by Holling C. Holling (Boston: Houghton Mifflin, 1941), has been produced on film by the National Film Board of Canada. The film tells the story of the adventures of a little homemade toy boat that was carried by the current through the Great Lakes down to the mouth of the St. Lawrence River. At the end, the film suggests that the little boat is going on to further adventures, perhaps in the fjords of Norway or in some other distant place. Children can react by inventing what might happen next to the boat that is called Paddle-to-the-Sea.

Films like *Paddle-to-the-Sea* that have been based on children's books have a definite place in the writing program; they tickle ears, eyes, and imagination, and many of the films available are of a high quality. Those from Weston Woods are a particularly exciting means of stimulating thinking. Children can write reflective content after seeing and hearing Robert McCloskey's *Time of Wonder* (New York: Viking Press, 1957) on a Weston

Figure 3-1. *"How the Frog Got His Spots," a story by Diane Ginter, a second-grader.*

Woods film; they can describe what a storm is like, report on a vacation they have taken, or summarize the story. After seeing and hearing Claire Bishop's *The Five Chinese Brothers* (New York: Coward, 1938), children can write expressive content in which they state opinions about whether the five brothers were dishonest. After seeing and hearing Marjorie Flack's *The Story of Ping* (New York: Viking Press, 1933), first-grade children can invent and write other stories about Ping.

The sound filmstrips that Weston Woods (Weston, Connecticut) produces can be used in much the same fashion. The selection and possibilities for written content are extensive.

The Red Carpet—lower elementary children can write inventive content: What happened to the red carpet when the astronauts came to town?

Mike Mulligan and His Steam Shovel—middle elementary children can write conceptual content: Why did Mary Ann lose her usefulness?

The Camel Who Took a Walk—lower elementary children can write projective content: What would have happened if the Lady Camel had not turned around?

Hercules—middle elementary children can write inventive content: the story of another object that outlived its usefulness.

Make Way for Ducklings—lower elementary children can write reflective content: an experience the mother duckling had with her babies.

Lentil—middle elementary grade children can write expressive content: Would you like Lentil for a friend? Why?

In addition, there are filmed materials such as *Let's Write a Story,* by Churchill Films that are designed and organized to encourage children to produce inventive idea-content. Open situations are projected to which children can bring their own background as they react with ideas. Youngsters in third, fourth, and fifth grades react well to this film, which takes them to an amusement park and along a beach with a friendly little dog as a companion.

MUSIC AND LITERATURE

"Ebb Tide" makes one feel as if one is standing in the sand, watching the sea race in and out. George Gershwin's *An American in Paris* brings one the sound of taxi horns in Paris. In Tchaikovsky's *1812 Overture,* one hears the cannons of war. One eighth-grade class produced some of its best written work in reaction to Ferde Grofés *Grand Canyon Suite.* The youngsters really felt as if they were standing in the desert, witnessing a rising storm and the quiet that follows. They enjoyed the musical suggestion so much that they told their friends in other sections about their experiences and these students asked their teachers if they too could "write from the Grand Canyon."

Less sophisticated musical selections also have the potential to stimulate ideas. Little songs like "The Dipsy Doodle Dragon" and "The Unicorn," recorded by Peter Pan Records, are effective with younger children. These songs describe the dragon or the unicorn in such a way that the child is encouraged to invent a story about the imaginary animal. The words from such songs as "My Favorite Things" can also prove to be an idea-triggering suggestion for some children. After singing about favorite things, a child can let his imagination fly free and write about his unusual favorite things.

A little poem like "The Bug" by Ailene Fisher can stimulate children to talk about what they have wondered.[1] After listening to the piece, one second-grade group wrote a poem about their wonderment:

I've Wondered

I've wondered why the grass is green.
I've wondered how the nighttime comes.
I've wondered why my baby brother always cries.
I've wondered why I'm always wrong.

Such stories as *Madeline* by Ludwig Bemelmans (New York: Viking Press, 1939), *Homer Price* by Robert McCloskey (New York: Viking Press, 1943), *Pippi Longstocking* by Astrid Lindgreen (New York: Viking Press, 1950), and *It's Like This, Cat* by Emily Neville (New York: Harper & Row, 1963), have main characters who are truly individuals, and can suggest ideas for inventive content. What other trouble could Madeline get into? What other things could Homer concoct? What else could happen to Pippi? The

---

[1] Aileen L. Fisher, "A Bug," in *The Coffee-Pot Face* (New York: The Junior Literary Guild and Robert M. McBride and Company, 1933), p. 51.

answer may be a plot for a story. A teacher can also read a story to her class and stop before reading the ending. "What do you think is going to happen?" she can query. "Let's write our own ending."

Children can also write expressive content as a reaction to stories they have read. We can ask upper-elementary grade children such questions as: Would you like Madeline for your friend? Why? Was it right for Juan de Pareja (Elizabeth Borton de Treviño, *I, Juan de Pareja* [New York: Bell Books, 1965]) to be treated as he was? Is *And to Think That I Saw It on Mulberry Street* (New York: Vanguard, 1957) as good a Dr. Seuss book as *Horton Hatches the Egg* (New York: Random House, 1940)? This type of question may spark a reaction in a one-paragraph paper written individually or by a total class that has heard a story.

The same kinds of critical questions can be directed at poetry and music. Rather than frowning upon the child who rejects a particular poem, the teacher can help the child explore his reasons for disliking it. The dislike may become a well-formed idea for written expression. Likewise, a child's dislike for a musical composition may be the nucleus of an idea. To dislike the *Grand Canyon Suite* is a perfectly valid reaction. The reaction is also an idea to be expressed in composition.

Thinking about stories they have read, children can also write the idea-content that is classed as reflection. Children can tell in their own words an incident in a story. Books that are episodical, composed of separate stories about a main character, are effective stimuli in this context. For example, the children in grades four or five can retell a happening in one of the following stories:

Eleanor Estes' *The Middle Moffat* (New York: Harcourt Brace Jovanovich, 1942),
Robert McCloskey's *Homer Price* (New York: Viking Press, 1939),
P. L. Travers's *Mary Poppins* (New York: Harcourt Brace Jovanovich, 1934),
Beverly Cleary's *Henry Beezus* (New York: William Morrow, 1952).

Marguerite, a fifth-grade girl, retold one chapter of *A Wrinkle in Time* by Madeleine L'Engle (New York: Ariel, 1962) in her review:

One day a boy named Calvin O'Keefe was delivering newspapers at the most unusual house. It was owned by Mrs. Whasit. Meg and Charles Wallace were approaching the house to discuss a matter. Suddenly and mysteriously they were propelled into her house. She had two other friends called Mrs. Who and Mrs. Which. Right in front of their eyes they changed like magic. Then they told Charles and Meg that they would help them find their father. For this they had to go into the 5th dimension of space called tesseract or a Wrinkle in Time.

Reviews like Marguerite's can be shared with other youngsters who may decide that they too would like to enter the fifth dimension.

Chrissy Frassinelli.   April. 27, 1971

Pippy Longstocking was nine years old.
She lived alone in a little yellow
house.
She had good climing trees if
you ever wonted to cline trees.

Figure 3-2. *A child's picture and composition motivated by the reading of* Pippi Longstocking.

Upper-grade children can describe a character in a book. They can write character sketches of—

Jennifer in E. L. Konigburg's *Jennifer, Hecate, Macbeth, William McKinley, and Me, Elizabeth* (New York: Atheneum, 1967),

Long John Silver in Robert Louis Stevenson's *Treasure Island* (New York: Charles Scribner's, 1911),

Charlotte in E. B. White's *Charlotte's Web* (New York: Harper & Row, 1952),

Sara in Betsy Byars' *The Summer of the Swans* (New York: Viking, 1970),

Claudia in E. L. Konigburg's *From the Mixed-up Files of Mrs. Basil E. Frankweiler* (New York: Atheneum, 1968), and

the girl who lives on Scott O'Dell's *Island of the Blue Dolphins* (Boston: Houghton Mifflin, 1960).

They can summarize stories such as—

Elizabeth Enright's *The Saturdays* (New York: Holt, Rinehart & Winston, 1940), *The Four Story Mistake* (New York: Holt, Rinehart & Winston, 1942), or *Then There Were Five* (New York: Holt, Rinehart & Winston, 1944),

E. C. Spykman's *A Lemon and a Star* (New York: Harcourt Brace Jovanovich, 1955) or *The Wild Angel* (New York: Harcourt Brace Jovanovich, 1957),

Marjorie K. Rawlings's *The Yearling* (New York: Scribner's, 1938).

THINGS

Specific objects brought into or made in the classroom have the potential to trigger ideas.

Hats.   Make a collection of hats: a helmet from World War II, a football-player's helmet, a beret, a bridal headpiece, a mountaineer's hat, a black fedora, a wide-brimmed Mexican sunhat. In discussions with the class, encourage the children to think about the possible stories that the World War II helmet could tell. Ideas can be expressed orally. Then each child may select one of the other hats as the object of his writing.

Coins.   Borrow a collection of coins from exotic countries: Thailand, Turkey, India, and Austria. Give the children time to look at the coins. Then talk about one coin—"The Indian Rupee's Tale." Each child may select one of the other coins as the object of his writing.

Pollutants.   Assemble objects or representations of objects that pollute —a light bulb, a model car, a cigarette, a model airplane, a bottle of insecticide, a box of detergent. With the children, talk about how each of these materials adds to the pollution of the environment. Each student tries to think of one practical idea for conserving the environment and writes a paragraph expressing his idea. Children who individually have trouble thinking of an idea are grouped into idea-pairs to write a paragraph together.

Bags.   Collect different kinds of bags: an orange bag, a beach bag, an airline bag, a hat bag, a garbage bag, a grocery bag, a bag bearing a foreign label. Children can talk about what these bags have seen and where they have been. Ideas stimulated in discussion are recorded in written form.

Miscellaneous objects.   Place a heterogeneous assortment of objects in a grab bag. Without looking at what they are selecting, children choose three or four items from the bag. The children must invent a story around these items. This activity can be carried on individually or in groups; the written activity can be preceded by improvised dramatics or talk.

Examples of objects that may be placed in the grab bag are a piece of cellophane, a ping-pong ball, a carrot, a marble, a glove, a coin, a twig, a feather, a raisin, a bill for a pair of shoes, a used bus ticket, a piece of cotton, a comb, a spoon, a paper clip, a calling card. To lead toward the activity and build interest, have the bag available for a period of several days; children can bring in objects to be included.

A collection of taped commercials.   Tape a series of radio commercials. Play the tapes to an upper elementary class. Students talk about some of the techniques used by writers of commercials. They devise a list of products to be advertised: Oh Ho, a new breakfast food; Caterpillar, a low-slung sportscar; Zing, a new toothpaste; Cho-Chunk, a new candy bar. They work in groups to write commercials that they intersperse in a radio program they may be producing.

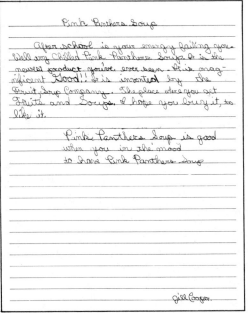

Figure 3-3.   *A commercial written by Jill Cooper, a fifth-grader.*

CHARACTERS

The characters children have met as friends on television or in cartoons can spark ideas for writing. Children know how cartoon characters operate, and they know what these characters typically say. It is, therefore, rather easy to take their friends on further adventures. This is particularly true for young children who have spent many hours watching TV. The world of Snoopy, Charlie Brown, Tweetie, Bugs Bunny, Felix the Cat, and Popeye the Sailor Man is a real one to them.

Leslie, a child in kindergarten, dictated into a tape recorder her story about her friend, Bugs Bunny.

Bugs Bunny Goes South

Bugs Bunny was walking, and a duck came up and said, "Hi, pal. Are you flying South for the winter?"

"No, I am not," said Bugs Bunny. "Bunnies can't fly!"

The Duck said, "I will take you. Just hold on to my hand, and we will go." So they went to the South Pole for the winter.

Asked to tell about Oscar of Sesame Street, she dictated:

Oscar

Oscar lives in the garbage can. He sings nutty songs sometimes. He pops up out of his garbage can when other people are talking.

About Charlie Brown and Snoopy, she recorded:

Snoopy

Charlie Brown was walking one day. Snoopy came up and waved to Charlie Brown, but Charlie Brown said, "Get out of here, Snoopy," because Charlie Brown didn't want Snoopy that day.

Having worked with characters whom they know as television friends, children can be encouraged to invent stories about imaginary characters they have not encountered in film or book. Examples are—

Hippo, the River Horse,
Herman, the Hermit Crab,
Lester, the Lonely Lobster,
Jennifer, the Jumping Green Grasshopper,
Freddie, the Talking Blue Parrot,
Leopold, the Lion Who Curled His Hair,
Agile, the Acrobatic Spider.

Names of animals can also be printed on slips of paper: the gorilla, the bear, the duck, the horse, the bee, the ant, the rhino, the egret, the porpoise, the woodpecker. Children select two slips of paper by reaching into a character grab bag. Around the two animals they must concoct a yarn. The result at times can be amusing as gorilla meets bee or duck encounters rhino.

Mix-and-match puppets lead to a similar activity. Youngsters in groups select four characters from a list of characters they have been building all week: a hippie, a hold-up man, a grandmother, a witch, a human umbrella, a mixed-up horse, a policeman, a good fairy, a rabbi, a little girl, a laughing loon. Children in groups make paper-bag puppets, write a puppet show, rehearse, and "do their thing" for the rest of the class.

TITLES

Some children can take off into the realm of invention when given a push by a title that catches their imagination or that relates to some aspect of real-life experience. Not all titles will spark imagination in all children; titles relevant for one child may "turn off" other children. The list given below, therefore, is only suggestive of areas that may appeal to children. A teacher can use it as a basis for devising her own list.

Help! The World Is Cracking!	Foul Ball
The Night the Clocks Stopped	Run!
Caught in a Trap	Street Fight
Smoke in the Forest	Man on the Moon
The Ghost Who Lived over the Bedpost	Lion on the Loose
One Drop More	Overdose of Heroin
Panic or Pleasure	Pollution Does Us In
We Made Headlines!	I'll Get Even
Hurricane Alert	Run for Your Life!
Knocked Out in the Fourth Round	Champion in the Ring
All Alone	Lost in the Crowd
Stand Up and Be Counted	Lost in the Woods
Friend or Enemy?	Excitement at the Station
No School Today	I'm a Man
My Gang—the Greatest!	Left Out

One way to handle the title approach to written expression is to construct an eye-appealing bulletin board that can be captioned "In the Mood To Invent?" A box of cards is attached to the board; each card in the box bears a title. In his free time, a child may go through the cards and select one on which he wants to write. When he finishes a story that he personally likes, he pins it to the bulletin board. Every few days the teacher and a committee of students replenish the supply of cards in the box. Which cards "sell" gives some indication of where student interest lies.

WORD BULLETIN BOARDS

The teacher who finds that her children react positively to bulletin-board motivation can reorganize the activity just described to focus on words that can be combined and recombined in different idea-stimulating patterns. "Help Yourself to an Idea!" the bulletin-board caption read in one fifth-grade classroom. Over a large pink bull-shaped pocket affixed to the board and filled with possible descriptive word-cards was the subcaption "Descriptive Word Bullpen." Over a similar orange-colored pocket filled with possible object word-cards was the caption "Object Word Bullpen." During free work periods, children reached into the pockets to draw out words they could combine to make a story.

> **Descriptive words:** *running, playful, frightened, brave, noisy, shy, lazy, mixed-up, shrewd, unhappy, oversized, lost, fantastic, soft, coughing, tired, wordy, hungry, forgetful, worn-out, sneezing, talking, naughty, walking, foolish, hopping, strange, tiny, friendly.*
>
> **Object words:** *football, piano, spring, furnace, ant, whale, balloon, watermelon, radiator, elephant, fly, mosquito, nut cracker, nickel, dime, dollar bill, spoon, doorbell, river, baseball bat, apple tree, light bulb, banana, water faucet, elevator, rocket ship, violin, toad, horse.*

In this activity, children may select as many different words as they want. They may take one object word and one descriptive word, two descriptive words, two object words, or two descriptive words and one object word, building word combinations that are rather far-out: the worn-out, sneezing whale; the playful spring and the noisy watermelon; or the football, the banana, and the water faucet.

Another variation of this activity moves an "Action Word Bullpen" onto the bulletin board in addition to the descriptive words and object words or in place of the "Descriptive Word Bullpen":

> **Action words:** *galloped, burst, chattered, tripped, flew, froze, acted, leaped, hatched, blossomed, laughed, smashed, prayed, ripped, yelled, whispered, careened, roared, slid, crept, cried, smiled.*

Again the children build their own combinations by drawing word-cards from the pens.

Word phrases can be lettered on elongated cards and attached to a similar type of participatory bulletin board called "Pick a Pair." The word pairs can be combinations of verbs: *ripped* and *roared, slipped* and *slid, ranted* and *raved, tumbled* and *twisted, huffed* and *puffed, zipped* and *zoomed.* The pairs can be adjective combinations: *sleek* and *smooth, slow* and *steady, creepy* and *crafty, cold* and *clammy, tough* and *terrible, rough* and *tumble.* The pairs can even be object words that carry on make-believe dialogue: *the kangaroo* and *the ostrich, the water buffalo* and *the fish, the iron* and *the dish towel, the pelican* and *the eagle, the skate* and *the ski, the lawn mower* and *the horse, the bicycle* and *the baboon, the moose* and *the antelope, the lead pipe* and *the umbrella, the organ grinder* and *the apple.*

As children complete a story in reaction to a phrase, they may, if they wish, mount their product on the board. If the display copy of all stories is written on paper the same size, one story can be placed on top of the one previously displayed, turning the series into a book of short stories that children can read at their leisure and that can be sent to other classes to be shared with other children.

OCCASIONS

Although adults enjoy holiday occasions, most children are absolutely enthralled by them. They count the days until Halloween, look forward to their birthdays, and build excitement in anticipation of a coming Hanukkah or Christmas celebration. Their birthdays, Thanksgiving, Valentine's Day, Christmas, Hanukkah, Halloween, the fourth of July, Rosh Hashana, and the New Year are high points in their year. Teachers can build writing activities upon this natural excitement of childhood. Occasions can be used to trigger almost every kind of writing activity.

Reports. A birthday child is asked to write about one exciting, terrible, sad, or happy happening in his life, and later on during his day he is asked to share it with other boys and girls. He can report the "where and when" of his birth, or he can report on his life—"The Story of Me, Myself, and I." A Polaroid camera is a helpful addition to this type of writing activity. Another student in the upper grades or the teacher in the lower grades can take a birthday picture of the child, which is projected with the opaque projector when the birthday youngster shares his report with the class. The picture is attached to the finished report that goes into the classbook: "This Is Us."

As a holiday occasion approaches, older children can find out how the holiday originated. Individually or in groups, children can write reports: "Where Did Halloween Come From?" "What Does Hanukkah Mean?" "Where Did Santa Claus Originate.?" "Why Do People Put Up Fir Trees at Christmas?" "What Is the Meaning of Thanksgiving?"

Poetry. For Valentine's Day, children can make their own valentine cards to send to other children and to carry home as gifts. Working with red, white, and black construction paper, every child designs his own cards. Inside he tucks a verse, humorous or serious, that carries his feelings. Little poems can be written as the message within a birthday card to be sent to a relative, the teacher, or a friend. A birthday-card group can make cards to be given to each child in the class on his birthday. Likewise, children can design Hanukkah and Christmas cards to send to friends and family that carry holiday wishes in verse which the children have written either individually or as a class.

In Susan Haumacher's fifth grade class during the December holiday period, the children decided to have their own holiday fir tree that they would decorate with balls they made themselves. The balls were cut from construction paper, were covered with glitter, and contained holiday verses that the fifth-graders had written. One little girl made her tree decoration in the shape of a menorah and inscribed inside:

> Menorah
> Jewish symbol
> proudly burning candles
> like eight fireflies
> Hanukkah.
>
> LISA ROPER

Lisa also wrote inside an icicle-shaped ball:

> ice—
> frozen clear
> dripping from trees
> fun for ice skating
> slippery

Another child designed a ball in the shape of a snowflake and wrote:

> Snow
> White Flakes
> Falling to Earth
> Beautiful Crystal Ice Stars
> Winter
>
> WENDY HALSEY

Story and play. Children's interest in holidays can be channeled into writing inventive or realistic stories and plays. In many instances, children can devise their own make-believe or real topics for writing and then for sharing as the entertainment at a class holiday party. A group of children can perform a play they have written, or an individual child can read his story. One fifth-grade youngster who invented her own title wrote:

Getting It Together as Santa Mouse

Scweek, Scweek, Scweek! I'm Santa Mouse! Did you ever hear of me? I live at the North Pole with Santa Claus. I dress up just like him, except I have whiskers by my nose—you know like a dog does? On Christmas Santa yells out:

On Dasher, on Dancer, on Prancer and Vixen, on Comet, on Cupid, on Donner and Blitzen.

I'm Santa's little companion. I stick with him and the other reindeers, but most of all Rudolph. I look out that all the elves do their work correctly not

wrong. I'm busy most of the time. But I'm the one who wraps all the gifts!
Not one or two but all the gifts! I also put the goodies in your stocking!
Scweek, Scweek, Scweek!
Merry Christmas!

JUNE NEILSON

For children who have trouble getting started, the teacher can offer
holiday topics that may spark ideas for a play or a story:

Thanksgiving
The Man Who Forgot To Be
    Thankful
No Turkey This Thanksgiving
A Pilgrim Came to Our Thanks-
    giving Dinner
What the Indian Said
Turkey, Cranberry, and Pumpkin
    Pie
I Was at the First Thanksgiving

St. Valentine's Day
The Valentine Card That Got
    Lost
A Broken Heart
A Valentine Card for Me
Nobody Loves Me
Mama's Valentine Wish
A Valentine Present for Paula

Hanukkah
The Candles Wouldn't Burn
No Candles in the Window
The Fifth Candle
The Hanukkah Candles Talk

Birthdays of Lincoln, Washington, Columbus, King
He Did It!
That Was the Day
A Man Who Changed the World

Halloween
The Ghost Who Lost a Shoe
No Trick or Treat! This Year
The Friendly Witch
The Broomstick that Wouldn't Fly
    Straight
The Orange Witch
A Goblin Who Didn't Want To
    Scare

Christmas
The Man Who Lost Christmas
Coal in His Stocking
He Gave on Christmas
He Didn't Want To Be a Chrismas
    Tree
The Christmas Carol That Was
    Flat
Santa—Lost in a Blizzard

St. Patrick's Day
I Wished on a Four-Leaf Clover
A Leprechaun Told Me
A Leprechaun Under My Bed
Leprechauns Are for Real

A Hero To Remember
One Hour in the Life of——
This Is Your Life, Mr.——

TRIPS

An actual visit to a locale may suggest a wide variety of writing
activities, letters, papers recommending a course of action, descriptive paragraphs, editorials. The visit may also provide much of the information
required for writing. Examples of trips are summarized below.

1. Visit any kind of industrial or commercial enterprise of unusual interest, such as a store that displays and sells Oriental rugs, an inn that dates
from Revolutionary or Civil-War days and retains some of the original flavor,
an antique shop, an airport for small planes, or a tree nursery. Suggest that
each child look for one thing that strikes his fancy or that he dislikes. Upon
returning to the classroom, have the children write:

- a thank-you letter to the manager;
- a letter to a student who did not make the trip, describing one aspect of the trip that was especially liked or disliked;
- a paper recommending how the trip could be improved another year;
- a paper describing a weakness or strength that the child sees in the enterprise.

2. Visit a geological or biological site, such as an area where erosion is rapidly eating away the land, an area where a forest fire has wreaked havoc, a river that shows obvious signs of pollution, an area where strip mining is evident, or an area where factories are polluting the air. Ask the children, "What measures can we take to prevent continued destruction of the environment?" Have children write paragraphs suggesting solutions. If their interest is great enough, have them write a letter to the editor of a local paper, describing what was observed.

3. Visit city parks or the school grounds to observe signs of vandalism and litter. On the walk, tally the pieces of litter seen. Look for flower beds and plots of grass that have been ruined by people walking through. Look for broken statues, railings, and windows. When you return, have the children write:

- a letter to a child who did not make the trip, describing what was seen;
- a position paper outlining a point of view, which is shared with other students in the class;
- a letter of protest to a park commissioner or a local paper, suggesting possible ways of correcting the situation;
- a script for a puppet show about what elementary school students can do to prevent the destruction of school grounds and parks. Do the show for other classes.

These assignments can be carried out individually in the upper elementary grades and as a total class in the lower grades.

NEWSWORTHY EVENTS

The world in which we live is in a state of constant change. Significant events occur almost daily. Today an astronaut walks on the moon, and tomorrow an earthquake rocks southern California. One day there is a partial eclipse of the sun; the next day a new mayor is elected. These and other world events are natural ways of stimulating children to report, to retell something read in the newspaper or heard on TV, and to summarize. A discussion of an exciting event and the children's reaction to it can lead to written expression almost without a teacher's suggestion.

Events close to home are, of course, most meaningful to children. For example, a group of inner-city youngsters in an upper elementary grade came into school talking excitedly about the explosion at a nearby Standard Oil Refinery. The explosion had been strong enough to shake their homes. The children recounted what happened and what they felt at the time, and then they expressed themselves in writing. One girl wrote:

The Explosion

When the explosion happened, it was about 12 o'clock at night. My aunt lives a few blocks away, and when it happened she fell on the floor. My cousin who lives with her was watching TV when all of a sudden he fell on the floor and he got up and said, "What happened?" My aunt said that a tank of gasoline exploded, so he immediately got in his car with my aunt and went to my house. There were a lot of people coming with children in their arms. My mother said that God surely looked after us.

Sports events may give boys in an upper elementary grade ideas for writing. Many boys follow the World Series, take interest in a heavyweight championship fight, or watch the football games on television. Then too, as children of suburbia are brought up learning to ski, sail, water-ski, skate, or bowl, they may follow related sports events on television. Depending on the geographical area in which she is teaching and the social group with which she is working, a teacher may find that a boy with no interest in imaginative writing may enjoy writing reports on sports. His topic may be a national sports event or a class or school game. His report may focus on one sport rather than another. However he orients his writing, his report may be included in the class newspaper as part of the sports section.

WORLD AND SCHOOL ISSUES

With children in the upper elementary grades, a discussion of world, national, local, and school problems can spark an idea for realistic writing. Children today are becoming more aware of the issues that confront the world, and they need to develop opinions that they can support in a rational way. Some widespread problems that have potential for stimulating discussion and writing include war, dope, crime in the streets, poverty, environmental pollution, juvenile delinquency, the draft, discrimination, unemployment, taxes, and inflation. Controversial issues relevant to the local school scene that may have significance for children are school regulations, cafeteria food, school elections, homework, length of the school day, and vacations.

An older elementary school child can express his ideas on pertinent issues in a position paper that outlines his reasons—

- why we should (not) send more men to the moon;
- why reusable bottles should be required;
- why there should (not) be a volunteer army;
- why we need peace;
- why a woman should (not) be president.

A series of papers by different children on the same issue, which express different ideas, can be turned into a newsletter and distributed to other classes. Students can also write editorials in which they analyze some facet of a problem, and these can be included on the editorial page of the school

Figure 3-4. *A fourth-grade child's position paper on pollution.*

newspaper. Students can write letters to national and local leaders, communicating their ideas on an issue. A group of children can compose a petition, which they can sign and send to a person who may be able to effect change—a senator, a representative, or a governor. A group of children can also write a script for a television or radio news special that outlines the dimensions of an issue. The program can be "released" to other classes. Still another kind of purposeful writing activity is the writing of a letter to the editor of a local paper on a current issue. Doreen Kunz wrote this letter to the Bergen County *Record*:

Recycling Glass

Editor, The *Record*

I am in the fifth grade and I go to Washington School. We are studying about pollution.

I read about the Coca Cola Company's collecting bottles to help pollution. I think they are doing the right thing. In our school we are recycling bottles to help pollution.

DOREEN KUNZ
SADDLE BROOK, NEW JERSEY

Teachers whose children have developed ideas and written on relevant world issues generally agree that a preliminary discussion by the whole class is necessary. Children need experience in analyzing issues in order to understand the diverse ways of viewing an issue and to project ideas about a problem area. Tape recordings of actual radio and television newscasts, round-table discussions, and speeches on a topic can be the sparks that will generate a discussion of an issue. Using the school tape recorder, the teacher can make recordings of controversial presentations. A controversial editorial from a local newspaper, a controversial speaker, or a crisis in the school may also spark discussion on an issue. The following two unedited papers were written in reaction to a picture showing a street scene in a poorer section of New York City.

What I Feel

I feel disgusted, we have food, money, a home, and they don't, they don't have a home, food, money, they don't have jobs. I would give all my money to them. I'm just lucky I have the things they don't.

CAMERON DAGGETT

What I Feel

I feel sorry for them. They don't have any room. No houses. I feel bad. I would like to do something for them. They don't have anything. No cloths. No money to have things. They don't have good schools to go to. The fathers need jobs to surport they're family's. They don't have enough experions. They haven't learned not much. They have no money. They have no toys or jobs or even homes. They have no money to have pleasure. They're going to get sick and thin. They'll start dieing and they'll be gone. No fun no houses. They won't have a life to live for.

JANINE SHEPPARD

Sometimes children begin thinking about social issues by listing words that an issue brings to mind. City youngsters living in a high crime area decided to write about crime in the streets. One seventh-grade girl listed as words that "crime in the street" brought to mind: *killing, fighting, mugging, shooting, cursing, kick, hit, punch, rock, suicide, rapping, jump.* She went on to write:

P——'s Streets

There is a lot of killing on the streets of P——, Governor and Main. You see of everything you didn't want to see. Every body there are bars on every corner. If you walk down the street they say something to you that's why people done like to walk on the street.

HANNA

Melvin listed and spelled his words: *stabing, chocek, suicide, mugging, poison, rapping, shooting, dope, stealing.* He wrote:

Violence

1. Down on Main Street there is a lot of stealing
2. People were mugged and, pocket books were snatched
3. There are a lot of killing around town.

School issues can be the focus of writing assignments in the upper elementary grades, especially in the eighth grade, where students are increasing their awareness of the intricacies of group interaction and are showing heightened desire to be part of the decision-making process. Topics that are relevant to this age group may include "Smoking in School," "Marijuana in the Halls," "Safety in the School," and "Cafeteria Food."

Working in an inner-city junior high school, a student teacher began with a picture of a school hall scene in which an older man is confronting a younger man. The writer's task was to relate this picture to some issue in the school and suggest a story about what might have been taking place. The range of ideas, as well as what individual children read into the picture, was amazing. Each child identified an aspect of the picture with a major concern he had. Here are two unedited stories that resulted:

What Goes on in School Today

One day the principal was walking in the hall and he was going into the boys room when all of a sudden he opened the door and a boy about 6 feet tall was standing there looking straigh at him with a cigar in his mouth.

The principal said to him no smoking but the boy just ignored him so the principal kiked him out of school.

AN EIGHTH-GRADE GIRL

The Pusher

One day a boy came late to school. He was dizzy and walking like he was drunk. He had been smoking marawana. He's teacher quickly got him to the nurse, and got him to reality again. She asked him "Charlie where did you get that stuff? Is it being sold here on the play ground"? "Yes, Miss Smith, it is, a man out there told me I was his friend, he said if I took it I'd past my exams today". Quickly Miss Smith ran down to the principal's office and told him what was going on! The principal, Mr. Caufman called the police. 15 minutes later they had surrounded the playground. The dope pusher was surrounded, it was no way out. The pusher ran into the school and hide in the door frame of the boys room. The principal quickly ran to the door. "Bang" the gun had shot off the wall and hit the pusher in the leg. After that the police arrested him and took him away.

AN EIGHTH-GRADE BOY

Teachers accustomed to having youngsters write about daffodils, witches, and snow may at first be rather startled by the suggestion that young people should be expressing themselves and writing on such topics as these. Perhaps we teachers have been too much like ostriches, with our heads buried in the sand. We must perceive that if smoking, dope, and even unwanted pregnancy are part of an upper elementary student's immediate environment, these issues are the topics about which he can speak and write most meaningfully. For him they are relevant.

SCIENCE AND SOCIAL-SCIENCE CONTENT

Children actively involved in science-related investigations will find written expression a natural outgrowth of their investigation. For example, youngsters in the middle elementary grades can set up a bird-feeding investigation. They can make different kinds of food available to birds in several different ways: crumbs, squash seeds, and cooked spaghetti can be scattered on the ground; peanut butter, beef fat, and pork fat can be rubbed on the bark of a growing tree; an actual feeding platform can be constructed, and bird seed can be placed on the platform. Children, of course, keep records of what they do and what they observe. Their records will include written statements, diagrams of the birds, and charts indicating the amount of food put at each bird-feeding station. This can be organized as a group writing activity, with one youngster serving as the recorder each day.

Children in Brenda Bryant's third grade in Camden Street School in Newark, New Jersey, produced the following statements as they observed fish in an aquarium.

Our fish were living in an aquarium.
We had four fish and three died.
In our aquarium we have only one fish left. It is a red fighter fish.

Later, hypothesizing about the cause of death, they wrote:

Maybe somebody was breathing over the fish.
Maybe somebody was feeding the fishes too much food.
The fish ate all the grass in the aquarium.

In a similar manner, children involved in a study of weather can make daily excursions out-of-doors to study weather conditions, such as cloud formations, temperature, humidity, and barometric pressure. They keep graphic and written records of their observations, and they write their predictions of future weather conditions.

Children carrying on an investigation of different ways to connect dry cells in a simple circuit can also keep written and graphic records of what they do and what happens. As the children try different patterns of connections, they diagram their circuits and explain with words the results. They may even formulate conclusions that can be drawn from the investigation. Again working in groups, the children may designate one child to be the recorder.

Youngsters in the lower elementary grades are more than enthusiastic when they encounter this type of investigatory recording activity. Susan Renna, a student teacher working in a suburban area, helped her third-grade youngsters study the behavior of solutions. Groups of children were given jelly jars, spoons, and possible solutes—sugar, salt, flour, pepper. The teacher poured measured amounts of cold and hot water into the jars for each group. The children then added a teaspoon of a possible solute to a jar of cold water and a teaspoon of solute to a jar of hot water. If the added solid dissolved, they added another teaspoon of the solute. Each group worked with a different solute; each group was responsible for keeping records of what was done and what happened. After the investigatory session the groups met as a class and developed a large chart of results. Finally they decided upon a conclusion, which they wrote together.

Working from scientific investigation, children have opportunities to produce varied content: descriptions, reports, comparisons, contrasts, explanations, hypotheses, conceptual schemes, designs. The written material they produce incorporates charts, graphs, tables, and pictures that the children design to support and clarify ideas. Children just beginning to play with written expression in the lower grades can work together to produce written records. Older children can carry on individual investigations and keep individual records of their activities. Because of the number of options that exist, scientific study has much to offer an elementary school writing program.

The content of the social sciences can make a similar contribution to the formation of ideas. Having studied some phase of history, a child can gain the skills of retelling by recounting a significant event. A fifth-grade girl who had studied the journey of the Pilgrims wrote:

The Pilgrims

Some of the people of England wanted to worship in their own way. They decided to go to Holland where they had religious freedom. In Holland the young English children were learning everything the Dutch way. So they decided to go to the new world.

They planned the trip weeks before. They also asked the King if they could go, and he finally said, "Yes."

On the way over some died, but most were alive. They had many terrible storms, and many thought that they would never live through it. They finally landed. The people made friends with the Indians who taught them many things.

Writing about social-science content is feasible at most grade levels. First-graders studying about community helpers can describe in brief sentences what each community worker does. Studying about their school, children can begin by talking about what the principal does, what the nurse does, and what the secretary does; their discussion can be stimulated by such picture series as that produced by Franklin Watts, "A Trip Through a School" (16 visual teaching pictures with teacher's manual by Lee Bennett Hopkins; see p. 224 for full citation.) After talking, children can write sentences telling about the people in their school.

In the middle grades, as children study about Indians, Eskimos, and the Japanese, they can summarize their knowledge in written form. In the upper elementary grades, youngsters can begin to write explanations of events they have studied: Why do people in different areas live the way they do? Why do people in some regions change their way of life? Why is there poverty in some areas of the world?

One activity related to social science that has high student appeal and has tremendous potential to stimulate varied ideas for writing is the production of a newspaper that resembles a newspaper published during some historical period. To produce a "period newspaper" children must use their knowledge of the past to write headlines, editorials, news stories, weather reports, the ladies' page, sports news, letters to the editor, political and social cartoons, comics, advertisements, and obituaries.

A particularly impressive job was done by Adelaid Lombardi, a sixth-grade teacher who had each child in the class select a part of the newspaper's staff that he wanted to join. Even the layout of the final paper was the responsibility of one group. This group took the pieces written by the children, cut them up, and pasted them on a large, newspaper-sized, four-page mock-up of a real paper. (See Figure 3-4.) The headlines on the front page of the Revolutionary War *Daily Express* announced "Flatboats Collide." This was the lead story:

> On the Mississippi River yesterday, four flatboats collided. A witness to the accident said that the four flatboats were traveling down the Mississippi when the flatboat at the head of the line made a sudden stop. The three flatboats behind it collided into the first boat. Two of the boats sunk and the other two were broken up. Seven passengers were killed and twenty passengers were injured. The injured were taken to Fort Sink Hospital. Funeral services will be held at St. James Church. After hearing of the incident, Governor Sweeney made a law forbidding flatboats to travel close together.

Other front-page stories were "Chief Dies in War," "National Road Crosses Country," and "Grasshoppers Kill Crops." On the centerspread were the classified ads, a political cartoon entitled "Stamp Out the Stamp Act," an announcement of an opening of a fair, an announcement of marriages and engagements, and the obituaries. There was also a version of "Dear Abby" called "Dear Alexandra."

Dear Alexandra,
    My hands are lobster red. That comes from washing dishes. What can I do?
                                    Reddy

Dear Reddy,
    I know what it's like so mix some lard and blueberries together and that will solve your problem.
                                    Alexandra

Dear Alexandra,
    My mother makes me work when I want to play. I'd like to tell her without getting her mad. What can I say?
                                    Work-hard

Dear Work-hard,
    You know making a new country takes work, so bare it.
                                    Alexandra

On the back page there were several news stories and a joke called "Revere Makes Mistake."

> Yesterday Mrs. Snyder walked into the General Store and asked if they had any red coats. The salesman asked the manager if he had any red coats. Paul Revere was in the doorway. The sales manager said, "The Red Coats are coming." Mr. Revere rushed out the door, rode down hill on his horse and yelled, "The Red Coats are coming; the Red Coats are coming."

A POINT OF VIEW

When a teacher defines the dimensions of the writing program in terms of writing poetry, stories, plays, and perhaps letters, children have a restricted writing experience in the elementary grades. Neglected is the writing of expository prose—reaction papers, reviews, laboratory reports, action reports, essays, petitions, research papers—which is a form of writing necessary for success in upper high school, in college, and in some phases of adult life. For that reason, a teacher must strive for a balance between structured activities that lead to creation of inventive content and activities that lead to the content of reflection, conception, and projection. Realistic writing stimulated by trips, by newsworthy events, by world and school problems, and by study of science and social science, has as significant a place in the writing program as does inventive writing.

search in reference materials

Sometimes we assume that ideas for writing will spring fully grown from our heads with little effort on our part, even as Minerva sprang from the head of Jupiter. Such an assumption is wishful thinking when writing involves complex content, especially in the areas of science and social science. Search—the process in which a writer saturates himself in source materials related to the general topic chosen—is a preparatory foundation for formulation of complex ideas.

What is involved in the search for ideas? First, a searcher thumbs through material, scanning here, skipping there, reading in detail something that tickles an idea already beginning to take form. He gets a spark of an idea and jots it down. He marks a portion of an article to which he wants to refer again. He skims through another reference, reading only a line here and there. Then the searcher sits and thinks, juggling thoughts, putting facts together, searching for the significant thread that will give meaning to what he writes.

A report that is nothing more than a sequencing of facts lifted verbatim from an encyclopedia results from an inability to use the search process for the formulation of ideas. For some children, search has erroneously degenerated into copying paragraphs of the reference encyclopedia in a notebook or on index cards. The paragraphs copied get juggled around and

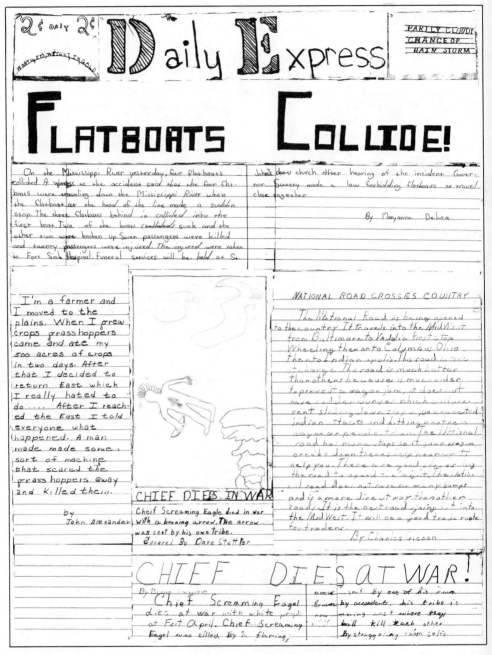

Figure 3-5. *A period newspaper by a sixth-grade class.*

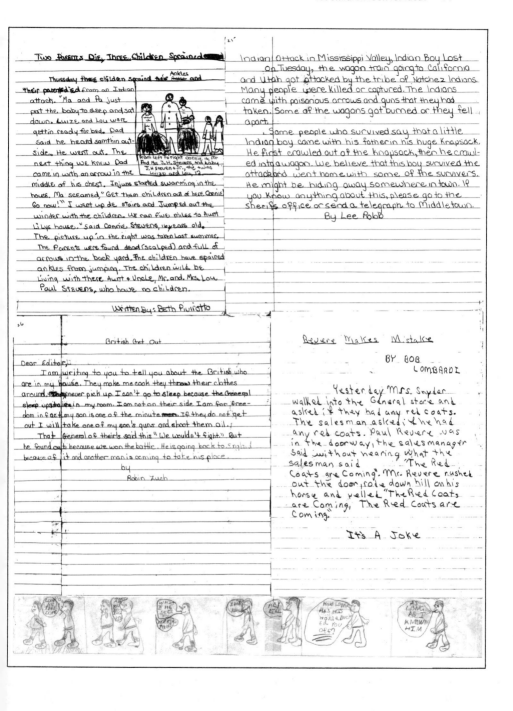

Two Parents Die, Three, Children Sprained

Thursday three children sprained their Ankles and
their parents died from an Indian
attack. "Ma and Pa just
put the baby to sleep and sat
down. Luize and Lou were
gettin ready for bed. Dad
said he heard somthin outside. He went out. The
next thing we knew Dad
came in with an arrow in the
middle of his chest. Injuns started swarming in the
house. Ma screamed, "Get them children out of here Connie
Go now!" I went up de stairs and Jumped out the
winder with the children. We ran five miles to Aunt
Lilye house." said Connie Stevens, 16 years old.
The picture up in the right was taken last summer.
The Parents were found dead (scalped) and full of
arrows in the back yard. The children have sprained
ankles from jumping. The children will be
Living with there Aunt + Uncle, Mr. and Mrs. Lou
Paul Stevens, who have no children.

From left to right Connie, 16, Mr.
And Mrs. J.H. Stevens, and baby
J.H Stevens Jr., the twins
Luize and Lou, 12

Written By: Beth Piurizotto

Indian Attack in Mississippi Valley, Indian Boy Lost
On Tuesday, the wagon train going to California
and Utah got attacked by the tribe of Natchez Indians
Many people were killed or captured. The Indians
came with poisonous arrows and guns that they had
taken. Some of the wagons got burned or they fell
apart.
   Some people who survived say that a little
Indian boy came with his father in his huge knapsack.
He first crawled out of the knapsack, then he crawled into a wagon. We believe that this boy survived the
attack and went home with some of the survivers.
He might be hiding away somewhere in town. If
you know anything about this, please go to the
sheriffs office or send a telegraph to Middletown.
         By Lee Robb

British Get Out

Dear Editor,
   I am writing to you to tell you about the British who
are in my house. They make me cook they throw their clothes
around. They never pick up. I can't go to sleep because the General
sleep upstairs in my room. I am not on their side I am for freedom in fact my son is one of the minute men. If they do not get
out I will take one of my son's guns and shoot them all.
   That General of theirs said this "We wouldn't fight." But
he found out because we won the battle. He is going back to England
because of it and another man is coming to take his place.
         by
         Robin Zuch

Revere Makes Mistake
         BY BOB
            LOMBARDI

   Yesterday Mrs. Snyder
walked into the General store and
asked if they had any red coats.
The salesman asked if he had
any red coats. Paul Revere was
in the doorway, the salesmanager
said without hearing what the
salesman said   "The Red
Coats are Coming". Mr. Revere rushed
out the door, rode down hill on his
horse and yelled "The Red Coats
are Coming, The Red Coats are
Coming."

         It's A Joke

actually become the report. To avoid such misunderstanding, we must teach children in the upper elementary grades (the fourth through the eighth grades) how to search for ideas.

SOURCES TO SEARCH

The child searching for an idea related to a general topic such as pollution, Israel, evolution, or life in the Middle Ages should scan such magazines as *National Geographic, Consumer Reports, Popular Mechanics, Time,* and *Life.* He can scan newspapers, pamphlets, and books. He can consult encyclopedias, but an encyclopedia should not be his only source.

To encourage children to use varied sources, the teacher should use a variety of references directly in her teaching. If the class is considering a problem of current social interest, she can read a comment from a recent news magazine or illustrate a point of view with pictures from such a magazine as *Life.* She can refer to editorials and articles in newspapers. If the class is studying a scientific topic, the teacher can refer to up-to-date material, including pictures, in *Scientific American.* For social-science investigation, she can use the maps that accompany *National Geographic* and such illustrated, oversized volumes as *Life's Picture History of Western Man, The World We Live In, The History of Russia, The History of China,* and the volumes in the various Heritage Series. She can consult the *World Almanac,* atlases, road maps, weather maps published by the U.S. Weather Bureau, general encyclopedias, and such specialized volumes and series as *Encyclopedia of American Biography* or Van Nostrand's *Scientific Encyclopedia.* In addition, books other than textbooks can be made available to the children for them to read a chapter or even a page. Instead of the teacher putting together a "reading table" of books on a unit of study, several children can go to the school library, check the card catalog, browse where the appropriate books are shelved, and return to the classroom with numerous references for use on the "unit reading table."

READING FOR SEARCH

How can we teach children the techniques for saturating themselves in source materials? One answer is to have reading periods in which children thumb through magazines, looking here and there but not reading word by word. Good for this purpose are old copies of *National Geographic,* in which pictures play a large part in the communication of the message and scanning can produce rapid understanding. Also, have the children play at "reading" a magazine article. They should try to get the sense of an article by reading only the first or last sentence of every paragraph. They can try the same technique with books: play at "reading" a book by reading only one sentence at the top of each page, one in the middle, and one at the end. Such weekly newspapers as *Our Weekly Reader* and *Junior Scholastic* can also be used to teach rapid skimming. Instead of reading in detail, suggest that the children first flip through the entire issue to discover what kinds of articles the week's issue contains and to determine which articles they would like to read in detail. On library trips, suggest that children skim through several books before selecting a book to bring back to the class for a thorough reading.

Another technique for teaching rapid skimming is first to collect newspaper articles on a topic such as pollution of the environment. Most newspapers have two or three articles in every issue, so a collection can easily be compiled by teachers and student scouts. Distribute an article to each child. The child looks at his article for only three minutes; then he must pass it to the child behind him, who gets it for three minutes before he in turn gets an article from a child in front. The process, which almost becomes a game, can be repeated five or six times, so that every child will have looked at five or six articles in fifteen or eighteen minutes. In the period immediately after the scanning, every child orally talks about something that interested him in one of the articles. Then the teacher can follow up with the question: "If we were to write a paper on pollution to send to the other fifth grade, what would be the main message we would want to get across?" Ideas can be written on the board or fed into a tape recorder. If each of the articles has been numbered, children can also record the article or articles that they consider a particularly valuable source.

OTHER SEARCH TOOLS

Searching for ideas naturally takes one to written materials, but it is just as natural to consult other kinds of sources. Children can attempt a systematic interview, talking to people in the community with the assistance of an interview guide that has been planned by either a small group or the total class. Discussions with war veterans, writers of children's books, executives of electrical utility plants, or politicians can give children meaningful ideas for writing.

Children can systematically observe social phenomena. They can observe changing habits of dress and grooming, they can study at first-hand the characteristics of different neighborhoods, or they can observe the littering habits of people by recording behavior from the vantage point of a street corner. Again, both the procedures attempted and the results of the investigation can produce ideas for writing.

Search can take children to filmed materials. Encourage children to check the lists of films and film strips available on the subject chosen for writing. Suggest that they study a film in depth, rerunning it several times to develop a greater understanding. Encourage children to find people with 35mm slides or home movies that might give them greater insight into a topic. Help them to analyze what they are seeing, to find meanings they can express in written form.

Search can involve listening to recorded materials. For example, a child writing on Hawaiian life could search collections of island music done by such performers as Alfred Apaka, Mahi Beamer, and Haunani Kahalewai (Decca Records, *The Best of Alfred Apaka;* Capital Records, *Island Paradise*). From "Koni Au," "Hawaiian War Chant," "Papio," "Aloha Oe," and other songs, a child can begin to know his subject and perhaps discover a theme for his writing, whether that writing is prose or poetry.

TIME

As children grow older and become concerned with researching an idea, we must encourage them to dig deeply into materials and ideas before beginning to compose the paper. While children are carrying on these preliminary search activities, the teacher's role is that of a sounding board. She talks with children individually about facts uncovered, helping them to identify the significance of the facts. Talking about what they have read sometimes enables children to put the pieces together into a relational scheme. In the upper grades, talking to other students about an embryonic idea can serve the same function. Idea-pairs—two students who talk over ideas before writing—can be established at the start of a search-saturation period.

One of the major problems to be overcome is the inclination of some students to start writing or copying immediately, to write down facts from the first article they encounter. Sometimes pretending to be detectives in search of evidence is a technique useful in getting children to prowl around in material. Conversely, some teachers have a built-in feeling that children are not being productive unless they are putting words on paper. One of the authors recalls a lesson in "creative writing" conducted by a student teacher. After less than five minutes had gone by, several fourth-graders were still studying the picture that was to be their inspiration. The student teacher prodded, "Come on! Get to work!" As teachers, we must remember that contemplating or pondering is work too!

Work takes time. When we ask children to search for ideas by saturating themselves in source materials, time should not be limited. All children should not be required to finish a paper in the identical time period. One child may take two hours to search for an idea; another may take two days or two weeks. When we recall that Thomas Gray, the great English poet, lay for six months beneath a giant yew in an old country churchyard at Stoke Poges collecting impressions for "Elegy Written in a Country Churchyard," we should not get impatient with children who spend considerable time searching for ideas and contemplating them.

summary thoughts

How can such activities as the ones just described be integrated into the ongoing work of classrooms? Of course, the teacher can build a lesson or series of lessons around any one of the suggested ideas. But there is another, perhaps more functional, alternative. Writing activity can be included among the options from which students can select during individual "seatwork" sessions. For instance, a student may choose to write on a title displayed on the bulletin board, select a picture from the picture set stored on the windowsill and describe it, listen to a story told on a Weston Woods tape and react to it, or work with a group of other students on a "period newspaper" in progress. He may check a plant growth experiment and record data, write his birthday report, or with three or four other children wheel a motion picture projector into the hall to view a motivational film. Such options as these turn routine seatwork periods into meaningful learning-activity times and can involve children in written expression daily and continuously.

4 let children record

Compare the typical composition (see Figure 4-1) written by first-grade youngsters just learning to put words on paper with the talk of an average first-grade child. The children's written compositions show discontinuity of thought, rather simple structures, and words accidentally left out; the speech of first-grade children is more logically developed, employs more complex linguistic structures, and exhibits few accidental deletions. Such a comparison suggests that the young child who is verbally recording his ideas on paper does so less clearly and less completely than when he speaks. For him, written recording is hardly efficient.

Written recording is inefficient for the young child because its production requires a visual, symbolic representation of ideas: the child must physically construct letters, and he must build letters into words. Yet at this stage he is only being introduced to manuscript skills, and his knowledge of the written representations of the words within his speaking vocabulary is extremely limited. Even when he has learned to control the pencil in order to produce all the letters in manuscript form, he is handicapped by his slowness. As he struggles to form each letter in manuscript, he focuses on that letter and may in the process lose the substance of his thought. Of

The World is red i Like The World red
it is funny The way it azk
The World is NIEe GOUP AT The World
i LiKe it
GiSS WantiDid   Ellen

browny was
a horse.
he lived in farm
he littie the
Farm veary veary
much

Figure 4-1. *Compositions by two first-graders.*

course, he also continues to work under the handicap of his limited spelling ability.

These factors suggest that ways of recording less bound by the child's skill in manipulating a pencil and in spelling words should be employed preliminary to and parallel with a child's construction of a written record. In Chapter 4, four ways of recording are explored: concrete representation of ideas, individual dictation of ideas, group dictation of ideas, and tape recording. In addition, ways of helping children to make the transition from what is primarily an oral form to the more typical written form of composition are described.

concrete representation

The young child's major way of recording his impressions of the world is concrete artistic representation. This form of recording is especially meaningful to him, for the young child is oriented more toward the concrete than toward symbolic abstractions. The recording of words on paper produces only a symbolic record, whereas a picture, a clay sculpture, or a shoe-box diorama gives a more concrete representation of the world.

Impressions of first-hand experiences can be recorded visually. Children can take their box of crayons, their drawing paper, and their drawing boards outside with them as they experience the world first-hand. Sitting on a grassy site, they can pictorially describe clouds, trees, birds, and the movement of the wind. Standing in a playground and watching a busy street, they can pictorially describe cars, pollution, policemen, shops, buildings, and people. Clustered by a cage at the zoo, they can represent their impressions of lions, zebras, antelopes, monkeys, bears, and other fascinating animal life. Back in the classroom they can draw descriptions of the hamster, the canary, the turtle, and the rabbit kept as class pets.

It is rather exciting to see how seriously young children can become involved in visual interpretation of real things of the world. On a recent visit to the Mikimoto Pearl Island in eastern Japan, one of the authors happened upon an entire school out on an expedition to record ideas in picture form. The children walked around the display area; then each child selected the site from which he would view the scene. The little ones seemed to cluster around the place where the diving girls jumped into the water to search for oysters; they were intrigued by the action. The older ones tended to settle before the statue of Mikimoto. Shortly, most of the children were actively producing a visual record of their trip.

Stories and reports can also be told in picture form. When a child comes to school bubbling over with excitement about an event he wants to share with his teacher, he can be encouraged not only to relate his story to the teacher, but to tell it through a picture that can be shown to other students. When a child travels into the realm of fantasy and relates ideas about Halloween witches, fairy princesses, and make-believe animals, he again can be encouraged to record his ideas in picture form for sharing with other boys and girls. When an incident happens in the classroom, children can project their impressions of the incident in visual form.

Children realize that ideas can be told through pictures when the teacher uses books that have pictures but no words at all. For instance, *My Schoolbook of Picture Stories* (Holt, Rinehart & Winston, 1967), with pictures by Eleanore Mill, presents a number of different classroom situations told only through pictures. Ellie Simmon's *Family* (New York: David Mc-Kay, 1970) describes through pictures the coming of a new baby to a family. Children "read" the pictures to find out what is happening to the story characters. This type of early "reading" activity can motivate children to "write" their own book of pictures, depicting things that happen in their classroom. Every child can contribute a picture to a class-events book, or an individual child may compile his own book—*Me*. In *Me* the child depicts events that have personal meaning for him: the coming of a new brother, an argument with Mama, a fight with Josie, a trip, the acquisition of a new family pet, moving, getting a new dress, a favorite toy. Whenever the child feels like it, he adds another page to his book.

Through a related technique, children can gain a notion of sequential development in story-telling. If all the children have participated in a class trip, the talk can center on things that happened on the trip when they return. When a child tells about an incident, he stands at the side of the room. The next child to tell about an incident from the trip stands next to him, either in front or behind, depending on whether the incident occurred before or after the one related first. As other children tell happenings, each stands in a relative position in line until all children have a place in the story-line. Those children who cannot think of a different incident stand next to a child who has told about a well-liked part of the excursion. The children return to their seats, and every child pictorially expresses his impressions of the part of the trip about which he spoke. All the children's papers may be taped together end-to-end in the order of the story-line; the strip of papers may be attached to rollers and run through a viewing box while each child tells about his own picture (see Figure 4-2).

This story-line type of activity can be carried on even more readily with small groups. A story-telling group clusters around the teacher; together, the children orally build a story. Then each child selects an incident in the story to put into picture form. Later the pictures are organized in a sequence that tells the story; they are taped together with an adhesive and are shown from a viewing box.

As a child moves from kindergarten to first grade, pictorial representation of ideas continues, but with the added feature of written lines. The child composes one or two sentences on lined paper stapled to his art work. He

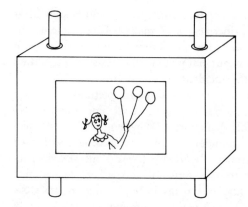

Figure 4-2. *A picture-story viewing box.*

tells his story first in picture form, then through the written word. Manu-script-drawing paper that has a large blank area at the top and several lines marked at the bottom is ideal for this purpose.

Even for children in the upper elementary grades, visual expression of an idea is a meaningful experience. First, many children in the sixth grade are still functioning in the concrete-operational stage, when a concrete referent is essential for the child if he is to handle abstractions with any degree of success. Second, concrete expression may facilitate thinking about an idea, may be a way to play intellectually with that idea. By projecting an idea visually, the youngster may be able to see new dimensions within a situation, and his idea may snowball. Third, there are some children who enjoy artistic expression more than written expression. If an experience has both artistic and written elements, the child who is uncertain of how to handle the verbal form may gain security by beginning with what he likes and can do well—artistic representation.

A student teacher with whom one of the authors worked tried a rather different writing-art experience that proved successful with upper elementary school youngsters. The teacher had her youngsters brainstorm, motivated by such questions as:

> Wouldn't it be funny if we had dog arms on our bodies? How do you think we would live if we did?
>
> What if an elephant had a giraffe neck? How would he look? How would he have to live?
>
> What if a lion had a trunk like an elephant, wings like a duck, and stripes like a zebra? Can you imagine how he would look? How would he have to change his way of living?
>
> Can you put together strange animal characteristics like this?

The teacher next projected some drawings of "ziberiches," fantastic animals that combine parts from several different animals, and the children suggested crazy names for them. Then came their turn: every child pulled five letters of the alphabet from a hat to form a crazy name for an animal he was to invent. Each designed a "ziberich" on drawing paper and wrote a short paragraph of inventive description about the "ziberich" he had created. Katie's invention was a "chyrn." Her drawing of a chyrn and her description are reproduced in Figure 4-3.

Another teacher had fifth-grade children use tempera paint and a dry brush to record their impressions of colored leaves that seemed to be tumbling in armfuls from the sky. In the manner of the Japanese brush stroke, the children mixed the paints on their brushes by dipping one side of the brush in one color of paint, the other side in another color. With a rolling motion of the brush demonstrated by the teacher, they produced impressionistic records of the showering leaves. Then the youngsters wrote short little verses in haiku form that expressed in words the feelings that their pictures communicated.

There are many, many ways to put impressions in concrete form: watercolor, felt pen, finger paint, clay, string dipped in paint, block prints, screen prints. Children can cut construction paper into various two- or three-dimensional shapes, cut portions of pictures from magazines and paste them together to make collages, combine real materials in inventive patterns, wind colored yarns to form weblike designs, or use their hands and feet as patterns. In so doing, their ideas may become clearer, enlarged, and even more exciting to them.

When encouraging art activities, the teacher must exercise one caution —not to force on the child a realistic, adult view of the world. Perceiving through the eyes of childhood, the child may represent snowflakes as green and blue upon a white background, rather than as white upon a green and blue background. He may represent sky as green and grass as blue. The initial reaction of the teacher may be to tell the child to use a blue crayon for sky, a green one for grass. Yet if she does this, she is insisting on a realistic interpretation of the world; she is forgetting that even as written content may be a reflection of the world or an invention that goes beyond the world, so artistic representation can have elements of realism and impressionism.

individual dictation

Children take pleasure in seeing their own words neatly typed on a page. Even though they themselves may not have printed the letters, they identify the story with themselves and feel a sense of both possession and pride. They perceive, too, that their words have value when recorded on the printed page; the words may be reread at a later time and shared with

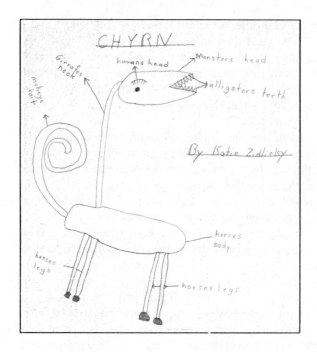

CHYRN

This is a Chyrn. It lives in the swamp in Africa. The trouble is, that when it walk its neck is so long that it breacks the branches off the trees. It eats leaves and small branches. It also eats small animals. It can run very very fast. It loves the sun when it is hot. When winter comes it goes to the ocean and goes and buries at the bottom under the sand. There he eats the fish and sand until it gets warm again.

Figure 4-3. *The chyrn, an animal invented by Katie Zidlicky of Matawan, New Jersey.*

classmates. They begin to comprehend that the spoken word has its counterpart on the written page.

The teacher of young children should set aside short periods of time to work individually with each child on written expression. She chats with the child about his ideas, encouraging him to think about his ideas, and culminates the individual session with him by taking dictation—recording word by word, sentence by sentence, what the child dictates. In short, she becomes the child's stenographer, inscribing the letters, words, and sentences that together form his story. If the child knows how to write each letter in manuscript, after dictating he may make a copy in his own handwriting. If he has only limited skill in manuscript, he illustrates his story, stapling the picture he draws to the story printed by the teacher.

When one of the authors was teaching first grade, she found that children looked forward to the time when they could sit with the teacher and dictate. After several dictating experiences, they obviously anticipated their turn and had almost prepared for it by thinking ahead about the content of their dictation. They had selected the topic on which they wanted to write before they came up to the teacher, and they began with relatively little encouragement from her.

The topics selected by the children reflected similar themes—animals, nature, "let's pretend"—as shown by the following samples taken from "Our Class Storybook," a first grade publication:

A Little Indian

Indian Two Feet wanted a horse, but he could not find one. He walked a long way. He went to the Chief. The Chief said, "If you keep on walking, you will find a horse."

BONNIE BOGERT

A Rainbow

One day we went for a ride, and it rained. Then, we went home. After that we saw a beautiful rainbow.

NANCY ADLER

Spring

In spring
The buds start coming out on trees.
In spring
The flowers begin to bloom.
In spring
The grass gets green.
In spring
The snow melts away.

SARA LEARY

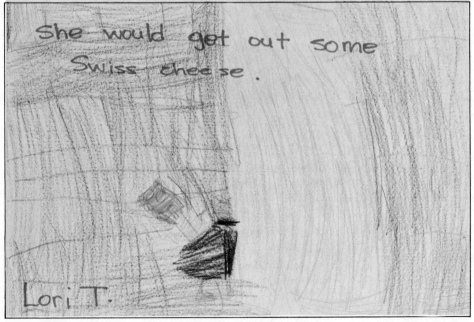

Figure 4-4. *Two young children's pictorial answer to the question, "What would Goldilocks do if she came to your house?" The words were written by the teacher, Donna Russo, according to the children's dictation.*

Fall Fright

As I was walking down the street,
I was scared right off my feet,
For I saw a witch
Who made me twitch.

SCOTT PURITZ

Jack Frost

When I got into bed, I heard noises coming from outside. I got up to look out of the window, but I didn't see anything. I went back to bed.

Since the noises continued, I tiptoed to the window again. As I looked out, I saw little people painting leaves red, orange, yellow, and brown. Jack Frost and all his helpers were making the trees colorful.

PATRICK ALBANO

A Bird

Once there was a bird who lived in the woods. He decided that he didn't want to live in the forest any longer because he didn't have any friends. So he flew to China.

On his journey he passed over a bridge. As he flew, he saw a castle. The Chinese people captured him and took him to the King. The King decided that the bird was valuable and made him his friend.

BOBBIE HIRSCHFELD

Needless to say, dictating to the teacher should take place within an environment completely free of pressure to produce. If a child cannot think of ideas to dictate, he can chat informally with the teacher about happenings in the classroom or at home, books he has been reading, or things he would like to do or have. When a teacher perceives that the individual child is not in the mood, or perhaps is not ready to dictate, she can adapt the situation to meet the child's unique needs. This child is channeled to express himself through a concrete, visual medium, while that child is channeled toward an overt acting out of feelings. In her work with beginning writers, the teacher's first objectives are to have the child relax, begin to enjoy verbal interaction with the teacher, and begin to express himself in ways that may culminate in written expression.

One advantage of this type of introduction to written expression is that a child does not associate failure or drudgery with his initial writing experiences. Encouraged by the personal attention of the teacher and her obvious interest in him, stimulated by the teacher's questions, which lead him to think in directions he would perhaps not have considered if left to his own devices, the child often does produce much more than he himself thinks that he can. Then too, the writing experience is not a laborious struggle for the child. He produces a story in short order without having to labor over the formation of each letter and without having to figure out which letters to record. At a time when the child's attention span is short, this is a definite advantage.

Some of the most relevant material that a child can read is material he himself has written. It has more personal significance than the stories found in the best basal readers. The words are most assuredly within the child's speaking vocabulary, so understanding of the conceptual content is not a problem. Therefore, after Bobbie dictates his story, the teacher reads it aloud to him and has Bobbie read it back to her. He is encouraged to share his story of birds, Kings, and China with his friends, reading it from the page printed by the teacher. He can put his page into a folder and read it again later to another group of classmates. Dictated writing inherently has this additional value: the product can be used as content for personal reading.

A few teachers may question the amount of teacher-time that individual dictation requires. Although the time spent with each child is probably no more than five minutes per composition, it takes well over an hour when five is multiplied by the twenty-five students in an average-sized class. Yet this time need not be grouped within one seventy-five minute block; it can be spread across several days. The teacher may work with one child as the rest put on their coats. She may fit three students in during a drawing session. After all, every teacher should include some one-to-one verbal interaction within the daily program, and what better way to structure that interaction than to focus on primary language development in speaking, writing, and reading.

We know one teacher who attempts to overcome the time problem by training linguistically competent sixth-grade children to take dictation from her kindergarten children. She believes that both groups of children gain from the experience. First, the little children gain because they have many more opportunities to dictate: the sixth-graders come for a half-hour each week, and with five sixth-graders participating, every little child has an opportunity to dictate at least every third day. Second, the sixth-grade youngsters must exercise their recording skills—punctuation, spelling, capitalization, and handwriting—and at times must even refer to the dictionary. Because he is producing a written record for someone else, the sixth-grader may have even more reason to produce accurate copy than if he were writing something for himself.

Dictation is not a technique limited to the beginning school years. Some youngsters in the upper elementary grades can gain from dictation. First, a youngster with a learning disability involving eye-hand coordination may have trouble simply forming letters. An eighth-grade boy with whom one of the authors worked recorded only indecipherable scratches on his paper; he did this so other youngsters would think that he was writing. Dictation became his major way of completing written assignments required in the content areas. Second, a child who has an extremely short attention span may gain from dictation work. If left at his seat to work alone, this type of youngster probably cannot concentrate for the length of time required to produce most forms of written communication. Oral dictation to the teacher focuses his attention on the task at hand, while the accompanying conversation with the teacher may help him to project an idea to be recorded. Third, a youngster may have trouble projecting the ideas of written content. Perhaps his mind freezes when he takes pen in hand because he has a mental block associated with writing. Dictation may prove to be an approach that circumvents the block.

group dictation

The youngsters in the kindergarten at the West End School in North Plainfield, New Jersey, visited the Einstein-Moomjy salesroom to see the Oriental rugs and the many different kinds of carpets. Before they left, Mr. Moomjy gave each child a small sample of carpet to take back to school. When the little ones returned to their classroom, they talked about their excursion and about all the things they could do with their carpets. Then the children talked about how they could begin a thank-you note to Mr. Moomjy and suggested possible sentences to be included in the letter. From the many suggested, the children chose two sentences to write in their letter:

Dear Mr. Moomjy,
  Thank you for the rugs. We enjoy using them.
                            Your friends at West End

As an individual activity, every child drew a picture depicting what he would do with his carpet and signed his name to his drawing. The drawings and the letter were stapled to a large piece of brown paper and were sent to Mr. Moomjy.

This type of group dictation experience can be continued in the first grade. Patrick brought his toy airplane to school to share during show-and-tell. After he had shown his classmates how his airplane could fly, the children as a group suggested lines to write about it. The teacher recorded the children's words on experience-story chart paper:

Up and down!
See Patrick's airplane
      up
Go
        and
          down.

On another occasion the children in the same first-grade class talked about the fish in their class fish bowl. Afterward they dictated a report to the teacher; individual children suggested lines, and the total group decided which lines should be recorded by the teacher.

The Fish Tank

We have three fish in our fish tank. The fish are orange. We have two snails in the same bowl.

One day these first-grade children were talking about the possibility of a snowstorm. Using their tremendous excitement as a stimulus, the teacher gathered her first-graders around her easel and recorded these lines with them:

Snow

The air is cold.
The sky is gray.
The wind is blowing.
Will it snow today?

After an excursion that took them down to the railway station and for a short ride on the train, the children dictated:

Our Trip

We went for a walk to the train station. We saw an old furnace in the middle of the waiting room. The station man gave us little tickets. We had a good trip on the train.

In each of these instances, after the teacher had recorded the communication on large-sized charting paper mounted on her easel, her first-grade children volunteered to read the lines of story, poem, or report. The class communication was read several times; then each child made a copy to include in his volume of the class-events book.

A second-grade teacher gave many of her youngsters their first experience blowing bubbles and followed it up with a group dictation. With the typical bubble-blowing equipment—bubble pipes and soap solution—the youngsters blew iridescent bubbles into the air on a morning when the sun was streaming into the room. As the bubbles danced up into the air, the children called out their impressions and the teacher recorded:

Bubbles are fun.
We like to blow
    big
    bubbles.

They burst on our shoes.
They pop on the ceiling.
They make rainbows in the air.

Bubbles are fun.
We like to eat
    big
    bubbles.

An inner-city fourth-grade class reacted to a rainy day and dictated the following piece of free verse to Joan Soroka, their teacher:

Rain

Rain means it is wet outside.
Puddles form on the ground.
People sink in the mud.
Umbrellas must be opened.
Thunder can be heard.
AND I HIDE IN THE HOUSE!

Similarly, a fifth-grade teacher in a semirural area of New Hampshire helped youngsters record their impressions of an ice storm that had covered that part of the world with a blanket of glaze.

Ice Day

Icy branches
Sparkle in the sun.
Trees
Bend down to touch the snow.
Roads
Are slippery with ice.

A rather different approach was employed by a sixth-grade teacher. He encouraged his youngsters to keep a running record of the growth patterns of tomato and radish seedlings, which the students were growing on a table near the window. To determine the effect of competition between different species on the development of each species, the youngsters planted a box of radish seeds, a box of tomato seeds, and a box of radish and tomato seeds. In each case, the same number of seeds was planted. The seeds were planted the same number of inches apart, and each flat was given an identical growing environment—the same amount of water, the same temperature, and the same exposure to sunlight. Whenever groups of children worked on the project, they dictated what they were doing and what they observed to a student recorder, who entered the data in the "Experimental Log":

Log—Effect of Competition on Plant Growth

April 2: We planted radish seeds in Box A. We planted thirty seeds in all. Each seed was placed one inch away from the next one. We poured on two cups of water.

R	T	R	T	R	T
T	R	T	R	T	R
R	T	R	T	R	T
T	R	T	R	T	R
R	T	R	T	R	T

R = radish
T = tomato

Figure 4-5.

We planted thirty tomato seeds in Box B. Each seed was placed one inch away from the next one. We poured on two cups of water.

We planted fifteen tomato seeds and fifteen radish seeds in Box C. Each seed was planted one inch from the next one. We poured on two cups of water. This is the way we did it. [See Figure 4–5.]

April 4: We added one cup of water to each box. We turned each box so that the opposite end was toward the window.

April 6: We added one cup of water. No seeds have begun to germinate.

April 9: We added one cup of water to each box. Some seeds have germinated. [See Figure 4–6.]

Box A	11 seedlings germinated
Box B	8 seedlings germinated
Box C	9 seedlings germinated

etc.

Figure 4-6.

The log was kept during the total period of the experiment, which was most of April.

Group dictation activities contribute much to a child's learning. First, there are always things going on in an activity-centered, open classroom that can supply the content for written expression. The children experience and then project ideas about experience. A natural outgrowth of experiencing and thinking is recording ideas on paper. If the teacher can perceive the writing potential inherent in most classroom situations, writing becomes an integral element of the developing curriculum. Writing is not a contrived or artificial process, and children can begin to see that written expression is a normal facet of living and that recording ideas is valuable. Second, group dictation is not at all a time-consuming activity. Most of the pieces presented in this section were written in less than ten minutes; one, the recording of experimental observations, took place concurrently with the activity and in the context of a subject area. The technique of group dictation makes possible the inclusion of more informal writing experiences in the curriculum than would be possible if the teacher relied totally on individual approaches. Third, participation in group dictation encourages cooperation among children. The children are involved in a common endeavor. If their written record is to be used for some formal purpose—to consider in drawing conclusions, to send to the station agent, to include in a class-events book, to be shared with youngsters in other classes—they tend to pull together to achieve that purpose. Fourth, as with individually dictated materials, the materials produced by groups can be used as reading matter by the children. It is reading matter that is highly meaningful and relevant.

tape recording

Modern technology supplies the teacher of written expression with devices that aid her in building writing-recording experiences for children: the audio-tape recorder and the video-tape recorder. They are effective ways for individuals and small groups to record ideas. Their applicability extends throughout the elementary grades.

AUDIO-TAPE RECORDING

Consider first the use of audio-tape recording with the very young child. After a child has explored an idea individually with the teacher, the teacher may propose: "Let's tell your story on tape so that later we can share it with our class." With a youngster of this age, the simpler and lighter cassette recorders are most efficient, because after a child has recorded, he himself can operate the machine to tell back the story. The cassette has an added advantage: as a child gains in idea-creation, he need not rely so heavily on the teacher to record for him. He can use the machine as a teacher-substitute, turning it on by himself when he gets an idea, recording his ideas, and listening to his product.

The older child can also use the tape recorder as a self-instructional recording device. On his own, he can orally try out an idea with which he is toying, then listen, consider, reorder his thinking, and perhaps try again. After he has projected his idea in a way that meets his own approval, he transcribes on paper the thoughts he has recorded on tape. Some children actually find this a more productive way of writing than the more typical way of recording ideas directly on paper. The pens of these children cannot keep up with the speed of their thoughts, so ideas get jumbled as they wait in line to get written down, and points are forgotten. When expressed into the tape recorder, children's ideas can spill out and be recorded as fast as tongues can move. Likewise, children handicapped by lack of spelling, punctuation, and capitalization skills are not affected by their handicap at the point in composition when idea-generation is most significant. How to spell a word, how to place a comma, and which letters to capitalize are not concerns to the composer working with a tape recorder. The major concern is with thinking through and developing ideas to be expressed.

There are limitations as well as advantages in the use of tape recorders as a device for encouraging the expression of ideas that will eventually be transcribed into written form. The child with a speech problem may prefer playing with ideas on paper rather than on tape. His awareness of his speech problem may hinder any kind of reflective, conceptual, projective, expressive, or inventive ideas that must first be expressed orally. The child with the short attention span who needs the questioning presence of the teacher to keep his mind centered on idea-production may similarly be less successful using the machine. The insecure, too, may not be able to project ideas with only a mechanical teacher-substitute to record his ideas for him. He may need the immediate personal reinforcement supplied by an empathetic human being. On the other hand, another shy child may have just the opposite reaction. He may fail when dictating ideas to a human being but succeed in expressing himself when the recording device is an inanimate object that is totally within his control.

VIDEO-TAPE RECORDING

Video-tape recording can play a parallel role in the writing program. Video-taping can be used to record children's ideas projected through action and dramatization. Several children may want to have their improvised group dramatization of a story recorded on tape to share later with other classes. An individual child may want to have his pantomiming sequence recorded for later viewing on class TV. Children may want to be recorded on video tape as they express themselves with physical action in response to a musical selection, as they dramatize a poem, or as they tell an original story, complete with props that communicate—pictures, dioramas, flannel-board figures, or puppets.

Generally, children are highly motivated when given the opportunity to express impressions before TV cameras. With a total lack of inhibition, children will gesture wildly, dance expressively, contort both face and body, hop in rhythm, dress themselves in costumes that carry them into make-believe. Their anticipation can be so great that they can hardly wait to see themselves in playback. They can be as enthralled watching the unprofessional rendition of a story they have invented as they are watching Sesame Street on TV.

A number of well-respected companies in the electronics field are currently marketing a video-tape recorder/camera outfit that is relatively simple to operate and is not excessively expensive. For example, the Sony Videorover II is priced around fifteen hundred dollars, which is not excessive when compared with other similar expenditures made by school districts. It is a completely portable system that can be moved easily from one classroom to another. It can be operated by one person, so the teacher of young children can handle the operation without assistance. The camera weighs only six pounds; the video-recorder weighs under nineteen pounds. Both are compact pieces of equipment, no more cumbersome than most regular-sized tape recorders. The equipment records both picture and sound that can be played back on a self-contained monitor. With the addition of an optional piece of equipment (a radio-frequency modulator), the tape can be viewed on a regular TV set. As compared with earlier models, this type of video-tape recorder is completely unthreatening; one need not be an electronics expert to manipulate camera and recorder. The teacher, as well as upper grade youngsters, can operate the equipment without encountering insurmountable problems.

To propose use of video-taping in public school classrooms is not to dream the impossible dream. Some urban and suburban school districts have already moved in this direction and have video-taping cameras functional in their classrooms. One reason the purchase of video-taping equipment has proved feasible is that it can be used for multiple purposes: teachers prepare short segments of instruction on video tape for later viewing by students; teachers tape short episodes of their own classroom performance to analyze later as a means of improving their own instruction; children are encouraged to tape group activity; and equipment can be taken on nature walks to record sights and sounds.

Technological devices such as audio- and video-tape recorders give the teacher an alternate way of recording children's impressions. For some youngsters, that way can be more productive than the traditional way of self-recording with pen and paper. In this respect, teachers need to be aware of all the available options and should route youngsters in directions that are in accord with individual ways of thinking and producing ideas. One child in the sixth grade may end up pounding a typewriter; another may produce his most original work by dictating to a tape recorder; a third child, even in the upper grades, may write his best ideas by dictating to a teacher; and still another child may be most productive sitting quietly alone in a corner with a felt pen in hand. Even in recording ideas for written expression, children have individual differences that teachers must respect.

recording with pen and paper

Not only do young children differ in the recording technique that is most productive for them; they also differ in their readiness to move from recording via dictation to recording via pen and paper. Some children are ready to encode their own ideas very early in the first grade; they have both the requisite manuscript skills and the ability to project ideas on their own. Other children are not ready to encode until later in their primary school experience. Instruction in written expression in the early primary years must take into account such differences in readiness.

The beginnings of individual encoding of ideas can occur in the context of dictation to the teacher. If the child gives the teacher a sentence to inscribe that contains a word that the child himself is able to write, the teacher may ask, "Lillian, do you want to write a word into your story yourself? I will help you with the letters." Building on this type of situation, the teacher may suggest on another occasion: "Lillian, I bet you can write that sentence yourself." Again, as the child tries to inscribe his own words, the teacher may help him by telling him the letters to write. In this way, individual inscribing becomes a natural, sequential outgrowth of previous writing-recording activities. It also occurs in a setting that is more likely to result in success for a child than having him struggle alone at his desk.

Group dictation can also lead to individual inscribing. Working with a group of youngsters who have shared a series of community dictation sessions and who have indicated a readiness to inscribe, the teacher may read a story, stopping before the end. She may ask her children, "How do you think the story will end?" Instead of recording their suggestions, she encourages them to talk about their ideas: "Let's each of us try to write down our own ending today. If you have trouble writing a word, look up, and I will write it for you on a card." If the introductory writing group has only six or seven youngsters in it, the teacher can move from one to the next; with felt pen, she can record on individual index cards the words that children request. The children can keep their word cards alphabetically in a shoe box and accumulate them from one writing session to another. During a later work period they can even be encouraged to draw a picture on their word cards to illustrate the meaning of the word.

Small group instruction in writing based on individual differences in encoding skills is carried out in much the same manner as group instruction in reading. Group A begins by talking about an experience with the teacher; then the youngsters in that group record verbally on paper with the help of the teacher. Their follow-up activity may be a related art experience, the writing of a second draft of the story they have just composed, or the illustration of their word cards. Group B begins by making a visual expression of their ideas through a drawing; then the youngsters in that group attempt to write down individually the idea depicted in the drawing. In the latter activity they work with the teacher, who stays close by to help with difficult words and to chat individually with the members of the group having trouble translating their ideas into written words. Group C, however, may not be ready to inscribe. Group C may join Group A to talk about an idea to be expressed, but instead of attempting to encode, they are channeled toward artistic expression of the idea. Later these youngsters in Group C dictate individually to the teacher. Individual children may function outside the context of the groups. Some children may be perfectly capable of inscribing independently: they can think and write on their own. Another child may find himself a private corner of the room and dictate to the tape recorder. Later he may encode his ideas on paper as he listens to the machine play them back. Figure 4-7 below depicts such a scheme for group and individual writing activity.

This scheme can be easily modified so that it is functional in the upper grades. Groups of youngsters in the idea stage of written production can meet with the teacher to talk about their ideas while other youngsters work individually at their seats on second drafts of compositions already begun, on artistic interpretation of ideas, or on finishing a display copy of a poem. Other groups of youngsters for whom recording is a struggle meet with the teacher, who gives assistance with the encoding process. The upper grade teacher can also work with the individual child while other children are working on written drafts at their seats or at the tape recorder. Youngsters in the upper grades differ considerably in their skill to handle encoding of ideas, so the need for individual and small group instruction is just as essential as in the lower grades.

	ACTIVITY I	ACTIVITY II
Group A	talking–writing under teacher guidance	art activity carried on independently
Group B	art activity carried on independently	talking–writing under teacher guidance
Group C	talking about ideas (merged with Group A)	art activity carried on independently followed by individual dictation to teacher
Individual Child	———————— individual writing activity ————————	
Individual Child	dictation into tape recorder	inscribing on paper

Figure 4-7. *The organization of group and individual writing activity.*

part I: content—a recapitulation

Many a teacher has encountered the child faced with the task of writing who complains, "I don't have anything to write about," or "I don't know what to say." Often the teacher is taken aback by the child's response to what she believes has been a clearly given assignment. Yet, isn't it highly improbable that a child who has had limited first-hand experiences, who has had little opportunity to think in a variety of patterns and to express his thoughts to someone else, and who has had little practice in recording ideas, will face an empty piece of paper with anything other than "I don't know what to say"?

To write, the child *must* find something to say. For this most fundamental of reasons, the core of any ongoing writing program must be activities that give children something to talk about, encourage children to think about all kinds of things, stimulate curiosity and the desire to discover, encourage children to express ideas both nonverbally and verbally, and aid them in recording their emerging ideas. The teacher who searches for an answer to the question, "What do I do when I teach children to write?" would do well, if she hopes to reach the I-don't-know-what-to-say child, to reformulate her question into "How do I help children to create, to experience and express, to search for ideas, to record so that ideas are not lost in the process?" By zeroing in on the latter question, the teacher is beginning at the beginning—with the *content* of written expression.

PART **II**   # CRAFT

The ablest writer is a gardener first, and then a cook. His tasks are, carefully to select and cultivate his strongest and most nutritive thoughts, and, when they are ripe, to dress them wholesomely, and so that they may have a relish.

J. C. Hare and A. W. Hare, Guesses at Truth

let children design

> *True ease in writing comes from art, not chance,*
> *As those move easiest who have learn'd to dance.*
>
> *Alexander Pope,* Essay on Criticism

An eighth-grade class was studying available vocational options before selecting courses to be taken in high school. Steve Rabin, a bright young man, thought that he might want to be a doctor. He found several references on the work of a doctor, studied them, and wrote the following report:[1]

Doctor

More people enjoy good health and live to an old age than ever before. This is because of modern medicine and the medical profession. I want to be a doctor. The main reason is because I like helping people.

Doctors diagnose diseases and treat people who are ill or in poor health. Doctors generally examine and treat patients in their own office and in hospitals, but they also visit patients at home when necessary. More than one third of the doctors are general practitioneers.

In offices through out the country, you will have to get a license to practice medicine. In every state it is required.

To qualify for a license, a candadate must graduate from an approved medical school and pass a licensing examination. Licensing examinations are given by State boards. Although doctors licensed in one state can usually

---

[1] Spelling, punctuation, and usage are reprinted in the child's form.

obtain a license to practice in another without an examinations, some states don't allow this.

Besides curing illness a doctor has to know to prevent illness and also how to help prevent illness from spreading.

Among the qualifacations needed for success are a strong feeling that you want to be a doctor, above-average intelligence and an interest in science. A doctor must also have good judgement, he must be able to decide quickly in an emergency and remain calm.

He must also be healthy and strong. There are many hours studying and long hours in the hospital. He is also in contact with many deseases.

In order to be a doctor you have to have four years of college in premedical study. This includes courses in English, physics, biology, and chemistry in a good college. In your last year of college you take an examination called Medical College Admission Test. This helps you get admitted to a medical school. In the medical school you spend the first two years in labrotories, and classrooms learning basic medIcal sciences. During the last two years, students spend most of the time in hospitals and clinics under the supervisim of experienced doctors. They learn to take case histories, perform examinations and recognize diseases. To become a specialist, you must pass another examination. After you pass the examination you work in a hospital from two to four years under your specialty. . . .

Bibliography

1. Encyclopedia of Career, Hopphey E. William. Duble Day. 1967
2. Doctor, Alverez C. Walter. Deagon Press. 1964
3. Should You Be a Doctor, Whiteman Mel. Grosset and Dunlap. 1965

What weaknesses are evident in Steve's composition? Although the boy apparently spent considerable time in preparation and search, it is obvious that he had not been helped to organize his ideas in a manner that assures effective communication. First, the overall structure of his report needs improvement. Ideas that belong together are handled in more than one location, which results in a discontinuity of thought. Similarly, one idea does not build upon previously developed thoughts and does not lead toward successive ideas; the result is lack of direction. Second, paragraphs are internally weak. They appear to ramble on rather than focusing on a main point to be communicated. The purpose of certain paragraphs is unclear, leaving the reader with the question, "What is the writer trying to communicate?" Essentially, Steve's major writing problem is a thinking problem. He has not mastered the thought processes most essential if a relevant idea is to be communicated effectively. In this respect, he has not mastered the craft of writing.

thinking for writing

Thinking for writing involves ability to discriminate between what is significant in the context of the idea to be communicated and what is insignificant. Basically, the writer must consider two questions: What are the essential elements of my idea? What examples, details, and/or points are needed to support the essence to be communicated? Encountering these questions, the thinker-writer discards one point while identifying another for inclusion in his communication. He gets "inside" his idea to the extent that he himself comes to know its overall significance.

Another facet of thinking for writing involves ability to perceive the psychological value of an idea and the component aspects of the idea. The thinker-writer asks himself, "What do I hope to achieve through my writing? Do I want to excite, calm, impress, cause to think, arouse to action, transmit information? What will be the psychological impact of the ideas and feelings that I am communicating?" Encountering these types of questions, the thinker-writer decides what might be a psychologically sound way of introducing his ideas to the reader, organizing an argument, presenting facts, relaying emotion, and ending a written communication.

The thinker-writer must also identify the logical and emotional relationships inherent in his idea if he hopes to communicate it effectively. First, he perceives which thoughts logically belong together, which facts relate to main ideas, how one idea relates to another, and how one idea can build upon a previous idea to form a sequential framework of thoughts. Second, feeling-laden ideas can emotionally relate to one another, and the writer must be able to perceive these emotional relationships within the material with which he is working. He senses that certain types of ideas communicate similar moods, and this similarity of mood may influence the organization of his writing.

Organizing one's thoughts for expression in written form is not just an analytical process involving the identification of significant elements, of the psychological value of an idea, and of the relationships inherent within ideas. It is, more essentially, a creative process involving the projection of a unique design for the expression of that idea. The mind goes beyond the existing material to reorder and to assemble a new structure. Designing a vehicle for expressing one's idea can be as creative a cognitive activity as devising the idea itself. The designer mentally tries out different arrangements; he plays with his idea, organizing the elements first this way and then that; he places ideas in juxtaposition, turns them over, juggles them, and reorders again. The result is an original design for communicating thoughts.

How can we teach children the skills associated with the organization of thoughts for written expression? This chapter suggests two approaches: one is related to teaching the requisite thinking-organizational skills, and the other is related to teaching specific aspects of paragraph development.

teaching for thinking

When the writer attempts to build a vehicle to express his thoughts and feelings, he does not employ a step-by-step procedure. He does not necessarily begin by identifying the significant elements in his idea, considering the psychological import of his idea, studying the relationships inherent in his idea, and finally projecting a design for communication, in that order. Rather, he is analyzing and designing in an interactive way as he builds his ideas and searches for related ideas. He may perceive a minor relationship in the data of experience with which he is working. This perception colors his conception of what is significant; this, in turn, determines which elements he selects and which he rejects. Consideration of the psychological value of his material may cause him to restructure the relationship that he originally perceived, which, in turn, may make the thinker-writer include additional elements and cast out ones selected previously.

To teach children the thinking skills requisite for the construction of a written piece is not, then, to teach them a sequence of steps to be performed; rather, it is to help children acquire specific skills that they can draw upon in a flexible way when needed. These skills are listed below:

- skill to distinguish significant and less significant elements;
- skill to distinguish elements having different psychological values;
- skill to analyze the logical relationships within an idea;
- skill to perceive emotional relationships important in the communication of a feeling or mood;
- skill to design a vehicle for the expression of an idea.

In essence, the teacher's job is to teach children how to handle ideas.

PERCEIVING RELATIONSHIPS

To design a structure for communicating ideas, the thinker-writer must identify ideas that belong together because of a common element. The thinker-writer builds idea-pools—clusters of thoughts belonging together on emotional or logical grounds. These idea-pools develop into paragraphs in which related ideas are organized together.

To build idea-pools, children must be able to perceive similarities and differences among ideas. This ability is a cognitive skill that can be developed rather systematically. First-grade children can sort blocks of different colors, sizes, and shapes into groups that share a similar characteristic. Likewise, they can sort word-cards into related piles. Words—*ax, bird, hammer, apple, banana, saw, giraffe, grapefruit, alligator, orange, baby, seal,* and *bee*—can be sorted into piles that share a similar first letter, or into piles labeled tools, animals, and fruits. Children should be encouraged to study the words to discover possible relationships and different ways in which the word cards can be grouped—for example, the number of letters in the word, the number of letters repeated within a word, or the number of vowels in the word.

As children move through the primary grades, they should encounter grouping activities that require finer discriminations. By the third grade, youngsters can look at shells, leaves, or rocks, and make piles of similar specimens. Moving from the concrete to the more abstract, they can group related idea-cards. For instance, three major categories can be given by the teacher: why I want to be a doctor, what doctors do, and what kind of preparation doctors must have. Children classify other sub-idea-cards within these categories: doctors prevent illnesses from spreading; I like people; doctors must attend a college; doctors must carry out an internship; I want to work with people; some doctors specialize in certain areas of medicine; doctors help people who are sick; I enjoy science. As children place their cards in a major category, they have to explain why that card belongs in that location.

Children can also categorize according to emotional feeling or mood. "Let's group together happy occasions. Let's build another group of sad occasions" can be a suggestion given to a first-grade class. Youngsters in the third grade can be asked to form idea-clusters based on the quiet times-noisy times dichotomy, or on the boring events-exciting events dichotomy. Fifth-grade youngsters can project word-pools on peace and war, honesty and dishonesty, or fear and bravery.

To develop skill in perceiving related elements, youngsters need numerous opportunities at every level of their schooling to classify according to similarities and differences. These opportunities should involve concrete materials, words, and ideas. They should also involve both logical and emotional relationships. Through such a developmental sequence of experiences we can teach children some of the thinking processes so fundamental to the design of a piece of written expression.

ANALYZING IDEAS FOR ORGANIZATIONAL CLUES

Sometimes inherent in an idea is an organizational scheme that the writer can use to build the framework for his writing. The scheme may not be apparent at first glance; it may be uncovered only by detailed analysis of the idea. This is especially true of ideas that, once proposed, have an internal logic all their own. It is true to a lesser degree of ideas that result in highly imaginative poetry.

For example, an eighth-grade boy proposes that if Britain had lost the battle with the Spanish Armada, then North America would have been Spanish-speaking. His basic idea is what logicians call a conditional inference. A conditional inference begins with a statement of conditions—the "if" part of an idea. It is followed with a statement of consequent—the "then" part of an idea. It is supported by evidence—rules, examples, generalizations, and data that connect the inference to the conditions. The eighth-grade boy analyzes his conditional inference about language and determines that he will organize his brief paper into two parts: a statement of the idea (if-then) and a statement of the supporting evidence assembled. In short, the if-then proposal logically suggests the overall organization for constructing.

Similarly, a student reads a short story and wants to write a brief paper that says it is not a good story. Her thought is a value judgment, an evaluation of the story. Evaluation is a complex process, consisting of three major tasks: (1) preparing a set of criteria by which the value judgment will be made, (2) assigning a value judgment in terms of the predetermined criteria, and (3) finding specific incidents, facts, and/or examples that conform or do not conform to the criteria. The student, writing a critical book review based on knowledge of the process, decides that first she will explain what it takes for a book to be considered good. Then she will express her judgment of the book and support her judgment by telling how the book did not meet her original criteria. Once again, the internal logic of her idea supplies the organizational framework for writing.

Children can learn to ask themselves questions through which they can analyze ideas such as these. The teacher can assist by initially supplying some guiding questions. For instance, the teacher might ask, "Why isn't the story any good?"

The child responds, "Because it isn't exciting."

"Do all stories have to be exciting?"

The child answers, "No."

"What other things do you like to find in a story? Which of these did you not find in this story? Give me examples of places where the story was dull and colorless. Jot them down. If we want to share our evaluation with the other students, what things would we need to write down?"

It is almost impossible to encourage every child to analyze ideas in this fashion unless the teacher is working on a one-to-one basis with a child and his idea. Of course, we can try to get children to understand the logical structure of such processes as evaluating, inferring, and comparing, by analyzing ideas as a total class. An entire class can propose criteria by which to evaluate anything—teachers, movies, television broadcasts, political candidates, or books. It can also sort out evidence to support a proposed conditional inference. In like manner, the class can compare, contrast, define, report, explain, classify, and describe, led by the guiding questions of the teacher. But to learn to construct a written piece, the individual must eventually study his own ideas and perceive an effective framework for expression. In the final analysis, to teach the craft of writing, the teacher must keep on the go, moving from child to child, asking questions that "push" the child "inside" his idea so that the child comes to know the significant elements within it.

The teacher, too, can suggest specific writing experiences that require children to think through the significant elements within contrasts, inferences, and classifications. The teacher's assignment can be a series of questions.

1. What do you think of this candidate for political office? Would you vote for him? not vote for him? Why?
2. What would happen if there were a Third World War? Why do you think this would happen?
3. What similarities exist between a grasshopper and a frog? What differences exist?
4. Do you think the Mets will win the Series? Why? Why not?
5. What do you think of this school regulation? Do you approve of it? disapprove of it? Why?
6. Do you predict rain for this afternoon? Why? Why not?
7. Would you prefer going to a ball game or going swimming? What do you like or dislike about a ball game? about swimming? What is the basis of your choice?

PROJECTING CREATIVE PATTERNS
OF ORGANIZATION

A book of poems written by a relatively new poet, Lee Bennett Hopkins, has a unique feature. The poet uses the manner in which a poem is blocked on a page, the size of the letters, and the style of print to help communicate his ideas. In a poem called "Fire-Escape Follow-the-Leader," Hopkins dances words across the page. Down goes d Ladder goes L In

$$\begin{array}{ll} o & A \\ w & D \\ n. & D \\ & E \\ & R. \end{array}$$

another poem, "Game Time," the poet blocks a numerical 1, 2, ... 7, 8 hopscotch pattern into his verse. In a third poem he puts his key words, PLAY STREET—AREA CLOSED, in the bold print typical of a street sign. His is a creative way of managing the visual effects of size and space. He has manipulated his ideas to the point where his form fits his message.[2]

The teacher can encourage a child to look for such creative ways to organize ideas. A child may be writing a cinquain but end up with something totally different. Poor cinquain? No! Maybe something totally original, a pattern all his own. Another child wants to write his short story as a poem. Another child wants to write his paper on war in red. A fourth child wants to write up and down rather than across. The teacher should encourage each of these children to experiment.

To the writer searching for a creative, unusual design in which to

[2] Lee Bennett Hopkins, *This Street's for Me!* (New York: Crown Publishers, 1970).

express ideas, use of the traditional outline as a means of organizing thoughts may be more of a drawback than an advantage. The construction of an outline, complete with Roman numerals and upper- and lower-case letters, is a highly systematic process. The structuring of such a complete, precise outline before beginning to write very possibly may prevent the fluid change in both ideas and organizational design so essential in constructing a written piece.

Anyone who has worked extensively with ideas on paper knows that the act of organizing changes the idea itself. The process of actually putting words on paper triggers related ideas, while at the same time portions of the original idea no longer seem to "hold water" or seem appropriate. Similarly, the details and ramifications of the idea begin to emerge, and different dimensions of the problem appear more significant.

An essential outgrowth of change in idea is change in the original concept of how to organize that idea for written communication. As the writer begins, he has in mind a tentative design. The design may be the rather vague notion: in the first part of the piece I will consider X, in the second part Y, and in the third part Z. The tentative design for other writers may be a listing of points to be included in the approximate order of presentation. But in our experience, rarely does the final organization resemble in detail the original tentative one.

Sometimes, too, the writer must actually attempt several organizing patterns before he settles on one within which he can function. He tries this; he tries that; he eliminates; he reorders; he puts this first, then last; he combines; he divides; he reassembles; he jots notes on paper; he restudies his data. Then he evaluates his options and begins to compose.

When teachers work with children in designing a framework for ideas, teachers may give the impression that designing is a very straightforward process. Children may be required to produce a precise outline before beginning to write. They may be required to follow it to the letter. They may even be evaluated on how closely the final product matches the original outline. No wonder children sometimes produce such unimaginative frameworks, for the act of construction has been transformed into a boring academic exercise, stripped of excitement and elation.

It is the teacher's attitude that either encourages or discourages experimentation and change. We must view the final dimensions of a written piece as an emerging product to be projected even as the writing progresses. We must accept differences in the way children approach construction, allowing this child to begin with a mental design of what he intends, encouraging that child to jot down the points that he wants to include, helping another child with a highly systematic orientation to employ a traditional outline as a base for construction. We can encourage children to modify any kind of initial, projected design as they write, and we can help them construct a first draft replete with cross-outs, write-overs, cut-outs, arrows indicating location, and stapled additions.

SELECTING A TITLE

It is within the overall design of a piece that title selection must be perceived. Words selected for the title of a piece are among the most important to be written. These words can give a capsule view of the idea. They can give some indication of the organization of what follows, or they can express the theme of the piece. They can indicate for whom the piece is intended, or they can be tricky, attention-getting devices.

The writer does not necessarily begin composing by constructing a title. His title may emerge in the process of actual writing. As the words of a composition or a poem begin to take form on paper, the dimensions of the ideas to be expressed become more obvious to the writer. He sees where he is going, and he constructs his title to communicate this direction. Then too, the writer may arrive at his title only after the piece is written. He reads and rereads what he has written, until he can identify the one, two, ten, or twelve words that express the essence of his writing. A title may also come from an association of words put together somewhere in the piece that in retrospect summarizes the whole piece perfectly.

With a child writer, we often put the cart before the horse. We begin by having him neatly write a title across the top of a paper. Then he must fit his ideas into that predetermined package, which is a rather impossible task. The product may be inconsistent with the title. The child may find that he cannot write on that title.

We suggest having a child compile a list of possible titles as he writes on a subject he himself identifies. Have him leave several blank lines at the top of the paper. When an inspiration strikes, have him jot the possibility at the top. After the piece is completed, encourage him to study the alternatives and perhaps add a few more. Have other children read the alternatives, indicating which one "turns them on," and then make a selection. A title constructed in this way is more likely to capture the essence of the written piece than one constructed initially to fit the requirements of an assignment.

ORGANIZING IDEAS FROM
RESOURCE MATERIALS

Watch young scholars at work in a library accumulating data for writing. Pens are being pushed as rapidly as possible across the paper as page after page of material is copied on index cards or in notebooks with little attempt made to sort the significant from the insignificant, the relevant from the irrelevant. Watch young college students, and many times you observe the same phenomenon, for the fallacy of hand copying is being perpetuated at every level of instruction at a time when copying machines are available at lower and lower costs. Do we, as teachers of composition, really believe that professional writers of serious material spend their preparatory time copying? How do they handle sources of data?

One way is to accumulate most of the related sources in one location. References that circulate are checked out of a library. Appropriate passages are copied by machine. As the writer skims his sources, he checks or slips in book markers to indicate particularly pertinent selections. These markers may be keyed in some way so that they indicate the specific topic of the selection. On the material that he has machine-copied, he underlines key points and makes notes in the margin. He may even classify all his references according to subtopics of his idea, dividing his references into piles of related material. Impressed by some really significant point, he may summarize that point on notepaper and react to it by adding his own ideas below his summary. He may copy with quotation marks a line or two that really hits the nail on the head. But the professional writer usually doesn't arrange his reference material in the traditional outline form—I, A, 1, and a.

Children can learn professional skills in handling resource materials by assembling their own collection of references relevant to their writing ideas. A class trip to the town library can supply every child with four or five books or periodicals. A letter sent to an appropriate agency can produce free folders and pamphlets. An interview with a scholar from the area of study can result in first-hand data. A questionnaire, prepared and distributed by the writer, can likewise produce data. Each child can have a particular section on the book shelves reserved for his materials. Book marks and pads of yellow paper can be made available for students working with a collection of source materials.

Children in upper elementary grades four through six can benefit from lessons on how to identify significant elements, how to summarize, and how to quote from sources. If all the students receive a weekly newspaper or magazine, this material can be the base for a lesson. After the children have read an article rather rapidly to themselves, the teacher can ask, "What is the main idea this author is telling us? What facts does he use to back up his idea? Which of his sentences really express his ideas in a nutshell?" Each child can then write a brief summary, one or two sentences, and jot down one "quotable quote"—words that have a high communication potential. As time progresses, the teacher can try having summaries written without preliminary discussion to see which children need further practice in summarizing and in selecting "quotable quotes."

To handle material in the manner just described requires some ability to perceive relationships. Younger elementary school children can hardly be expected to manage the tasks of organizing numbers of sources to support ideas. Even average middle school children in grades four through eight have trouble manipulating extensive amounts of reference materials. Therefore, though in elementary school we begin to have children support their ideas with references, we must do it within reason, asking for no more than four or five pages of fifth- or sixth-graders, and six to seven pages of seventh- and eighth-graders. If we ask for more, we will probably end up teaching children how to plagiarize, for they may well resort to copying directly from their sources rather than designing a framework of their own.

structuring paragraph patterns

Another aspect of expressing ideas in prose form is actually composing paragraph patterns that fit together to communicate the writer's idea. Composing is, first, an artistic endeavor: the writer may have an internal feeling about the way ideas should fit together. He may sense when paragraphs do not develop smoothly and when a different arrangement of thoughts or a change in pace is necessary. Composing is also a technical endeavor: the writer knows that paragraphs generally are built in certain patterns and applies his knowledge sometimes in a rather systematic way. When children have neither the artistic sense nor the technical know-how, their written work exhibits the same disorganization within and between paragraphs that is seen in Steve's report, "Doctor."[3]

In general, teachers, have not stressed patterns in their instruction. For instance, Steve's teacher gave him an *A* on his paper and made no suggestions for improvement. She probably was impressed by his extremely neat, precise penmanship, his obvious use of source materials, the length of his paper, and the level of word usage. Similarly, when some teachers-in-training have been asked to identify Steve's major weaknesses, they have jumped on his spelling of *candidate, qualifications, research,* and *supervision;* they have noted his usage of *an examinations,* his failure to underline titles, and his inconsistent use of pronouns, *he* and *you.* Yet problems of spelling, usage, and punctuation are relatively minor compared to the larger problem of building paragraph patterns. In this section, ways of helping children develop paragraph sense are considered.

ORGANIZING PARAGRAPHS

One of the most typical writing experiences in the first and second grades is writing the "news of the day." Children contribute sentences about what has or will happen that day; the teacher prints the sentences on the board, and later, as seatwork, the children copy the "news of the day" as a penmanship exercise.

In one second-grade class we visited, the news went something like this:

[3] See page 105.

Peter got splashed by a car.
It was raining this morning.
Linda didn't come to school.
Janie fell in a puddle.
There was a large dark cloud.
Maxie was late to school because he found a big lake on the road.

The teacher recorded the sentences in the order given, and the children proceeded to copy the piece in the same way.

Writing experiences such as the "news" are golden opportunities to teach children paragraph development. The teacher can continue the lesson with questions: "We seem to have two kinds of sentences here. Which sentences tell us about things people did this morning? Which sentences tell us about the weather this morning? Which kinds of sentences—about people or about the weather—should we rewrite first? Why? What sentence will be our beginning sentence? Let's put *1* in front of that sentence. What sentence will be our second sentence? Let's put a *2* in front of that. What will be our third sentence? Why? Let's put a *3* in front of that." The children can then rewrite the sentences following the order of the numbers:

It was raining this morning. There was a large dark cloud. Peter got splashed by a car. Janie fell in a puddle. Maxie was late to school because he found a big lake on the road. Linda didn't come to school.

What is being taught now is not only the projection of ideas for writing, but the perception of relationships among ideas as well. Whenever children write prose together, they should first be urged to share whatever ideas they have. After expressing their ideas, children can go back, as in the previous example, and order the ideas together.

Working with very able children, a teacher might strive for a tighter organization of the ideas by asking, "What sentence does not tell us something that happened to us on our rainy day?" Children may identify the sentence about the black cloud as one that does not "fit" with the others. If they identify a sentence as "not belonging," the children can delete it from the paragraph.

A paragraph is considered by most authorities to be a series of interrelated sentences that project a single idea. Often the idea of a paragraph is set forth in a sentence, the topic sentence, and it is this idea that gives unity to the paragraph. All other sentences must in some way be related to the idea in the topic sentence. Through activities such as the one just described, young children can begin to understand the structure of a paragraph.

Older children can work with more sophisticated paragraph patterns. For example, sometimes a writer constructing a paragraph builds inductively toward his idea, putting several details in sequence and ending with a sentence that ties up the whole. At other times, he builds deductively: he states his point and then marshalls the details to support it. At still other times, he sandwiches his topic sentence between two layers of related material. Sometimes, too, the topic sentence remains unwritten. The writer assumes his audience can perceive the interrelationship among the component sentences. There are obviously many ways to put a paragraph together.

To help children develop paragraph sense, we can give them two topic sentences that are similar, but not identical, and have them write a paragraph about each. What related thoughts would we put in the first paragraph? What thoughts fit better into the other? We have tried this technique even with college students who have trouble organizing paragraphs. At the college level we have used these two sentences: "The parking problem at the college has become a major concern of both students and faculty"; "The spring season has made the parking situation at the college almost impossible." In the first paragraph, students include details to prove student and faculty concern: letters to the editor of the school paper have appeared; students have spoken to their professors about being late to class; professors have discussed the situation in faculty meetings; student sit-ins are being considered. In the second paragraph, students include details to show how the spring season has added to the problem: showers have turned parking lots into pools; grassy areas used for parking have become mud fields in which a student can lose his car; walking from the more distant lots is hazardous as a student tries to avoid water-filled potholes.

Examples of similar types of exercise sentences for use in elementary school are—

A–1. People are becoming more concerned about pollution of the environment.
   2. We are rapidly turning our rivers into cesspools of pollution.
B–1. To play in the snow is fun.
   2. The snowstorm struck last night.
C–1. Dogs should not be allowed to run loose.
   2. A dog is a boy's best friend.
   3. A boy who has a dog should be willing to take care of it.
D–1. Boys are becoming more style-conscious.
   2. I like (don't like) long hair on boys.

This type of exercise more closely replicates the actual task of writing unified paragraphs than the traditional exercise of underlining topic sentences in paragraphs from a grammar book. If children are to be asked to underline topic sentences, they should work with paragraphs that they have written themselves. They underline to determine whether each paragraph they have constructed expresses one central idea.

Another kind of exercise for teaching unity of thought within paragraphs was reported to us by a third-grade teacher, Miss Elaine Winters.

Miss Winters constructs paragraphs that contain one sentence unrelated to all the others. Her students take turns donning a detective's cap to identify the sentence that does not belong in the paragraph. She then has the children focus on paragraphs that they themselves have written to detect the "intruders."

SEQUENCING IDEAS

In constructing an effective paragraph, the thinker-writer must sequence his ideas so that one point builds naturally toward the next. As early as the first grade, children can work with sequential patterns. They can be asked to line up objects according to size. Later on they can make time lines on which they line up events chronologically. At the same time, a teacher can help children recap recent events. As a class, they can list events, starting with those that happened last. A teacher can have children orally recount processes by asking, "What do we do first? next? then? after that?" Teachers can have children give directions orally by asking. "What is the best way to get to Route 208? What do we do first? Then what? Finally?"

Experience-story charts can be used to introduce children to the notion of sequencing ideas. One second-grade teacher took her children on an excursion to the neighborhood stores. Upon returning, the children, together, wrote a report of their trip.

Our Walk to the Stores

Our class went on a walk today. We visited some stores. First, we went to Priscilla's Candy Shop. The lady gave us chocolate candy. Then we went to the pet store. We saw dogs, monkeys, birds, and an alligator. After that we went to the florist shop. We watched a lady make a bouquet. We saw roses, orchids, and big ferns. Our class had fun on our walk to the stores. We want to go again.

That the teacher helped the children sequence their ideas by asking guiding questions is obvious in the tight organization of the paragraph. She probably began by asking, "What did we do today?" and followed up with, "Where did we go first? What happened at the candy shop? Then where did we go? What happened there? After that what did we do?" Hers was an introductory lesson in the craft of writing that stressed intuitive understanding. She was teaching the craft not by giving and explaining definitions and rules, but by having the children experience the process.

A related technique is to have children play with scrambled paragraphs in which sentences have intentionally been disorganized. The children order the sentences. A teacher can take paragraphs from student textbooks, rearrange the sentences, type them on a sheet with the primary-story typewriter and make a transparency, which can be projected for class or group analysis. It is good to choose paragraphs involving different kinds of content, so that students get practice in ordering different kinds of ideas. With older children, scramble more complicated materials, such as passages from the *Declaration of Independence.*

Still another way to help children sequence ideas is to cut up a comic strip into its component segments and scramble the segments. The children must put the segments into a logical order. Sometimes it is fun for children to work with several scrambled comic strips that bear the same title and involve the same characters. Now the task is more complex; children must group the segments that belong together before sequencing them.

Very closely related to the sequencing of ideas is the construction of smooth transitions between ideas placed in juxtaposition. As the writer orders his ideas, either consciously or intuitively, he builds his transitions according to the nature of the relationships he perceives in his material. He may make a point and then want to modify it in some way, so he writes "However——," "Nevertheless——," "On the other hand——," or "Regardless of this——." He may express an idea and then want to add a related thought, so he interjects "Also——," "In like manner——," "Likewise——," or "Similarly——." He may make a generalization and follow it with a particular instance, so he states "For example——," "An instance——," or "Specifically——." He may be describing a sequence of events, so he writes "First——, Next——, Then——, Last——."

A simple technique we can employ to help children with transitions is to delete transitional words from a paragraph and have children fill in the deleted words.

> John liked Susan._____he did not want to take her to the dance. He had very good reasons. _____ he did not have the money. _____ he did not have a suit._____he had not even the slightest knowledge of how to dance.

There are, of course, many ways of filling in the blanks. As children propose additional possibilities, lists of alternate transitional words can be recorded on cards to be kept available for reference during writing.

Children can also be asked to combine sentences, forming different transitional patterns that communicate approximately the same message. Take the first two sentences of our John-and-Susan paragraph. How can we combine the sentences and still communicate his liking and his not wanting to go to the dance? Children will propose—

> Although (or though) John liked Susan, he did not want to take her to the dance.
> John did not want to take Susan to the dance even though he liked her.
> Despite his liking for Susan, John did not want to take her to the dance.

Such patterns as these employ subordinate clauses and phrases to make transitions.

Another type of exercise involves rewriting sentences in which *and* and *so* are used as primary transitional elements. For example, rewrite the following:

> Bill Hamilton went fishing in the river and fell in and lost his catch so he turned his fishing trip into a swimming trip and went home wet and without fish.
>
> Our family went on a picnic in the woods and we played games together and we built a fire and we cooked our dinner over the fire and then we sang songs until the fire burned out and the sky got very dark so we had to go home.

Still another kind of exercise useful in developing skill in thought transitions is the chain story. A chain story is one in which each child begins a story but writes only the first paragraph. Then the story is passed on to another child, who adds to it. After a short time period, the story is passed to still a different child, who continues the story.

Smooth transitions are important in this context as a child picks up the theme started by someone else. To aid in the process, the teacher can supply charts that list—

- words to consider if you want to change story direction: *on the other hand, nevertheless, however, whereas;*
- words to consider if you want to continue with the same story direction: *also, now, the next, in the same way.*

The teacher can also suggest that the child identify a key word or words in the material written by the previous student and for continuity repeat these key words in the portion he is adding.

Experience seems to indicate that chain stories on which three children work are more effective pieces of writing than stories to which numbers of children add a section. Perhaps there is a psychological reason for this: children retain a sense of possession for a story and do not look at the activity as simply a game. There may also be a structural reason: short stories typically do have a beginning, a middle, and an end. Each child in a group of three can more readily perceive how his section relates to the whole. Three language-disadvantaged children in the fourth grade wrote the following chain story after enjoying several previous experiences with this activity.

The Bogey Man

One night as I was in bed I saw a shadow...it was very big. Mommy! Mommy! I called, but no one came. And then I reliezed it was the Bogey Man! He crept closer and closer. A bogey a bogey I'd scream if I could. *Next Child:* I got out of bed. I jump out the winow. I got lost out there. *Next Child:* There I saw a man. He had a cape it was scarey he said I'm the boogy man. Then the cape fell off. I found out it was my father. I screamed oh daddy you scared me halve to death! He put me in bed and the next morning he explained.

THE END!

Although the three children show lack of ability to work with sentence units, it is most apparent that they are beginning rather effectively to handle the sequential development of an idea within a paragraph.

summary thoughts

Integral facets of any ongoing writing program are encounters with the paragraph patterns and thought processes so fundamental to written expression. Therefore, the teacher who decides to design a writing program into her classroom curriculum rather than to teach isolated "creative" and "functional" writing lessons must, by necessity, include work with the individual student; she must allow time to help the student analyze his own ideas and ways of organizing them. Similarly, the teacher must design into her program small-group skill-building sessions that are directly related to organizational and thinking problems children are having; she must allow time for children to play with paragraphs—putting sentences into logical sequences and perceiving relationships among thoughts. It is through such individual and group activities based on actual written work done in classrooms that children begin to acquire skill in manipulating ideas on paper.

6

let children put words together

*Words are the dress of thoughts; which
should no more be presented in rags, tatters,
and dirt than your person should.*

Lord Chesterfield, Letters

Ultimately the writer is faced with the task of selecting words and building them into units of thought that communicate his idea. This task is not one that occurs after the writer has formulated his idea completely, or after he has designed a structure for expressing that idea. It takes place concurrently with idea-formulation and design-structuring. Even as an idea begins to develop, it takes on verbal dimensions, and at times as the idea grows, the structures to express it become apparent to the writer with specific words emerging as key ones in communicating that idea.

To select the appropriate word and to generate a good English sentence are essential elements of writing if clear, precise expression of thought is to result. In the elementary schools, teachers can give attention to this craft phase of writing; they can help children to develop skill in handling words and sentence patterns.

selecting words

Our job as word-teachers is to give youngsters the building blocks of communication: the words to express emerging ideas. How is this to be achieved? Let us look specifically at techniques that can prove helpful in the elementary school situation.

FINDING WORDS TO EXPRESS EXPERIENCE

A storm had raged almost continually for several days. When it abated, Leslie, a four-year-old, came out to survey the damage. Picking up pieces of bark that the wind had pulled from the trees and scattered over the driveway, Leslie concluded, "The wind pulled the skin from the trees." Leslie wanted to communicate her reaction, but lacking the exact word to express her thoughts, she had extended the meaning of a word she did know (*skin*) to the one she required (*bark*).

One of the authors was with Leslie when the four-year-old discovered the "skin" of trees. She suggested, "Leslie, let's look at the trees where the bark has been pulled off." Together she and Leslie peeled off bark loosened by the storm, looked at the new surface, compared it with the surface still covered with bark, and picked up more pieces of bark from the lawn. During the whole experience, Leslie and the author talked about bark, what it looked like, how it felt, and what purpose it served.

Leslie, a child who likes to collect things, made a collection of different kinds of bark. A short time later, Leslie called out to her little friend who had come to play, "Look at all my pieces of bark." Leslie had acquired another building block of communication.

It is in the context of meaningful experience that vocabulary grows. A child experiencing a phenomenon and needing additional words to express ideas readily latches onto words interjected into the experience. Therefore, the very experience that supplies the idea-content for written expression may also be the source of a vocabulary to express the idea.

Talking about the experience is the bridge to that vocabulary development. For example, sixth-grade youngsters carrying on a plant growth experiment can be asked, "What do you hypothesize will be the outcome?" As the youngsters devise hypotheses, the word *hypothesis* will begin to appear in their speech patterns. At the first-grade level, similar types of language experiences are possible: children visiting an aquarium can talk about fins and gills, scales and barbs. They can describe the fish as streamlined, shiny, or slim; and they can assign inventive names to the fish that they like: Finny, Sword, Tiger Fish. At the third-grade level, youngsters who have experienced a particularly happy activity—a party, finger-painting session, a walk in the woods—can be encouraged to talk about happy-feeling words. The teacher, too, can interject her own happy-feeling words, words that the children can use on the spot to talk about their feelings. When a sad event occurs, children can be encouraged to talk about sad-feeling words, and into their conversation the teacher can again interject words that the children are obviously seeking.

The focus of vocabulary-building activity is initially oral. The teacher structures discussion so that children incorporate more and more words into their speaking vocabularies, for after all, when children begin to write, they are only putting on paper the thoughts that they have previously been expressing in oral form. The words that they speak are the words they tend to write into their compositions.

For this reason, discussion of a variety of experiences is essential. Observing fast-moving vehicles on a busy city street can be the springboard for using action words. Touching different types of materials, such as cotton, silk, and sandpaper, can be the springboard for using texture words. The accidental falling down in the playground and skinning of a knee can be the springboard for using pain words. Watching different chemicals burn in a flame can be the springboard for using color words. Fighting with a friend can be the springboard for using mad words. It is the teacher who must uncover for her children the language potential inherent in an experience.

Vicarious experience can also lead to new words. One of the authors observed a kindergarten teacher discussing with a group of children a picture of a lady rolling out cookie dough. Many of the children had never seen dough in its uncooked state and did not know what it was. Several children who had had the experience explained to the others. As the group made plans to make dough the next day, children who were among those not originally knowing about dough were using the word in a natural way.

Recordings of popular songs can also serve as a medium for encountering and assimilating new words. Recordings like Simon and Garfunkel's "You Can Tell the World" or "Sounds of Silence" can stimulate interaction with words. Children can listen to the way words have been put together, talk about words and silence, and even sing along with the recording star.

Upper grade children add words to their speaking and writing vocabularies through study of the content areas. A fifth-grade class was observed discussing geologic change after a six-week period during which they had studied geologic processes. Words like *erupt, submerge, crater, fissure,* and *alpine* were used naturally by the youngsters as they talked about the experiences they had had within their unit. The teacher of this class had as one of his unit objectives that the children assimilate these basic words in their functional vocabulary. The culminating discussion indicated that he had achieved his objective.

Beginning with relevant words when working toward a writing activity can be an especially useful technique with youngsters who have a limited verbal facility. A group of seventh-graders from a city school were observed as they shared a common experience and talked about words they could use to express their ideas about the experience. During the discussion the teacher also informally mentioned words that the students might find necessary to express ideas. The students kept a pencil in hand during the talktime and jotted down the words they might want to use in the writing period to follow. If a student did not know how to spell a word, he was urged to put it down in a way recognizable to him. During the actual writing session, the teacher circulated quickly from student to student, correcting the spelling of words on each student's list, so that by the time the student wanted to use a word, he could simply copy it from his own list.

A youngster who speaks a nonstandard dialect of English and who has a limited standard English vocabulary has a special need for a vocabulary-building language program based on experience and talk. He needs to encounter words in situations that have meaning to him so that new words are gradually assimilated into his speaking vocabulary and will eventually appear in his written work. Experiencing words should be an integral part of his daily school program, so that whenever possible he will be able to relate abstract words to some concrete experience in the real world.

PERCEIVING THE STRUCTURE OF WORDS

That words in and of themselves can be intriguing to the human mind is made evident by the existence of numerous word games and puzzles: the daily crossword puzzle, anagrams, and games like Scrabble can keep the mind involved and active for hours. As a means of increasing children's facility with words, a teacher can take advantage of the interest words engender by building activities in which children encounter the structural relationships that exist within and among words.

Grapheme-phoneme relationships. It is helpful for a writer attempting to encode to understand the relationship between phonemes and graphemes in the English language. When we teach children to spell, what we fundamentally do (if we adhere to a linguistic approach) is teach children different ways in which speech sounds are encoded—in other words, the different graphemes through which a phoneme can be represented.[1] Children encounter specific situations in which certain graphemes tend to be used. Moving from specific examples, children discover generalizations for themselves: /f/ is represented with the letter *f* or the letter *ph* when the sound occurs at the beginning of words, but never with *gh*; /f/ coming at the end of a word is more likely to be represented by a double *f* than by a single *f* if the preceding vowel is short; /k/ followed by an *i* is represented by the letter *k*, whereas /k/ followed by an *a* is represented by the letter *c*.[2]

[1] A grapheme is a letter or a group of letters through which a speech sound is represented: the letter *r* is a grapheme as is the letter group *wr*. A phoneme is a significant speech sound of a language. On paper, a phoneme is indicated by a letter or letters enclosed within two slashes: /sl/ or /ey/.

[2] The teacher who wants to pursue grapheme-phoneme relationships is referred to Fred Brengelman, *The English Language* (Englewood Cliffs, N.J.: Prentice-Hall, 1970).

The older child who has not acquired a rudimentary skill in manipulating such grapheme-phoneme relationships is severely handicapped as he begins to record his own thoughts on paper. Essentially he is language-disadvantaged. For instance, Gayle, a girl in the third grade, wrote "I Kope you cowld canem to my birtday waday 7, 1971 an Maine 200." Timmie, a boy in the same grade, recorded "I hope yue come to oue pony. We well have a pig kake and we well have somd fize."

How can teachers help children like Gayle and Timmie? First, both these children need experience with the full range of phonemes employed in the English language so that they themselves can produce the sounds. They would benefit from listening-speaking lessons in which they encounter the speech sounds and reproduce them orally. One lesson for Timmie would involve distinguishing the two consonant sounds, $/p/$ and $/b/$, as in pig and big. He could listen to words beginning with $/p/$ and $/b/$ and sort them into two groups. His lesson would also help him understand how speech sounds are recorded on paper; he would work with the graphemes used to represent $/b/$ and $/p/$.

Granted, activities like those suggested for Timmie are typically conducted in kindergarten and the first grade; they are not "third-grade experiences." Yet Timmie is not functioning at a theoretical level called the third grade. He is language-disadvantaged through no fault of his own—he probably had limited exposure in his early years to the full range of American English phonemes and as a result has not acquired skill in encoding. Much of his writing activity, therefore, must still be oral; he records via tape or via dictation. Simultaneously, he must be developing encoding skills in a systematic program geared by his teacher to his personal deficiencies.

On the other hand, the child who has acquired a knowledge of linguistic interrelationships can apply his understanding to the encoding of words that he is writing down for the first time. If he is uncertain how to spell a word, he writes it in the most logical way he can, drawing on the knowledge he acquired previously in inductive spelling lessons. When he has finished recording his thoughts, the child can reconsider the letters he has written, checking in the dictionary to assure accuracy. Of course, to be overly concerned with using the correctly spelled word can be a handicap as one begins to compose a written piece. Stopping in midthought to go to a dictionary can cause one to lose the primary thought altogether. To write down an approximation, or even leave a blank to be filled in later, appears to be a more productive option.

Having children acquire skill in handling the different graphemic representations of a speech sound aids in final dictionary checking. Children often raise the question, "How can we look up a word in the dictionary if we can't spell it?" Working with grapheme-phoneme relationships, children have an available *modus operandi*: they write down as many graphemic representations that adhere to the generalizations they know; then they check the possible representations in the dictionary, looking up each in turn.

Structurally related words and word units. Understanding some of the patterns that exist within English words can also be an aid to the writer attempting to record his ideas. Some of these understandings can be acquired much in the manner of a game. For instance, children in the fourth grade are given these two sets of words:

Pattern A	Pattern B
days	flies
buys	cries

They must determine in which of the two patterns other related words belong: *journeys, blueberries, plays, armies, ladies, monkeys, valleys, alleys, assemblies.* Then they must add *s* or change the *y* to *i* and add *es* to the following words: *dry, lay, boy, joy, alloy, injury, jury,* and *strawberry.* The word puzzle to be solved is "In what cases do we change the *y* to *i* and add *es*?" The child can apply this understanding as he checks words about which he is uncertain.

A child's vocabulary is also improved if he understands the internal structure of words, the meaningful units or morphemes of which words are composed. For example, a child who knows what happens to the meaning of a word when *un* is affixed in the initial position may be able to add other words to his functional word repertoire with little difficulty. In the middle elementary grades the child can play with *un-* opposites: happy-unhappy, pleasant-unpleasant, able-unable, and cooperative-uncooperative. The teacher can begin the word game by printing the *un-* opposites on cards, mounting the cards on a bulletin board, and having a child explain how the second word differs from the first. A stack of similar cards can be made available to the children so that over a period of a week they can search for other *un-* opposites to print on cards and add to the board. If the game is played team-style, a team gets a point for each *un-* opposite uncovered by a team member. A team has a right to challenge any words added by the other side. A successful challenge gives the challenging team three points.

A similar word game can be played with other structural units, such as *dis-, con-, in-, -ment, -tion ,-ance, -ness,* and *-ful.* In each case the children build on words with which they are already familiar. They increase the number of words on which they can draw as they speak and as they write, and they increase their understanding of structural spelling relationships— how these morphemes are added to other morphemes. The latter understanding can be applied as children attempt to use words in their writing.

Structurally similar words can also be encountered as a group. Playing orally with relationships within such words, youngsters incorporate the words into their functional vocabulary. One fun example involves the words in which /ey/ is represented as *et* because of a common French origin. Children can begin with words like *buffet* and *bouquet* supplied by the teacher. Their job is to uncover structurally related words (and they are allowed to refer to a dictionary). The search can go on for several days as children add related words to a bulletin-board chart. Similar game-search activities can take place with words that contain units like *photo, phono, therm,* or *graph*; with contractions like *it's, don't,* and *shouldn't*; with hyphenated words; with words of similar foreign origins. The objective is more than just having the youngsters develop an understanding of the structural relationships among words within their language. The objective is that the youngsters have an increased facility with words as a medium of communication.

FINDING SYNONYMS FOR OVERUSED WORDS

Children can begin to realize the power that words can have by working with synonyms. Synonyms usually do not have exactly the same meaning; fine distinctions exist. For example, "I hate him" is a perfectly acceptable form and follows a typical linguistic pattern:

I	hate	him.
subject	verb	object

However, there are other ways of constructing the same sentence.

1. I detest him.
2. I abhor him.
3. I abominate him.
4. I loathe him.

Each communicates a slightly different shade of meaning. Webster's clarifies these differences.

> *Hate* implies aversion often coupled with enmity or malice; *detest,* violent antipathy; *abhor,* profound, often shuddering, repugnance; *abominate,* strong detestation, as of something ill-omened or shameful; *loathe,* utter disgust and intolerance.[3]

To come to a more concrete and functional understanding of synonyms, children can play with a simple sentence: "The man walked down the street." Children can volunteer to pantomime the sentence, keeping in mind another verb that tells more precisely how the man walked. Children will

---

[3] *Webster's New Collegiate Dictionary,* 2d ed. (Springfield, Mass.: G.C. Merriam Co., 1949), p. 379.

stagger, limp, hobble, and stumble. Others will guess the verb that describes the activity. Here are examples of other sentences to be pantomimed:

1. The teacher *looked* at the boy.
2. The boy *swam* through the water.
3. The lady *got out* of the car.
4. The horse *trotted* down the street.
5. He *drove* his automobile through town.

Youngsters can also be encouraged to keep lists of possible substitutes for words they typically overuse. What word can we substitute for *interesting*? for *pretty*? for *nice*? Answers may result in a "class thesaurus," which the children construct together. As they compose, junior high school youngsters can refer to Roget's *International Thesaurus,* a volume that many professional writers find more valuable than a dictionary. Younger children can refer to *In Other Words: A Beginning Thesaurus* and *In Other Words: A Junior Thesaurus* by W. Cabell Greet, William Jenkins, and Andrew Schiller (Glenville, Ill.: Scott, Foresman, 1968 and 1969). In a sense, when we expect children to write without such an aid, we are expecting them to do better than the professional.

For older elementary school children, a thesaurus can actually become a fun book to take along on an excursion. A group of sixth-graders got carried away with words after they had listened to the sounds at a busy intersection. The thesaurus supplied them with words like *whiz, buzz, zip, screak, screech, crump, jangle, clash, clatter, rattle, clank, whoop, squeal, whine, wail, whistle, blare, rasp,* and *hiss,* which appealed to the children because of the onomatopoeic sounds. When the children returned to their classroom, they concocted sounds, by voice and by rubbing objects together, that were actual examples of the words found in the thesaurus. They made a tape in which words and sounds were juxtaposed. Through their own activity, the words became meaningful symbols for actual events.

FINDING COLORFUL EXPRESSIONS

Certain word combinations add color to a written piece. These combinations include colloquialisms, dialect, slang, figures of speech, play on words, and informal usage of language.

Colloquialisms. In American English we can "fly off the handle," "dress a turkey," and "face the music", and when we do, we add another dimension to our language. Children delight in looking at idiosyncracies of our language if they are presented as colorfully as in Peggy Parish's *Amelia Bedelia* (New York: Harper & Row, 1963) or Eth Clifford's *A Bear Before Breakfast* (New York: Putnam, 1962). Based on the material supplied in books such as these, children can make their own dictionaries of favorite idioms and add to them day by day. They can keep these homemade dictionaries as ready references as they write.

Dialect and slang.   When writing, we sometimes attempt to convey a mood, develop a character, or describe a geographical region by employing dialects, slang, or jargon. For instance, C. S. Forester uses the distinctive jargon of the sailor in *Captain Horatio Hornblower*:

> "Hard-a-starboard," he rasped at the quartermaster at the wheel, and then to the hands forward, "Smartly with the braces now!"
> With the rudder hard across the ship came round a trifle. The fore topsail came round. The jibs and fore staysails were set like lightning.[4]

We can encourage children to do the same by supplying them with references when they attempt stories that might require slang or jargon. References in this case are books written in the desired style—sometimes novels, sometimes short stories. Second, we can encourage children to write realistically by our own attitude toward slang and even swearing. One of the authors vividly remembers being told as a child to write "proper English" when she tried to construct a story about the sea. Now sailors do not always use "proper English." Instead of insisting on inappropriate standards of word usage, teachers should help a child find material that will give him a rather accurate impression of the speech characteristics of a group of people.

Figures of speech.   William Strunk and E. B. White in *The Elements of Style* recommend that figures of speech be employed sparingly, as too many can be "more distracting than illuminating."[5] Employed sparingly and in appropriate contexts, however, figures of speech can be effective. For example, Carl Sandburg turned to metaphor when he made fog into a cat in "Fog," as did Alfred Noyes when he wrote "The road was a ribbon of moonlight." In contrast, Wordsworth turned to simile when he wrote "I wandered lonely *as a cloud*," as did Coleridge in his line "I pass, *like night*, from land to land." Most of us have used the hyperbole when we have made such gross exaggeration as "I was so hungry I could have eaten a horse" or "I was so embarrassed I thought I would die."

In playing with simile, metaphor, and hyperbole, children should not be required to distinguish them; to know the difference between a simile and a metaphor does not result in effective use. Emphasis should be on encouraging children to try their hands at writing figures of speech. For instance, we can project beginnings of lines to be completed by children in

---

[4] C.S. Forester, *Captain Horatio Hornblower* (Boston: Little Brown, 1951), p. 71.
[5] William Strunk and E.B. White, *The Elements of Style* (New York: Macmillan, 1962), p. 66.

numerous ways. Suggest "as lonely as a ——," and children will add "but-terfly," "a man standing on a barren desert," "a solitary spaceman," and "an undersea diver." Suggest "as happy as ——," "as peaceful as ——," "as warlike as ——," "as unhappy as ——." The possibilities are endless as children themselves take over the game to propose similar base phrases for similes. Children can also play with these beginnings:

> The man walked like (as if)——.
> The girl sang like (as if)——.
> The girl danced like (as if)——.
> The boy drove like (as if)——.
> The man worked like (as if)——.
> The child ran like (as if)——.

Play on words. We can all remember one type of riddle that we especially appreciated as children—the riddle that is essentially a play on words. "We've all heard the one":

> Why does an elephant have a trunk?
> *Answer:* Because he couldn't carry a suitcase.
> What is green and goes ding-dong?
> *Answer:* A green ding-dong.
> What is black and white and red all over?
> *Old answer:* A newspaper. *New answer:* A skunk with diaper rash.

These riddles base their humor on the double meanings that some words have.

Children are a storehouse of play-on-word riddles. The riddles they know can be recorded in a class riddle book and can stimulate the invention of original riddles. The riddles that children invent can be shared with others in the class during a riddle-upmanship contest, and the best one's can be carried to other classes. Such an activity encourages children to play with words in humorous ways.

Literature supplies numerous examples of humorous uses of words of the same or similar sounds (puns). In "Faithless Sally Brown," Thomas Hood played with the words *toll'd* and *told*:

> His death, which happen'd in his berth,
>   At forty-old befell.
> They went and told the sexton, and
>   The sexton *toll'd the bell.*[6]

[6] Thomas Hood, "Faithless Sally Brown," in *Poems of Thomas Hood,* ed. William Cole. Copyright 1968 by William Cole; reprinted by permission of Thomas Y. Crowell Company.

Oliver Herford played with the sound of the word *speak*:

> My sense of sight is very keen.
> My sense of hearing weak.
> One time I saw a mountain pass,
> But could not hear *its peak*.[7]

In "John Burns of Gettysburg," Bret Harte played with the word *mead*:

> The very day that General Lee,
> Flower of Southern chivalry,
> Baffled and beaten, backward reeled
> From a stubborn *Meade* and a barren field.[8]

Older elementary school children take delight in such word usage. One of the authors vividly recalls an incident with an eighth-grade class she was teaching. She began a statement with "Now, I grant that——." The children snickered. "What's wrong?" she queried. "Grant grants," one boy replied. What had struck the funny bone of these bright children was Miss Grant's use of *grant*. With children like these, we can capitalize on their natural enjoyment of the humor in certain word-sound combinations. We can record "Grant grants" on a Pun Board to which students add puns that they identify in their reading, that they themselves invent, or that they hear television comedians interject into a situation. The current crop of humorous televison programs is a gold mine of examples of the playful use of words, and upper grade children can be motivated by TV humor to try their hand at writing "Laugh-In"-type skits. These skits can be assembled into a rapid-moving humor program that engenders laughter through jokes, play on words, satire, facial expressions, and flashes of color and motion.

Informal Usage. Given the two sentences "I wish that I *was* rich" and "I wish that I *were* rich," which usage is "correct"? According to *A Dictionary of Contemporary American Usage,* *was* is quite acceptable even in formal writing. Actually, we no longer think of a particular usage as correct; rather, we distinguish levels of acceptability: formal, standard, and nonstandard. Then too, some usage that was considered nonstandard in the past is today considered standard because of its general use in conversation.

Why insist on outmoded levels of usage in writing by children? Too

---

[7] Oliver Herford, "My Sense of Sight," in *Home Book of Verse for Young Folks,* ed. Burton E. Stevenson (New York: Holt, Rinehart & Winston, 1956); reprinted by permission of Louise Kramer and Richard Slayton.

[8] Bret Harte, "John Burns of Gettysburg," in *Bret Harte* by Joseph B. Harrison (New York: American Book, 1941). Copyright 1941 by American Book Company; reprinted by permission.

often we put ourselves in the position of the rat in the following argument from *The Wind in the Willows*:

> The Toad, having finished his breakfast, picked up a stout stick and swung it vigorously, belabouring imaginary animals. 'I'll learn 'em to steal my house!' he cried. 'I'll learn 'em, I'll learn 'em!'
> 'Don't say "learn 'em!" Toad,' said the Rat, greatly shocked. 'It's not good English.'
> 'What are you always nagging at Toad for?' inquired the Badger rather peevishly. 'What's the matter with his English? It's the same what I use myself, and if it's good enough for me, it ought to be good enough for you!'
> 'I'm very sorry,' said the Rat humbly. 'Only I *think* it ought to be "teach 'em," not "learn 'em." '
> 'But we don't *want* to teach 'em,' replied the Badger. 'We want to *learn* 'em—learn 'em, learn 'em! And what's more, we're going to *do* it, too!'
> 'O, very well, have it your own way,' said the Rat. He was getting rather muddled about it himself, and presently he retired into a corner, where he could be heard muttering, 'Learn 'em, teach 'em, teach 'em, learn 'em!' till the Badger told him rather sharply to leave off.[9]

Teachers should be familiar with what is considered standard usage in informal writing in order to avoid such unnecessary controversies, as "It is I" instead of "It is me," or "Does everyone have his book?" instead of "Does everyone have their book?" We must remember that we generally split infinitives, dangle prepositions, employ *like* as a conjunction, and say "different than."

This point relates particularly to the written expression of a youngster who comes to school speaking a nonstandard dialect of American English. The dialect that this child speaks differs from standard American English in several basic respects. First, the child's vocabulary includes words and expressions not found in a standard dictionary or words employed in ways other than a dictionary suggests. Second, his dialect has structural patterns that differ from those typically employed in standard informal usage. To insist that this child speak and write in only standard American English patterns and with standard vocabulary is to ask the impossible and is, in essence, to reject an element of the child's culture. Walter Loban's words are relevant here.

> Pupils need to learn standard English in addition to the social class dialect they know, Cajun, Appalachian, or whatever it may be. (We are not here concerned with *regional variations* of English but with *social class variations.*) If such pupils do not learn a second kind of dialect, standard English, they will be forever prevented from access to economic opportunity and social acceptance. We can learn to grant full dignity to the child and to the

9 Kenneth Grahame, *The Wind in the Willows* (New York: Scribner's, 1954), pp. 233–34. Copyright 1908, 1933, 1953, 1954 by Scribner's; 1961 by Ernest H. Shepard; reprinted by permission of Scribner's.

language spoken in his home. At the same time, we must help him to acquire the established standard language so he can operate in society as fully as he may wish. He would, of course, be free to make the choice of not using his second dialect. . .

Loban, however, proposes—

> In the kindergarten and in the earliest years of school, the emphasis should be upon the child's using *whatever dialect of the language he already speaks* as the means of thinking and exploring and imagining. Language is also more than a tool of thought. It is a way of expressing emotions and feelings. It is a way of adjusting to other people, of expressing solidarity with the human race. Language has many purposes among which one of the most important, and certainly the most important to the teacher, is the use of language as a means of developing the powers of reason. But it is not the only one. If the child speaks a dialect and says, "Them magnet's pickin' up the nails," we do not need to worry about "them magnet's" at this point. Let him say, "them magnet's." That usage will not interfere with the crucial cognitive processes. If we do not first encourage the child to use his own language in its full range, we may diminish his desire to use language in school.[10]

The dialectally different youngster in the upper elementary grades is systematically introduced to standard vocabulary and sentence patterns. The child begins to distinguish between what Gladney and Leaverton call "EVERYDAY TALK" and "SCHOOL TALK."[11] He listens to school talk, he imitates school talk, he distinguishes the elements of school talk from everyday talk, and he begins to differentiate the situations in which school talk can be used and those in which everyday talk can be used. What the child basically does is learn standard English as a second language.

The characteristics of the child's talk—his vocabulary and his sentence structure—will be reflected in his writing, of course. The child in the primary grades writes in his native dialect; as he becomes more familiar with standard English and situations in which it is used, he must decide whether it is appropriate to use his native or standard dialect, and he functions in terms of his decision.

LISTENING TO THE SOUNDS OF WORDS

Although selecting the precise word to convey meaning is important, a sense of sound is also vital to the construction process. Rhythm and rhyme

10 Walter Loban, "A Sustained Program of Language Learning" in *Language Programs for the Disadvantaged: The Report of the NCTE Task Force on Teaching English to the Disadvantaged*, co-chairmen Richard Corbin and Muriel Crosby. Copyright 1965 by the National Council of Teachers of English; reprinted by permission of the National Council of Teachers of English.

11 Mildred R. Gladney and Lloyd Leaverton, "A Model for Teaching Standard English to Non-Standard English Speakers," in *Elementary English* 45 (October 1968): 758–63.

can be used to heighten an effect the author is attempting to create. Alfred Tennyson rhythmically creates the effect of galloping horses in the following selection from "The Charge of the Light Brigade":

> Half a league, half a league,
> Half a league, onward,
> All in the valley of Death
> Rode the six hundred.

On the other hand, John Masefield uses repetition of phrase elements and rhyme to create his mood in "Sea Fever." By placing the same phrase at the beginning of each verse, the poet helps the reader to make the transition from one line of verse to the next. In the first stanza, examples of alliteration, in which the author repeats the same sounds are italicized. In the second stanza, words are italicized to illustrate the effective use of rhyme and repetitions.

> *I must go down to the seas again,* to the lonely *sea* and the *sky,*
> And all I ask is a tall *ship* and a *star* to *steer* her by;
> And the *wheel's* kick and the *wind's song* and the *white sail's shakings,*
> And a gray mist on the sea's face and a gray dawn breaking . . . .
>
> *I must go down to the seas again,* to the vagrant gypsy *life,*
> To the gull's way and the whale's way where the wind's like a whetted
> *knife.*
> And all I ask is a merry yarn from a laughing fellow-*rover,*
> And quiet sleep and a sweet dream when the long trek's *over.*[12]

A similar device that writers have used successfully is onomatopoeia, when a word is in itself the sound it describes. In "the burning wood *crackled* and *hissed*" or "the *buzz* of a bee," the italicized words are examples of onomatopoeia.

Writers have used their knowledge of phonics to create an effect. Knowing that some sounds are hard and some soft, a writer may select harder sounds to convey an impression of galloping hoofs, for example. Words such as *gate, galleon,* and *gusty* would more effectively create this impression than the softer sound of *g* found in *gem, gist* and *gypsy.* Likewise, words beginning with the hard sound of *c* might be more effective. Doubtlessly Alfred Noyes was not functioning by trial and error when writing "The Highwayman." He was keenly aware of the sounds of words in creating the desired impression. Listen to how he used the hard *c* and *g* sounds in the following passage:

> The wind was a torrent of darkness among the gusty trees,
> The moon was a ghostly galleon tossed upon cloudy seas.

[12] John Masefield, "Sea Fever," in *Collected Poems* (London: Macmillan, 1912). Copyright 1912 by Macmillan, renewed 1940 by John Masefield; reprinted by permission of The Macmillan Company.

> The road was a ribbon of moonlight over the purple moor.
> And the highwayman came riding—
>> Riding—riding—
> The highwayman came riding, up to the old inn-door.[13]

As we read poetry to children, we can help them begin to hear the sounds of rhythm, rhyme, alliteration, and onomatopoeia by having them play with verse in creative ways. Children can chant a poem together, beating out the rhythm with clip-clops of their feet, "conducting" with their arms as they might do to music, or catching the beat of a poem with bongo drums or castinets. They can draw a rhythm as Langston Hughes does in his little book *The First Book of Rhythms* (New York: Franklin Watts, 1954).

Use of alliteration can be encouraged in several ways. Tongue twisters like "Peter Piper" or "The Woodchuck Chucked" may be a good beginning. Follow up the reading by having children compose their own tongue twisters. Also, children very often discover alliterative effects for themselves. Ask children to listen to the sounds as you read a poem by a child, then one by a famous poet, both of which employ alliteration. The listening activity may help them understand the kinds of effects possible with words.

For children to attempt rhyme can be more of a liability than an asset at times. To achieve a rhyming pattern, children may select inappropriate words and settle for awkwardness of expression. For this reason, we should be hesitant about requiring rhymed poetry to be written by all students. Instead, we can introduce children to rhyme in Mother Goose, Dorothy Aldis, Aileen Fisher, and a host of other poets. We can also encourage young children to play with rhyming words by making rhyming flowers, as shown in Figure 6-1.

There are rhyming games like Go Fish, too. Rhyming words—*row, sow, low, show; pan, tan, van, man; ball, tall, call, fall; bake, cake, lake, fake; fat, cat, mat, rat*—are printed on cards. Children match rhyming pairs as they draw fish-word cards from a fish pool and as they take turns asking other players for cards they need to make a pair. Activities such as these may encourage a child with a penchant for rhyme to write in a multitude of rhyming patterns.

building sentences

Joe, a fifth-grade boy, described his friendship with a dog in this unedited story:

---

[13] Alfred Noyes, "The Highwayman," in *Collected Poems* (Philadelphia: Lippincott, 1906). Copyright 1906, 1934, 1947 by Alfred Noyes; reprinted by permission of J.B. Lippincott Company.

How My Friend King and I Met

One summer day I was walking to the store with my sister and a little boy. Suddenly a great big dog had our attention. There he was standing on the other side of the street. All of a sudden he came over to us, we petted him for a while then he looked very hungary and thirsty. So my sister went in the house and got some water the little boy got him some dog food because he had a dog all ready had a dog. Then we decided to call him King because he was so big. We played with him awhile, then he got tiered and layed down for a while in front of my house. After he fell asleep and woke up again. The little boy brought out a cracker, then we wanted to see if he could do tricks. So I saw if he would beg. So I took a cracker and threw it in the air and he jumped up and gupled the cracker up. The next day my father found an owner to the dog in the paper. When the owner came to pick him up. We saddly walk him to the car. Then said, "Good by King we will always remember you!"

THE END

Joe's story is a rather interesting one. The sequence of events that he recounts is easy to follow; his choice of words is appropriate in the context of

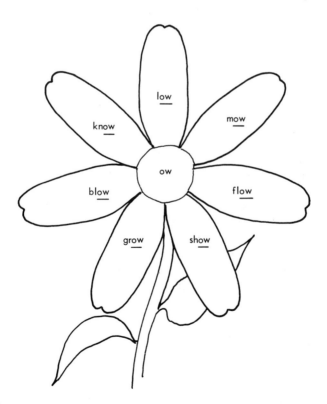

Figure 6-1.

his tale. But it is obvious to the reader that Joe lacks sentence sense: he tends to write two sentences as one—"All of a sudden he came over to us, we petted him for a while"—and he writes incomplete sentences—"When the owner came to pick him up."

Joe is not alone in his inability to perceive sentence boundaries. Writing incomplete and run-on sentences is a rather common problem that some college students even exhibit at times. What can the teacher of writing in the elementary school do to help youngsters like Joe? The following section projects an answer and also suggests ways of helping youngsters to develop variety in the sentence patterns they compose.

HEARING SENTENCES

One of the simplest and most effective techniques for helping children like Joe to develop sentence sense is to have them listen to their own writing. A young child can be asked to read his composition to the teacher. When reading the composition, the child will almost naturally pause at the end of the sentences he has written. The questions for the teacher to ask at this point are "Why did you stop there?" and "What punctuation mark do we use for a long pause?" The child can add periods wherever he naturally pauses for a "large-sized stop." Reading "When the owner came to pick him up," the child will tend to make only a "small-sized stop"; he can hear that a comma rather than a period is required.

Observing in a third-grade class, we saw a teacher draw upon this technique with a child who had written the sentence "Why was Peggy a stranger in the city?" with a period as end punctuation. The teacher had the child read the sentence aloud and then asked, "Why did you make your voice go up at the end?" The child's response was that the sentence was a question, and without prompting he added the question mark.

One way of preparing children to listen for and hear the natural rhythmic patterns in their sentences is to encourage flowing reading technique. Ask a first-grade child to read a sentence in the story that tells how Sally felt when she went to school. He will probably read the sentence not as a thought unit, but word-by-word. The teacher can suggest, "Boys and girls, let's read that sentence together just as if we were speaking it," and the young readers will read the sentence in a more flowing manner that communicates the overall meaning more clearly and helps them to perceive the relationship between written and spoken thoughts.

Oral exercises, likewise, prepare children to hear sentences in their own writing. The teacher of young children can read the following sentences:

The dogs are barking.
The girls are singing.
The elephants are running.

After that, the teacher can suggest, "I am going to read some groups of words to you. Some will be sentences like the ones I just gave; we can use them when we write. Some will not be sentences; we cannot use them as sentences when we write. Let's decide:

Barking in the woods
The horses are eating
Eating nuts
Running home
The boys are fighting

A similar technique can be used with run-on sentences. Run-on sentences can be read to children, who must determine where the first sentence ends and the second sentence begins.

All of a sudden he came over to us we petted him for awhile.
We gave King a cracker he jumped up and down.
The dog did tricks for us he sat up and begged for a cracker.
The dog fell asleep he woke up again.
The little boy got some water he gave it to King.

This type of listening exercise can be carried out most effectively with the aid of an overhead projector. After the teacher has read a run-on sentence and the children have heard the sentence boundaries, she can project the sentences and the children can put in the periods or pause markers.

Some of the relationships between punctuation and meaningful pauses within sentences can be taught in much the same way. A teacher can read aloud the sentences "John, your brother, is here," and "John, your brother is here." Children can talk about what the first sentence means, what the second sentence means, and how they determined the differences in meaning. If the teacher has the sentences printed on strips of paper or prepared for projection with the overhead, she can readily consider the relationship between pauses and comma usage.

One fifth-grade teacher has found choral speaking to be an effective technique for having children hear the relationships between sentences within a selection. The children, not the teacher, determine the intonations they will attempt, the points at which they will pause, the points at which they will carry their voices upward or downward. Children suggest interpretations based on the sentence structure and the punctuation used by the author. To interpret, they must analyze relationships and begin to perceive how sentence boundaries are indicated both in spoken and written form.

When the notion of listening for sentence boundaries has been developed, an upper grade child can independently use a tape recorder to listen for the sentence boundaries within his own writing. The child records his story on tape, reading it with as much expression in his voice as he can muster. Then he plays back what he has recorded, listening for sentence boundaries that he records on his written composition. If a tape recorder is not available, children can work together as listening-mates. One child reads a second child's composition to him while the second child listens for sentence boundaries.

When a child exhibits a lack of sentence sense, he may also gain from writing activities that focus directly on the sentence. The topic should be a limited one. Have the child in the lower elementary grades write a single sentence beginning with one of the following phrases:

- Happiness is——.
- I wish that——.
- A friend is——.
- Dogs are——.
- Thanksgiving is——.

A similar assignment for the upper elementary grade child is to write one sentence stating—

- your opinion of the food in the cafeteria;
- your reaction to a woman as President;
- your guess as to who will win the World Series;
- your reason for (not) wanting to be an astronaut.

Copying their sentences on a transparency with a wax crayon or special felt pen, children can project their sentences using the overhead projector. Ideas can be discussed.

GENERATING A VARIETY OF SENTENCE PATTERNS

The ability to carry out some of the higher thought processes implicit in different kinds of idea-content bears some relationship to the ability to handle associated sentence patterns. In conditional inference, for example, the thinker directly or indirectly is employing the complex sentence pattern "If——, then——." If he cannot manipulate that pattern, making a conditional inference is almost an impossible task. Likewise, to write in an interesting fashion requires an ability to handle different kinds of sentence patterns and expansions and transformations of those patterns.

With young children we begin with the simplest basic pattern identified by the linguists as a sentence: Noun-Verb. The teacher can present examples of sentences that fit the pattern: "The cat played," "The dog ran," and "The bird sang." Asked to think of other sentences that follow this pattern, children volunteer their own examples, which can be recorded on experience charts.

Lefevre has identified four basic English sentence patterns. Because children can systematically work with each of these patterns and can gradually come to a heightened understanding of the structures available within our language, the Lefevre scheme is presented here.

Pattern I: NOUN VERB ADJECTIVE OR ADVERB
Examples:
N V   The penguin hopped.
N V Adv   The water boiled violently.
N V Adj   The package arrived intact.

Pattern II: NOUN VERB NOUN
Examples:
N V N   The dog bit the mailman.
N V N   He patted the dog.
N V N   Mother forgot her sister.

Pattern III: NOUN VERB NOUN NOUN OR ADJECTIVE
Examples:
N V N N   I gave Mary a bicycle.
N V N N   She considered me an enemy.
N V N Adj   He made his wife happy.

Pattern IV: NOUN LINKING VERB NOUN OR ADJECTIVE
Examples:
N LV N   My brother was the winner.
N LV N   The spacemen became heroes.
N LV Adj   Some children are unhappy[14]

Youngsters should have plenty of oral work with the patterns as a basis for writing. The format for this oral work can be—

- projection by the teacher of examples of sentences that meet the specifications of a pattern: "She touched the stove." "She cleaned the floor." "The dog ate the meat." "Some boys lifted the rug."
- projection by the children of more examples of sentences that meet the specifications.
- some discussion of the structure of the pattern after the children have discovered for themselves the structure of the sentences given as examples.

Using the pattern as a model, youngsters eventually concoct sentences on paper.

As they concoct sentences, children can expand the basic sentence patterns. As they work within the simple pattern N-V and suggest a sentence similar to "The bird sang," the teacher can say, "Let's tell more about the bird so that we know which bird sang." Children may project:

[14] Carl Lefevre, *Linguistics, English, and the Language Arts* (Boston: Allyn and Bacon, 1970), pp. 180–81. Patterns I, II, III, and IV cited by permission of Allyn & Bacon, Inc.

> The happy bird sang.
> The bird in the apple tree sang.
> The blue bird on the window sill sang.

Eventually they generate sentences in which the verb component is expanded:

> The bird is singing.
> The bird is softly singing.
> The bird is softly and sweetly singing from its perch in the tree.

Oral activities in which sentence components are expanded help a child to acquire a sense of the word orders employed in standard oral English. Children who grow up speaking a nonstandard dialect of English may order their words differently and may need extensive oral work if they are also to become proficient in standard English word order. The same would be even more true of youngsters who are learning English in school but who speak a totally different language at home—Chinese, Spanish, or French. Whereas the child who hears standard word orders at home will use them almost automatically, the child who speaks a different dialect or a different language will require many more oral activities as a basis for writing standard English patterns.

One activity that is both fun and profitable in this context is building sentences from a given group of words. Print word cards: *elephants, the, ran, slowly, steadily, and, very, big, gray*. Each child in the group receives a card. Together they build a sentence from their words, placing adjectives and adverbs in appropriate locations in the sentence. Printed on cards, word groups such as *into the woods, through the fields,* and *of long grass* can be interjected into the sentence as children work with more complex structures.

Children build an intuitive understanding of what a sentence is through such activity. Instead of beginning with a meaningless definition of a sentence, they gradually acquire a sentence sense as they continually manipulate different kinds of sentence patterns. Emphasis is on generating a variety of sentences, not on naming kinds of patterns, identifying the pattern to which a particular sentence belongs, or defining patterns.

As children move out of the primary school, they can formally begin to handle linguistic procedures for combining the basic sentence patterns. Children can encounter pairs of closely related sentences:

> In summer we eat fresh vegetables. In winter we eat frozen vegetables.
> I cleaned the stove. Myra worked on the refrigerator.
> Sylvia is the ping-pong champion. She is my sister.
> The girl arrived. I like her.
> Too much waste is being dumped into our rivers. This pollutes the water.

Initially the children can try to combine the pairs by compounding: "In summer we eat fresh vegetables, and in winter we eat frozen vegetables." They can try their hand at building complex structures: "While I cleaned the stove, Myra worked on the refrigerator," or "I like the girl who arrived." They can work with the appositive: "Sylvia, my sister, is the ping-pong champion"; with the participle: "Dumped into our rivers, too much waste pollutes the water"; and with other more sophisticated structures. Again the stress is on producing complex patterns rather than on recognizing or naming them.

Another way in which children can play with sentence patterns is to manipulate simple transformations. The teacher suggests, "Let's make questions from 'The cat is playing.' 'The dog is running.' 'The bird is singing.' " Children propose:

> Is the dog running?
> Is the cat playing?
> Is the bird singing?

In so doing, they are transforming the basic Noun-Verb pattern into Auxiliary-Noun-Verb? and have projected another pattern in which they can build sentences. The same simple transformations can be done using any of the four basic sentence patterns in the Lefevre scheme.

Children can also play systematically with transformations of the basic patterns in imperative sentences. A Noun–Verb pattern becomes simply Verb, as in "Go!" "Run!" and "Play!"; a Noun–Verb–Adverb pattern becomes Verb–Adverb, as in "Run quickly!"; and a Noun–Linking Verb–Adjective becomes Linking Verb–Adjective, as in "Become Heroes!" when children try their hand at building commands from kernel sentences.

READING A VARIETY OF SENTENCE STYLES

Written English differs from spoken English in several important respects. First, there is a tighter, more logical organization in sentences written down to be read by someone else than there is in spoken sentences. Second, more diverse and sophisticated structures are employed in written communications. Third, there are fewer extraneous words.

Because written expression does differ in these respects from oral expression, contact with different kinds of written material can help a youngster achieve an intuitive understanding of English sentences recorded on the printed page. As teachers of writing, we must develop a parallel literature program that introduces children to the best literary styles available, so that they will be encouraged to read and to read more. To teach the skills of reading is not enough; we must turn children on to books so that they search for more and more books to read.

This is not to imply that teachers should help children analyze the sentence structure in books they are reading—not at all. That process would probably be more effective as a means of turning children off to books. What is being suggested is a literature enjoyment program in which children encounter books written by some of the great writers for children so that they almost intuitively know what to expect from Konigsburg, McCloskey, Dr. Seuss, and Sendak. They see these writers as human beings plying the writing craft in patterns typically their own, and they begin to use some of the ways of forming words into sentences that these professional writers use. Writing is, after all, an art. Knowledge of patterns and words carries the writer only so far. Then artistic sense takes over as the writer makes words flow rhythmically across a page and interweaves one pattern into another. This sense can hardly be taught; we can only hope that a child can catch it by brushing against the writings of those who have a unique facility with words.

summary thoughts

In concluding this chapter, the authors hasten to add that *building words into sentences and paragraphs is only one component of writing*. It is not synonymous with writing, as sometimes is assumed. To write means to play with ideas and then to capture these ideas on paper through words, sentence patterns, and paragraphs. Learning to write is not merely the study of those words, sentences, and paragraphs. If it becomes this in the classroom, then we are not really teaching children to write; rather, we are stressing craft and sacrificing the essence of communication—the idea. In so doing, we open our program to the charge of irrelevancy.

let children revise

Blot out, correct, insert, refine,
Enlarge, diminish, interline;
Be mindful, when invention fails,
To scratch your head and bite your nails.

Jonathan Swift,
On Poetry

Speaking of the "process of making poetry," Amy Lowell asserted that—

> a poet must be both born and made. He must be born with a subconscious factory always working for him or he never can be a poet at all, and he must have knowledge and talent enough to 'putty' up his holes—to use Mr. Graves's expression. Let no one undervalue this process of puttying; it is a condition of good poetry. Of the many first manuscript drafts of great poets that have passed through my hands in the last twenty-five years, I have seen none without its share of putty.[1]

Samuel Johnson talked of the effort of writing: "What is written without effort is in general read without pleasure."[2] Boileau in *L'Art Poétique* suggested continued revision as part of writing: "Hasten slowly; without losing heart. Twenty times upon the anvil place your work."[3] Ovid proposed discarding unsuccessful attempts: "Much have I written, but what I thought

---

[1] Amy Lowell, *Poetry and Poets* (Boston: Houghton Mifflin, 1930), p. 26. Copyright 1930 by Houghton Mifflin Company; reprinted by permission of the publisher.
[2] Samuel Johnson, *Miscellanies*, vol. 2, p. 309.
[3] Nicholas Boileau-Despréaux, *L'Art Poétique*, pt. 1, line 171.

145

defective I have myself given to the flames for their revision."[4] Some of these writers were concerned with poetry, some with prose. Yet there seems to be general agreement among successful writers that revision is a necessary part of writing. The writer cannot do without "putty."

On the other hand, creative ideas rarely blossom in an environment in which that putty is applied indiscriminately by someone else or specifically in which the teacher assumes the critical role and corrects papers before students write a revised copy. In "Toward a Theory of Creativity," in *Creativity and Its Cultivation,* Carl Rogers has proposed that the opposite role on the part of the teacher fosters creativity: the teacher must be accepting, understanding, noncritical, and open to new ideas.[5] First, according to Rogers, the teacher must accept the student as a person with unique and individual interests, values, goals, aptitudes, and abilities; as a person who has immense value in the total scheme of human events.[6] The ASCD 1962 yearbook, *Perceiving, Behaving, Becoming,* expressed Roger's point in these words: "Valuing the uniqueness of each person is basic to the release of creativity. Differences are accepted and welcomed."[7] Second, understanding means that the teacher tries to comprehend what the student is feeling, thinking, and attempting to say. This is empathy in its highest form and requires the teacher to remove himself from his own thoughts and take on his student's feelings and thoughts; to sense the need for achievement, affection, attention, and acceptance that the student is expressing; to sense the student's fear of failure. Third, by "noncritical" Rogers means that there is no external evaluation of the person. The teacher leads the student to find the locus of evaluation within himself. Fourth, a teacher must be open to new ideas and new ways of expression if the child is to feel "psychologically free." Rogers has contended that the student must have freedom to express himself, to chart his own course of action, and to identify those areas to which he has a commitment, if creative ideas are to emerge.[8]

A synthesis of the Rogerian conception of an open, noncritical environment as requisite for creative thought, and of the notion that successful writing results from a revision of what has been written, leads to two related conclusions:

- the teacher should not function as chief revisionist or evaluator; the child functions as his own revisionist or editor;
- a child needs to develop the skills that will enable him to revise what he has written.

[4] Publius Ovid, *Tristia,* Book 4, elegy 10, line 61.
[5] Carl Rogers, "Toward a Theory of Creativity," in *Creativity and Its Cultivation,* ed. Harold Anderson (New York: Harper & Row, 1959), p. 78.
[6] Ibid.
[7] Association for Supervision and Curriculum Development, *Perceiving, Behaving, Becoming* (Washington, D.C.: ASCD, 1962), p. 151.
[8] Carl Rogers, "Toward a Theory of Creativity," p. 80.

These conclusions imply how the teacher should not handle a child's written efforts. When reading and correcting children's compositions, many teachers actually revise for the child—reorganize, edit for punctuation, capitalization, and usage, rewrite awkward sentences, and make deletions. Receiving his teacher-edited papers, a child makes a final draft by copying the composition with the teacher's changes. That such a procedure is antithetical to both the nature of the writing process and the requirements of a noncritical environment is obvious. Is the child learning how to apply what Graves has called "putty"? Definitely not. The teacher is getting the practice in applying the techniques of language; at this point the child functions merely as copier: he copies his original work with the teacher's corrections. Is the child free from external critical consideration of his work? Again, definitely not. The child finds his paper decorated with red circles, notations, and carets that imply lack of success. Is the child acquiring an erroneous attitude about writing, that ideas once inscribed on a page need never be revised by the writer? Unfortunately, the answer to the last question is affirmative. The child is encouraged only to record his ideas on paper. He is not participating in the follow-through phase, the phase in which he places his work on "the anvil" for revision.

How does the teacher structure a writing program so that children assume the role of revisionist? An answer to that question has three facets:

- Helping children acquire the specific language skills they need to serve as their own editors.
- Helping children acquire the technical skills of editing.
- Organizing written activities to encourage revision.

The remainder of this chapter will focus on these three facets and will identify conventional usages that children may encounter in their writing.

helping children acquire specific language skills

For children to revise what they are writing, they must have some understanding of the way in which the English language is manipulated and some skill in handling the manipulations. For instance, a kind of writing elementary school children seem to enjoy is dialogue. They write conversation in their plots, creating the exact words story characters say to each other. Basically, recording direct quotation is a rather simple process, but unless children have some idea of how speech is written down, they will not be able to record the verbal interaction between story characters in conventional form. Direct instruction in the manipulation of conventional usages, therefore, is a requisite component of a writing program in which children take an active role in revising their own work.

DISCOVERY OF LANGUAGE GENERALIZATIONS

The standard ways in which written language is manipulated can be taught inductively by having children analyze examples of a specific language usage and discover for themselves the generalizations that describe the conventional usages. To see how specific language skills can be taught inductively, let us look at the teaching of direct quotations. Teaching inductively, the teacher would present a group of youngsters with a series of sentences in which conversation appears. These can be sentences that the children have just dictated to the teacher and that she has recorded on an experience chart.

> Mary said, "I liked the doughnut store best."
> Jackie asked, "Why did you like the doughnut store?"
> Mary answered, "I liked the smell of the doughnuts. They smelled so good."
> Tom added, "I liked the smell too."

The teacher can say to the children, "Let's read the words Mary said, the words Jackie said, the next words Mary said, and Tommie's words." After the children have read the words, she can help them analyze: "What marks show on paper the words each child said? What kind of pause marker do we use just before the spoken words? Where do we put our end punctuation?" To see if children can apply their understanding, she can have them finish sentences: Marty asked, —————, Joe answered, —————, Janie said, —————, Bruce replied, —————, Laurel wrote, —————. Working in editing-pairs, children compare their sentences to the models.

The second lesson in an inductive series involves the analysis of sentences of slightly greater complexity.

> "I liked the doughnut store best," said Mary.
> "Why did you like the doughnut store?" asked Jackie.
> "I liked the smell of the doughnuts. They smelled so good," Mary answered.

The initial focus is on how these sentences differ from the model studied before. When children have identified the differences, they can consider how they know which words were spoken words, what kinds of pause markers are used at the end of the speaker's words, and what kinds of pause markers are found at the ends of the sentences. Their next task is to apply their understanding by writing similar sentences.

Following this lesson, children consider more complex sentences.

> "I lost my pencil," said Mary. "My pen is also missing."
> "Where are we going?" asked Jane. "I want to go home."

With each lesson the children refine their understanding of conversational patterns.

APPLICATION OF LANGUAGE GENERALIZATIONS

Research indicates that study of conventional language patterns has had little carry-over in the past to written activity. One hypothesis is that teachers have conceived of writing as a "one-shot" endeavor, the child simply writing down his ideas to be corrected later by the teacher. Yet a child emotionally involved in his idea as he should be if he is to develop it in all its intricacies is not consciously thinking about commas, capital letters, spelling, and word usage. Actually, if he were to focus on details of construction, might he not lose the content of his idea? The teacher or researcher who hopes that a child will consciously apply generalizations as he writes is misconceiving the nature of the beast.

Writing is not a one-shot endeavor. There is another phase in which conscious application of generalizations may be more valuable—the revision phase that occurs *after* ideas have been captured on paper. It is at that point that conventional ways of spelling, punctuating, and using words are considered.

Then too, instruction in the conventions of language usage has often been given in a context totally removed from the writing process. The teacher, following her language text, teaches about direct quotations when the topic appears in the book, not when her youngsters show a need for the skill. Thus the lesson, given in isolation, has little effect on children's writing. The teacher who hopes for carry-over should help children to discover inductively how to manipulate conventions related to such matters as direct quotations only when children are attempting to write conversation in their stories. When children understand how quotations are typically manipulated, the teacher has youngsters focus their thinking on sentences that they have written themselves, encouraging them to revise their work in terms of the generalizations discovered previously. She guides the children with questions:

> Have I put quotation marks around all the words spoken?
>
> Have I used a comma after words such as *John said, Mary asked, Sylvia remarked,* when these words come before the spoken words?
>
> Have I put a period, question mark, or exclamation point inside the quotation marks when the statement, question, or exclamation comes at the end of the sentence?

Questions such as these are projected *after* children have written their stories, when they are in the revision stage. This approach is different from that in which the teacher keeps a chart at the front of the room and draws the children's attention to it before they begin to write their stories.

Writing Pointers

1. Put your title in the middle of the first line.
2. Skip a line between your title and your first words.

3. Indent the first line of the paragraph.
4. Leave margins on both sides of the paper.

When revision is considered a phase in the writing process, such a checklist (if the items were considered significant by the teacher) would be rephrased as questions to consider when preparing a revised draft—not as items to consider as one consigns ideas to the paper.

The same point can be made in reference to handwriting skills. Clear handwriting is important, but the writing of a first draft is not the time to perfect one's skills; that is the time to work with ideas—to develop ideas that begin to surface as one takes pen in hand. To warn children as they begin to write, "Watch your handwriting!" is to place a stumbling block in their way. Handwriting should be watched during the writing of a final draft.

helping children acquire editorial skills

The teacher who asks her students to work as editors without giving them any general pointers about how to proceed may find that they do not know where to begin. Where does a child begin?

The child should write knowing that a revision will take place. The child writes on every other line with margins so that he can add or cross out later on without problems of space. When he cannot think of a precise word, he leaves a blank to be filled in later with the aid of a thesaurus, another student, or the teacher. When he is absolutely uncertain of how to spell a word, he makes an interpretable attempt, noting *sp* over the word. If, on the other hand, his uncertainty is with some technical problem of usage— whether to capitalize, which kind of punctuation to employ, whether to use a possessive form—he indicates the site with a mark such as *u*. These items are the first to be checked as the child writer comes back to his composition on another occasion.

Another technique for a child editor is to listen to what he has written. As previously noted, reading orally and listening to what one has written are techniques helpful in identifying sentence boundaries and determining what punctuation to use. In addition, oral reading and listening can aid in identifying words omitted unintentionally from a sentence or letters simply left out. One second-grade child had written "The boys are in the street" as "The boys a in the street." Reading the sentence aloud to her teacher, the child promptly perceived her omission and said, "Oh, I forgot to finish the word."

Similarly, listening to what one has written helps one to identify words placed inappropriately in a sentence and jerky repetitive sentence patterns. Especially with rhythmic poetry, listening makes evident the interplay of sounds and the flowing rhythm of the lines. As a writer hears his own poem, he can carry the listening process a bit further, trying to conduct the lines with his hands or beat the rhythm with his feet. When editing his own prose, the writer simply listens while he silently mouths his words, while another child reads his words to him, or while the tape recorder plays back the words he has previously recorded.

Another editing technique is outlining to check the overall organization of the piece. The child notes the main idea of each paragraph or stanza. He goes through his own manuscript and jots in the margin one, two, or three words that sum up each paragraph and stanza. Then he checks to see if similar jottings appear in several places in his piece, asking himself whether this helps to communicate the idea or whether the piece would move better with the related ideas grouped together.

A child looking at his own work may benefit from a knowledge of proofreading techniques. Instead of rewriting, he can insert these signs on his first draft:

new paragraph,

insert,

delete,

don't capitalize,

capitalize;

Having checked the areas of uncertainty, having listened to his piece, having checked the overall organization, the child can go through his composition and apply these five symbols. Likewise, instead of rewriting each editorial change, the child can circle a sentence and draw an arrow from it to a position in which it creates a stronger effect, cut paragraphs apart with scissors and staple them together in a more logical order, and number the sentences in a paragraph, indicating the desired order. The final draft is a compilation of all the necessary changes.

By the fourth grade, children can function as independent editors quite successfully if they have had a gradual introduction to editing procedures. In contrast, children in primary grades need greater teacher guidance; most editing has to be done in conference with the teacher. Since compositions at this level are relatively short, a great deal can be accomplished in a brief period spent with the teacher. As the child moves into the third grade, he is capable of greater independence; he can be introduced systematically to techniques of editing that he can gradually apply on his own.

encouraging revisions

Time is a factor in an author's revision of a manuscript. It is only after time has passed that an author can look at his own work with the impartial eye of an outsider. The next day he can delete words and phrases that only a night before seemed pure inspiration as he consigned them to the page. Children, too, should wait to revise; they should write today, revise tomorrow, and even revise again the next day. In the words of Quintilian, "Let our literary compositions be laid aside for some time, that we may after a reasonable period return to their perusal, and find them, as it were, altogether new to us."[9]

THE WRITING FOLDER AND THE EDITING GUIDE

As a way of encouraging a child to return to a composition "after a reasonable time," the teacher can have each child keep a writing folder of all work in progress. When a child begins a piece, he marks it *first draft* and adds it to his file folder. In the folder are pieces that are going through second and third revisions, as well as final drafts. These, of course, bear the designation *second draft, third draft,* and *final draft.*

The individual writing folder has certain advantages. The folder makes it convenient for every child to work at his own pace; all children need not be working on the same "assignment." One child may decide to revise something in which he is deeply involved today while another may begin a poem with which she has been toying subconsciously. Also, the folder system makes it possible for a child to go to the file during seatwork periods, locate his folder, and edit materials not yet in final draft. Finally, the file folder works well from a practical standpoint. After a period of revision, a paper may begin to look like a patchwork quilt—a sheet stapled here, half a sheet clipped there. Incidentally, no intermediary draft should be judged on neatness, for a paper under revision can hardly be kept neat as lines and paragraphs are added, deleted, and changed. Under these conditions, a folder helps to maintain order.

Still another way of encouraging revision is to help each child develop an individualized editing guide, a list of specific points to look for in revision. Usually a child has specific writing weaknesses. He may not differentiate between *there* and *their*; he may tend to write run-on and incomplete sentences; he may overwork the word *nice.* After the teacher has worked with the child on these points, they become items on his guide to be considered in the revision stage of writing. The child posts the guide on the inside of his writing folder. Initially a child's teacher, who is "senior editor," helps the child construct his guide, but as the writing progresses both the

[9] Marcus Quintilian, *De Institutione Oratoria,* book Y, chap. 4, sec. 2.

writer and the "senior editor" add further items. The writer can even acquire a "house editor," another child with whom he can pair for cross-editing.

It is impossible to include all the points of construction and usage on a child's guide. In revision a child is more successful if he focuses on four or five items related specifically to his major problems than if he attempts to look for a million and one possible openings for revision. His guide, therefore, should be simple, reflecting his own writing problems. Then too, some kinds of construction and usage are employed only in formal communication, and this level is hardly applicable in elementary school composition. A child should revise his writing in terms of what is acceptable in informal communication.

FUNCTIONAL SELECTION

All of a child's written work need not be revised. If the child is given an opportunity to write every day, he may produce much more than he has time to rewrite and more than the teacher has time to read. The key here is functional selection: after the child has written a number of pieces, he selects the ones he wants to share with others. He may decide to edit a news story, a report, an editorial, or a puzzle to submit to the class newspaper; to revise a story for the school magazine; to rewrite a poem for mounting on the bulletin board; or to revise a letter to send to a manufacturing concern. He may decide to reconsider a story to be shown to his classmates via the overhead projector; to edit a letter to send to a friend sick at home; to rewrite his verse that will hang on the holiday tree or will be printed on a valentine card; to revise his script for a TV, radio, or dramatic production. The teacher's job is to supply meaningful situations that encourage revision—the writing bulletin board, the school paper, the class magazine, the letter actually sent—making these integral aspects of class activity.

In expecting children to revise their own written expression, the teacher must change her philosophy if she believes that only perfect copy is to be displayed, posted, or included in a classroom publication. While a child is learning to edit his own work and is doing so in terms of four or five major concerns listed in his editing guide, other weaknesses in his work will remain. A teacher who views her role as a corrector would probably have edited out all the weaknesses so that the final copy is perfect copy. But the question to be asked here is "Who will benefit from the existence of such perfect copy?" Certainly not the child, who simply is copying his teacher's corrections. Of course, it behooves the teacher to communicate her philosophy to her principal and parents so that they will not expect only perfect copy to be displayed and carried home.

THE CONFERENCE AND GROUP INSTRUCTION

The keystone of a writing program in which children are encouraged to revise their own work is the teacher-pupil conference. The teacher must set aside time each week to confer with every child. Together they review compositions in the child's writing folder, identifying points to be included on the editorial guide, building specific language skills that the individual child may need to revise his pieces, comparing a first draft with a final draft, deciding which compositions should be revised, determining writing activities that the child might attempt, and formulating a series of writing experiences—an individualized weekly plan that the child will follow. Such conferences are essential if children are to edit their own work effectively, if children are to develop a desire to improve their writing skills, and if children are to work continuously and independently on writing activities.

It is in the conference setting that the teacher can work with each child at the child's level. She identifies a child's construction weaknesses in the same way as she attempts to diagnose his reading difficulties, and she focuses on related skill development. Teaching materials for each child are the sentences and paragraphs that the child is in the process of composing. For instance, the teacher individually leads a boy who has trouble organizing his thoughts to think through the organization of paragraphs. She may ask, "Steve, in your first paragraph what is the main idea that you are trying to get across?" Responding to his answer, she may suggest. "Write an introductory paragraph that says just what you told me." She may inquire, "Steve, what are you trying to do in your second paragraph?" Responding to his answer, she continues: "Look through the paper. Is there any other paragraph that does the same thing?" She stimulates him: "Do you think you could combine them into one better paragraph? Do you see any other paragraphs that belong together?" With this child the task is to help him develop a notion of the unity of a paragraph and to see similarities and differences among ideas. With another child in the same class, the task may be a different one. The task is always determined by the child's unique writing problems.

Of course, even as we teach reading in small groups, the teacher can gather together children who are functioning at rather similar writing levels and build specific language and editorial skills. For instance, children who need practice handling complex sentence patterns can join in adding *when if, because, who, that,* and *which* clauses to a kernel sentence. Children who have difficulty with sequencing can order "scrambled paragraphs" in a small group, and children who have trouble with such conventions as possessives, agreement of subject and verb, or capitalization of proper nouns, can discover relationships through inductive lessons organized by the teacher for a small group. Only rarely does an entire class reach the point where each member's weakness is common to the total class. Therefore, skill development, paralleling children's revision activity, tends to be an individual or small group activity.

THE TEACHER AS DIAGNOSTICIAN

If individual weaknesses are to be the focus of skill development, the teacher must first function as diagnostician. Before she can help the child attack his weaknesses, she must be able to perceive what his paramount problems are, such as word usage, paragraph organization, sentence structuring, or awkward expression. To do this, she must have an in-depth understanding of language. That a teacher who does not understand the writing craft will have trouble functioning as a diagnostician of student problems is evidenced by an actual example taken from a student's first draft. A little girl, who had written about Santa Claus getting stuck in the chimney, had inscribed: "Bonnie was awake in bed. She heard a thud." Her teacher revised the story for her by converting the period into a comma and marking the capital *S* with a lowercase *s*. The teacher had written a run-on sentence into the child's paper. How could this teacher possibly help children develop sentence sense until she had investigated sentences more thoroughly herself?

identifying the elements of revision

What are some of the points a student self-editor may consider as he begins to revise his own manuscript? In this section, the authors attempt to project many possibilities, knowing that no one child in the elementary school will ever be involved with this amount of detail. Some children will be considering rather elementary points, whereas others will be handling much more sophisticated aspects of styling. The authors, therefore, project these specific details to sketch the overall dimensions of revision that individual children may encounter from time to time.

ECONOMY IN WORD USAGE

Strunk and White state that—

vigorous writing is concise. A sentence should contain no unnecessary words ...for the same reason that a drawing should have no unnecessary lines and a machine no unnecessary parts. This requires not that the writer make all his sentences short, or that he avoid all detail and treat his subjects only in outline, but that every word tell.[10]

---

[10] Willian Strunk and E. B. White, *The Elements of Style* (New York: Macmillan, 1962), p. 17; © 1959 by The Macmillan Company.

To check economy, a self-editor may look for the following:

- needless duplication of adjectives:
  To be Miss America a girl must be both *beautiful* and *good-looking*.
  The *enormous, immense* building towers over the city.
- needless duplication of adverb and verb:
  The cold spring flowed *amply* and *abundantly*.
  He *stared* and *gaped*.
- unwarranted use of specific determiners and intensifiers, such as *the, very, quite,* and *so*:
  Sharon looked *so* radiant in her wedding dress; she was *very* happy and *very* contented.
  We will consider *the* specific components of the job.
- use of two or more words where one suffices:
  I *ascended up* to the fifth floor on an elevator.
  He used four words where one *could do the job.* (sufficed)
- use of several sentences where one suffices:
  Dorothy washed the dishes. She put the dishes away. Then she hung up the towel.
  After Dorothy had washed and put away the dishes, she hung up the towel.

PRECISION IN WORD USAGE

The dictionary is a basic tool for the student self-editor because it can be used to check both the spelling and meaning of words. Any word about which there is the slightest uncertainty is checked, as are words written with a full knowledge that the usage is unacceptable. The student editor should specifically check—

- words that he has rarely or never before employed in written expression
- words that he is using in a way different from previous usages
- contractions: *its* and *it's*
- homonyms: *to, too, two; their, there; compliment, complement*
- words the meaning of which are often confused: *affect, effect; desert, dessert; further, farther*
- words having two vowels coming together that might be reversed: *receive, believe, relieve, conceit, retrieve*
- words that may have silent letters: *pneumonia, receipt, crease*
- words of foreign origins: *buffet, bouquet, apropos, smorgasbord*
- words containing a vowel sound that may be represented by one of several letter patterns: *although,* beau, *doe, owing, mocha*
- words containing a consonant sound that is represented by more than one letter pattern: ph*one,* f*ox;* s*ent,* c*ease*
- words containing rather similar sounds: *our* and *are*
- plural forms of words.

APPLICATION OF STANDARD FORMS
OF WRITTEN EXPRESSION

There are numerous dictionaries and handbooks that enumerate specific points of usage. The teacher of composition would do well to keep as ready reference such guides as *A Dictionary of Contemporary American Usage, Oxford English Dictionary, The American Heritage Dictionary, American-English Usage, Dictionary of American Slang, Webster's Third New International Dictionary,* and *Webster's New World Dictionary* to answer student queries. Still, the average elementary school student will probably encounter only limited aspects of standard informal usage as he composes, which may include the following:

Usage

agreement of subject and verb:
  the girls sing rather than *the girls sings*
  he doesn't rather than *he don't*
  it rains hard rather than *it rain hard*

employment of past and future forms of verbs:
  yesterday it rained rather than *yesterday it rain*
  tomorrow it will rain rather than *tomorrow it rains*

selection of the appropriate participle form:
  he has gone rather than *he has went* or *he has wented*
  he has run away rather than *he has ran away*

use of double negative forms:
  he has no book rather than *he hasn't no book*

usage of specific words:
  he isn't rather than *he ain't.*

Closely related to standards of word usage are accepted notions regarding the capitalization and punctuation of written work. Children in the elementary school will probably write in patterns requiring the following:

Punctuation

selection of appropriate punctuation at the ends of sentences
  Help! Where are you? I am here.

use of the comma in compound constructions
  John, Jake, and Jack are pals.
  I will bring pie, cake, and doughnuts.
  He looked up, saw the gun, and ran.
  The clouds formed, the rain came, and rivers ran in the streets.
  Those plants are found in wooded areas, grassy plains, and mountainous regions.

use of the comma in subordinating ideas of condition, time, and reason at the beginning of sentences
  If you are happy, your face shows your pleasure.
  When I see a ghost, I run.
  Since he left, I have been working twice as hard.

Since he has none, he must borrow.
Because he was a track star, he could outdistance the thief.

use of the comma in nonrestrictive adjective clauses and appositive constructions
Miss Johnson, who is our fifth-grade teacher, is home today.
Janet, the star of the team, broke her leg.

use of the comma in direct address
John, come here quickly!
I want that done by tomorrow, John.

use of the comma and quotation marks in direct quotations
Coach Thompson asked, "How many boys can play?"
"All players must be in bed by nine," directed Coach Thompson.

use of quotation marks or underlining in titles
"Fog"   *The Last of the Mohicans*
Newsweek   *The New York Times*

use of semicolon in coordinating clauses
The girls took over the cooking chores; the boys built the fires.

use of period after abbreviations
Mr., Mrs., Ms., Dr.

Capitalization

capitalization of first words of sentences

capitalization of titles of designations
Dr., Mr., Miss, Mrs., Ms.

capitalization of countries, continents, states, cities, towns, and languages

capitalization of proper names
Jake, Overlook Hospital, Newark State College

capitalization of words in a title
Coming of Age in Samoa, "The Highwayman," *The New York Times*

CLARITY IN SENTENCE CONSTRUCTION

In checking clarity of sentence construction, the self-editor looks for—

run-on sentences:
A doctor must also have good judgment, he must be able to decide quickly in an emergency and remain calm.
Mary bought some candy, her favorite was chocolate-covered almonds.

incomplete sentences:
Running into a big, stone wall.
When we arrived at Kennedy airport.
All the people on the runway and in the airport.

misplaced and dangling clauses and phrases in sentences:
To learn to appreciate coffee, many cups need to be drunk.
When a child, the doctor took out my appendix.
After swimming in the lake, lunch was eaten.
Falling into the lake, we all rushed to pull him out.

VARIETY IN SENTENCE STRUCTURE

Perrin contends that—

series of sentences of about the same length and general pattern become monotonous. Varying the length helps avoid such monotony, but even more important is changing the order of elements in the sentence...the chief way to vary written sentences is to change the order of their parts.[11]

When we edit our own work, we can ask ourselves, "Do I tend to repeat certain patterns?"

Simple sentence:
Nixon was elected.

Simple sentence with a compound subject:
Nixon and Agnew were elected.

Simple sentence with a compound predicate:
Kay ran and jumped.

Compound sentence:
We have ants living in the kitchen, and spiders have made themselves at home in the basement.

Complex sentence:
Although he was only ten years old, he could speak three languages.

Compound, complex sentence:
Although he had been a captive for five years, he returned unharmed; he escaped by slipping across the border at night.

To achieve variety an editor can subordinate an idea of lesser importance in several ways. First, he can place an idea of lesser importance in an adverbial clause coming at the beginning or the end of the sentence.

Condition:
When the sun shines, I am happy.
I am happy *when the sun shines.*
If you learn to express yourself clearly, you may be more successful.
You may be more successful *if you learn to express yourself clearly.*

Time:
Since I have come, not one story has been written.
Not one story has been written *since I have come.*

Reason:
Since he is president, he has the final word.
He has the final word, *since he is president.*
Because he answered correctly, he won the jackpot.
He won the jackpot *because he answered correctly.*

---

[11] Porter G. Perrin, *Writer's Guide and Index to English,* 3rd ed. (Glenview, Ill.: Scott, Foresman, 1959), p. 181; reprinted by permission.

An editor can also revise a monotonous pattern by subordinating with an adjective clause, as in the following sentences:

> The story *that is my favorite* is "Jack in the Beanstalk."
> The man *who wrote the music* had been trained at Juilliard.
> The boy *whom I like* believes that women should be well educated.
> The President's nominee to the Supreme Court, *who had been approved by the Senate,* had taken his seat on the bench when the controversy began.
> The ensuing controversy, *which had repercussions around the world,* ended with his resignation.

A more sophisticated editor can turn to noun clauses and appositives for variety:

> **Noun clauses:**
> *That all the world will know the truth* is my only desire.
> *What he wanted most* was *what he could not have.*
>
> **Simple appositives:**
> Dr. Jacobs, *our former dentist,* now lives in Miami.
> My husband *George* is taking me to the Caribbean.
>
> **More complicated appositive forms** (generally not constructed by elementary school children):
> *A man who knows his way around Washington,* Bob will be able to get the job done.
> Many of these countries—*for example, Canada, Russia, and Sweden*—have longer winters than the United States.
> My teacher is an intelligent woman—*a woman with an understanding of literary criticism.*

The following are examples of other phrase elements that can vary a monotonous structure, though only the last has extensive application in elementary school writing:

> **Gerund phrases:**
> *Eating humble pie* is not a pleasant experience.
> *Taking a hot shower* is one way to relieve tensions.
>
> **Participial phrases:**
> *Typing his paper,* John discovered many errors in his first draft.
> *Having worked to the point of exhaustion,* he made additional errors.
>
> **Infinitive phrases:**
> *To understand that problem,* you must read an advanced text.
> *To go to India* is to have one's eyes opened.
>
> **Prepositional phrases:**
> The man was sitting *on the couch.*
> My mural came *from Japan.*

On the other hand, at times an author builds an effect by repeating sentence groups, as Eth Clifford does in *A Bear Before Breakfast* (New

York: Putnam's, 1962). Clifford repeats " 'Oh,' said Jack, 'Oh,' said Jean," every time his picture-story book children understand that their expectations based on literally interpreting figurative language will not be realized. " 'Oh,' said Jack. 'Oh,' said Jean," after they realize that no lady will actually come out of the clear blue sky. " 'Oh,' said Jack. 'Oh,' said Jean," after they understand that they will not really see a white elephant. Through repetition of the lines, Clifford alternates a mood of anticipation with one of disappointment.

STRUCTURE OF LARGER THOUGHT UNITS

When revising, a writer focuses not only on the words and sentence patterns he has employed, but also on the way he has structured larger units—the paragraph, the stanza, the material included under major and minor subtitles. The questions he can use as a guideline for self-analysis include the following:

- Does each paragraph have an internal unity? Does it have a point, fact, or thought that holds it together?
- Are there any sentences in a paragraph that do not seem to relate to the main point of the paragraph?
- Is an identical idea developed in more than one paragraph? Does this add to the effect? Should paragraphs be combined?
- Are paragraphs on related and similar topics grouped together?
- Are there any ideas that I need to develop in greater depth?
- Is there any unrelated or unnecessary material (paragraph, section, stanza) that should be deleted?
- Does the order in which I put my paragraphs appear natural to the reader? Would there be a more effective ordering of ideas? Would it be more effective to order ideas inductively (examples——→generalization)? Deductively (generalization——→examples)? Inductively/deductively (examples——→generalization——→examples)?
- Is there a natural progression of thought or feeling from one stanza of my poem to the next?
- Are there any natural breaks in the development of the paper that may require a subheading? Do the subheadings I have already used aid in communication of meaning?
- Does the title communicate the thought or feeling intended?

part II: craft—a recapitulation

In this section we have enumerated specific points that can be considered in retrospect as a child in elementary school studies what he has organized and written:

- economy in word usage
- precision in word usage
- application of standard forms of written expression
- clarity in sentence construction
- variety in sentence structure
- structure of larger thought units

Are all these details of equal importance to the child attempting to increase his proficiency as a writer? No. It is the opinion of the authors that the selection of words and the structuring of sentences, paragraphs, and even larger units, are most fundamental, taking precedence over questions of capitalization, punctuation, spelling, or form. After all, the way a writer puts words together into sentences, stanzas, paragraphs, and larger units is a major element of his individual writing style; the organization of major thought units is his own invention, his own brainchild. It is this ability, rather than skill in spelling, punctuation, or capitalization, that separates the good writer from the great. In the final analysis, the professional writer turns to a professional editor to check minor details. In teaching the writing craft to children it seems logical, therefore, to concentrate most on what is most central in the process, giving secondary attention to other aspects.

CONTENT
PART III AND CRAFT

"The time has come," the Walrus said,
"To talk of many things:
Of shoes—and ships—and sealing-wax—
Of cabbages—and kings—."

Lewis Carroll,
"The Walrus and the Carpenter"

let children
enter
the realm
of poetry

The forms of things unknown, the poet's pen
Turns them to shapes, and gives to airy nothing
A local habitation and a name."

Shakespeare,
A Midsummer-Night's Dream

What is it that we are asking children to do when we ask them to create within the realm of poetry? Carl Sandburg begins an answer in two of his definitions of poetry: "Poetry is the opening and closing of a door, leaving those who look through to guess about what is seen during a moment," and "Poetry is a series of explanations of life fading off into horizons too swift for explanations." For Christopher Morley, "Poetry comes with anger, hunger and dismay," whereas Percy Shelley writes in *A Defence of Poetry* that "Poetry is the record of the best and happiest moments." Voltaire adds, "Poetry is the music of the soul; and, above all, of great and feeling souls." To William Hazlitt, "Poetry is that fine particle within us that expands, rarefies, refines, raises our whole being," and to Thomas Chivers, "a perfect poem [is] the crystalline revelation of the divine Idea."

Poetry, then, begins with music in the soul, a feeling, an expansion of our being, an explanation of life too swift for explanation, but it is music, a feeling, an expansion, an explanation clothed in the beauty of words. Edgar Allen Poe writes that "I would define, in brief, the Poetry of words as the Rhythmical Creation of Beauty." Matthew Arnold makes a similar point: "Poetry is simply the most beautiful, impressive and widely effective mode of saying things." Whereas painting is "silent poetry" to Plutarch, poetry is "speaking painting." In essence, the poet paints his idea with a radiance of words that sing, shout, bubble, and burst forth upon the ear.

creating poetry

Plying his craft, the poet frequently takes a rather ordinary, everyday event and adds new dimensions to it. He builds images by looking at events from his own probing, individual perspective and by combining words in unique patterns. This A. E. Housman does in a little piece entitled "Eight O'Clock":

> He stood, and heard the steeple
>   Sprinkle the quarters on the morning town.
> One, two, three, four, to market-place and people
>   It tossed them down.
>
> Strapped, noosed, nighing his hour,
>   He stood and counted them and cursed his luck;
> And then the clock collected in the tower
>   Its strength and struck.[1]

A steeple sprinkling the quarters on the morning town; a steeple tossing down one, two, three, four; a clock collecting its strength to strike the hour —a mundane occurrence is transformed into the unique sounds and images of poetry.

THE IMAGES OF POETRY

That the unique image is essential to poetic expression can be seen in work by such diverse poets as Ogden Nash, Robert Frost, Carl Sandburg, and even Mother Goose. Instead of writing that the turtle lives within a horny shell, Nash humorously concocts:

> The turtle lives 'twixt plated decks
> Which practically conceal its sex.
> I think it clever of the turtle
> In such a fix to be so fertile.[2]

Working with a different event—birches weighted by ice—Robert Frost writes that—

---

[1] A. E. Housman, *The Collected Poems of A. E. Housman.* Copyright 1922 by Holt, Rinehart & Winston, Inc.; copyright 1950 by Barclays Bank Limited; reprinted by permission of Holt, Rinehart & Winston, Inc.

[2] Ogden Nash, "The Turtle," in *Verses from 1920 On* (Boston: Little Brown, 1940). Copyright 1940 by Ogden Nash; reprinted by permission of the publisher.

> When I see birches bend to left and right . . . ,
> I like to think some boy's been swinging on them.[3]

In a more serious mood, Carl Sandburg projects this image of life:

> The people is a polychrome,
> a spectrum and a prism
> held in a moving monolith,
> a console organ of changing themes,
> a clavilux of color poems
> wherein the sea offers fog
> and the fog moves off in rain
> and the labrador sunset shortens
> to a nocturne of clear stars
> serene over the shot spray
> of northern lights.[4]

In yet another vein, there are the images of Mother Goose:

> Hey, diddle, diddle,
> The cat and the fiddle,
> The cow jumped over the moon!
> The little boy laughed to see such fun,
> And the dish ran away with the spoon.

Turtles 'twixt plated decks, swinging boys and birches, people as a polychrome, spectrum, and prism, dishes running away with spoons—these are the kinds of images a child poet can discover too as he creates within the realm of poetry.

THE SOUNDS OF POETRY

An element essential to the building of these images is the sound of the words in which the image is clothed. "Hey, Diddle, Diddle" builds on the recurring sound of *d*, giving a sharp, staccato beat to the piece. Sandburg in "the labrador sunset shortens/to a nocturne of clear stars/serene over the shot spray" builds on the repetitive sound of *s*, the whole line sliding gracefully from tongue to ear. Sandburg constructs his images upon the sound of the *m* in "moving monolith," the *c* in "a console organ of changing themes, a clavilux of color poems," and the sound of the *p* in "people," "polychrome," and "prism." Although Housman relies upon alliterative effects to build his images, he also draws upon rhyme as a means of instilling his images with beauty: *steeple/people, town/down, hour/tower,* and *luck/struck.* As for

---

[3] Robert Frost, "Birches" in *You Come Too* (New York: Holt, Rinehart & Winston, 1959), pp. 30–31.
[4] Carl Sandburg, *The People, Yes* (New York: Harcourt Brace Jovanovich, 1936). Copyright 1936 by Harcourt Brace Jovanovich, Inc.; copyright 1964 by Carl Sandburg; reprinted by permission of the publisher.

Ogden Nash, he is a master of the sound/meaning relationships within words as he plays with such combinations as *eagle/ea-gull* in "The Sea-Gull":

> Hark to the whimper of the sea-gull;
> He weeps because he's not an ea-gull.
> Suppose you were, you silly sea-gull,
> Could you explain it to your she-gull?[5]

The beauty of such poetry is that of sheer good fun.

The cacophony of harsh syllables placed in juxtaposition can be an element upon which an image is constructed. The repeated croak of the frogs, "Brekekekex-koax-koax," echoes through Aristophane's "The Frogs." *Chimborazo, Cotopaxi, Popocatepetl* are the exotic-sounding names that clang upon the ear, creating associations of the faraway in W. J. Turner's "Romance."[6] Strange-sounding names add the magic of faraway to the poetry of Rudyard Kipling. He gives us a glimpse of the Moulmein Pagoda on the Road to Mandalay, and he introduces us to the steadfastness of Gunga Din in the heat of India. Lewis Carroll's magic of sound is that of jabberwockies, slithy toves, and frumious bandersnatches. His art is inventing words by combining adjectives such as *lithe* and *slimy* into *slithy, fuming* and *furious* into *frumious*. The result is a portmanteau word—one word that carries the meaning of the two originals—that is often jarring and strident, echoing and reechoing upon the senses, bringing a distinctive dimension to poetry.

Some poets also employ rhythmic word patterns to build beauty into the images of their poetry. There is a musical lilt to the lines of Robert Burns's "A Man's a Man for A' That":

> Then let us pray that come it may,
>   As come it will for a' that,
> That sense and worth, o'er a' the earth,
>   May bear the gree, an' a' that.
>   For a' that, an' a' that,
>   It's coming yet, for a' that,
>   That man to man, the world o'er,
>   Shall brothers be for a' that.

This same lilting quality is found in a myriad of poems, such as "The Green Grass Growing All Around, All Around" (author unknown), John Masefield's "Sea Fever," A. E. Housman's "When I Was One-and-Twenty," and Robert Burns's "Flow Gently, Sweet Afton." (See Oscar Williams, ed., *Immortal Poems of the English Language* [New York: Pocket Books, 1952].)

---

[5] Ogden Nash, "The Sea Gull," in *Verses from 1920 On;* reprinted by permission of Little, Brown, Inc.

[6] W. J. Turner, "Romance," in *The Dark Wind* (New York: Dutton, 1920).

VISUAL EFFECTS

Some poets use visual effects to add beauty to their poetry. Italics, capitalization, short line-long line combinations, indentation, punctuation— all may contribute to the image being projected. The overall arrangement of words into artistic patterns on a page may be an integral element of the piece. Likewise, the relationship of empty space to written word may be an important aspect in the design of a poem. "In Just—" by E. E. Cummings derives beauty from almost all these visual elements:

in Just—
spring   when the world is mud—
luscious the little
lame balloonman

whistles   far   and wee

and eddieandbill come
running from marbles and
piracies and it's
spring

when the world is puddle-wonderful

the queer
old balloonman whistles
far   and wee
and bettyandisbel come dancing

from hop-scotch and jump-rope and

it's
spring
and
        the
              goat-footed
balloon Man   whistles
far
and
wee[7]

To build an image of spring and childhood, Cummings runs the names of his playmates together, ignores the conventions of punctuation, turns to the dash for effect, spaces words purposefully on the page, breaks lines of verse into visual units, and even invents words like *mud-luscious* and *puddle-wonderful* to conjure up the delights of a childhood spring. A painter as well as a poet, Cummings designs with word, space, and concrete letters; he brings a unique dimension to poetic creation.

---

[7] E. E. Cummings, *Collected Poems* (New York: Harcourt Brace Jovanovich, 1923). Copyright 1923, 1925, 1931, 1938, 1951, 1953, 1954, 1959 by E.E. Cummings; copyright 1926 by Horace Liveright; copyright 1963 by Marion Morehouse Cummings; reprinted by permission of Harcourt Brace Jovanovich, Inc.

This chapter began with the question, What is it that we are asking children to do when we ask them to create within the realm of poetry? Certainly we are not asking them to produce at the level of a Housman, a Cummings, a Carroll, a Sandburg, or a Nash. But if poetry is image and word beauty wrapped in one, then we *are* asking children to search for unique images through which to express their ideas, thoughts, emotions, and explanations of life; we *are* asking them to play with words that communicate with the beauty of "smouldering radiance," becoming aware of the sounds, rhythms, and visual aspects of words.

As a way of encouraging children to experiment within the realm of poetry, a teacher can have children create images, sounds, and visual elements of poetry without expecting them to produce fully crystallized poems. Emphasis in this context is on generating images and on building sound-word and visual-word relationships. Children toy with words, word pairs, phrases, and clauses in what might be termed prepoetry writing sessions, their only task being to play with the sounds of words, to concoct visual patterns out of words, and to play with images that may express their ideas and emotions. How does the teacher begin? Specific suggestions in the form of capsule ideas are given in the following sections. Each suggestion or idea can be expanded by a teacher into an actual teaching-learning activity—a mini-lesson—for use in a classroom.

PREPOETRY EXPERIENCES:
CREATING IMAGES

1. *Image brainstorming.* With children working either as a class or in smaller groups, toss out a question: What is summer? Have the children respond with as many words or word combinations as they can concoct. Tell the children this is a no-limit fun game—their wildest thought is to be expressed. Record on the chalk board if it is a class activity; otherwise, have each child record his "storm of ideas" anonymously on paper. If the children are brainstorming in groups, have one child record the associations for the group.

In response to this activity, a class of sixth-grade students produced the following unedited lines:

School's over. It's mischief time. Forget everything you learned in school.
Hot, dragged out time of swimming and sunbathing, glad to get back to school.
The sun shining on the sandy beaches.
Watching the sky changing color.
Summer is too much when your in love very much.

Endless summer is never having to end.
Happiness with guess who at the boardwalk bench.
The school is done and over with its time to have that summer fun.

Several youngsters volunteered to combine the images into a poem. Their edited poem was entitled "Endless Summer."

Endless Summer

Forget everything you learn in school.
School is over and done till September.
Summer is just too much when you're in...love.
Endless swimming in cool lukewarm water.
Dragged out time for swimming and sunbathing,
Sun setting on the sandy beaches,
Watching the sky change its colors,
Happiness with guess who at the boardwalk bench.
　Endless
　　　　　　summer
　　　　　　　is
　　　　　never having to
　　　　　　　end.

Other questions that can be used to motivate sessions in image brainstorming are—

What is a fish?
What is a friend?
What is a cloud?
What is a mountain peak?
What is a mother?
What is a brother/sister?
What is an elephant?
What is a day?

What does vacation mean?
What does snow mean?
What does wintertime mean?
What does friendship mean?
What does Halloween mean?
What does Christmas/Hanukkah mean?
What does war mean?
What does peace mean?

What can we use a brick for?
What can we use a piece of thread for?
What can we use a spider for?
What can we use a blanket for?

2. *Image listening.* Read children poems that derive their appeal from the images painted by the writer. Below are examples of such poems and

names of anthologies where they can be found. The anthologies are listed in the annotated resource bibliography (pp. 218).

> "Dreams," "Troubled Woman," "My People" by Langston Hughes in *Don't You Turn Back: Poems by Langston Hughes,* selected by Lee Bennett Hopkins.
>
> "Never Too Late," "Cradle Moon," "The Sky" in *I Wonder How, I Wonder Why* by Aileen Fisher.
>
> "The Telephone," "The Freedom of the Moon," "The Road Not Taken" in *You Come Too* by Robert Frost.
>
> "Humpty Dumpty," "Little Miss Muffet," "Little Jack Horner" from Mother Goose.
>
> "Star Hole" by Richard Brautigan, "A Song in the Front Yard" by Gwendolyn Brooks, "How To Eat A Poem" by Eve Merriam in *Man in the Poetic Mood,* edited by Jay Zweigler.
>
> "The Listeners" by Walter De La Mare, "Pippa's Song" by Robert Browning, "Fable" by Ralph Waldo Emerson, in *Immortal Poems of the English Language,* edited by Oscar Williams.
>
> "Tree Climbing" by Kathleen Fraser, "Nobody Loves Me" by Charlotte Zolotow, "My Nose," by Dorothy Aldis, in *Me: A Book of Poems,* compiled by Lee Bennett Hopkins.
>
> "If I Were Teeny Tiny" and "What's the Funniest Thing?" by Beatrice Schenk De Regniers in *Something Special* by B.S. De Regniers.

3. *Image experiencing.* So they can experience an image in a physical, rather concrete way—

- have children imagine what a giant spider web would be like by building one with twine laced from tree to tree out-of-doors;
- have children imagine they are lost by following a wooden maze while blindfolded;
- have young children pretend to be a leaf buffeted in the wind, a jellyfish carried on the tide, a bird flying for the first time. This type of activity can be done to a musical accompaniment.

4. *Image fantasizing.* Give children the opportunity to imagine the fantastic. Build a lesson on what it would be like to—

- be one inch tall looking at the world
- be ten feet tall looking at the world
- sit on a cloud
- be all alone in a small rowboat at sea
- be a bee, sitting on a flower petal
- climb the side of a skyscraper
- push the earth with a giant bulldozer
- tunnel down an ant hill.

Either record each child's image on the board or have him do it anonymously on a sheet of paper. Later, have two or three youngsters write a poem by combining the suggested images.

PREPOETRY EXPERIENCES: CONSTRUCTING VISUAL EFFECTS

1. *Seeing poems.* Construct poetry broadside charts in which poems printed in manuscript on large sheets of oaktag are displayed, or project poems using the overhead or opaque projector. For this purpose, select poems that draw their special effect from a variety of visual devices.

> "Wind" by Eugene Gomringer in *Man in the Poetic Mood,* edited by Jay Zweigler.
> "Tug of War" by Kathleen Fraser in *Faces and Places: Poems for You,* edited by Lee Hopkins and Misha Arenstein.
> "The Tale of a Dog" by James H. Lambert, Jr. in *I Went to the Animal Farm,* edited by William Cole.
> "Therus" by Eve Merriam in *Man in the Poetic Mood.*
> "Monument" by E. M. De Melo e Castro in *Man in the Poetic Mood.*
> "Fiddle Practice" and "Miss Priss" in the *Monster Den* by John Ciardi.
> "Do You Remember" by Emmett Williams in *Man in the Poetic Mood.*

2. *Seeing pictures in words.* Give children the fun of concocting visual pictures with single words. Show them some examples as in Figure 8–1.

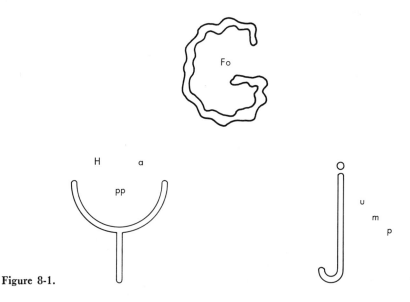

Figure 8-1.

Let youngsters select words that they can picture. The following words are workable in this context:

hippopotamus	flat	dot
endless	circle	motorcycle
ladder	snake	climb
zigzag	column	fall
candle	monument	help
electric	thin	hole
pyramid	fat	stop
mouse	chimney	banana

Children can also try to produce visual effects using the letters of the words in phrases: *giant step; waves, waves, waves; fir tree; apartment house; climbing up a tree; tiny ant; walking in circles; railroad train; head-on collisions; automobile tires; running downhill;* and *up, periscope.*

Figure 8–2 provides some examples to get children started.

3. *Building visual effects into poems.* Structure class activity so that there is time for writing-experience poetry charts in which young children dictate images in groups and the teacher records. As she records, the teacher should keep in mind that the way she capitalizes, punctuates, italicizes, and positions words on paper may heighten the effect. From her way of recording, children intuitively pick up some of the visual dimensions of poetry.

Older children can be encouraged to write the words of the poem

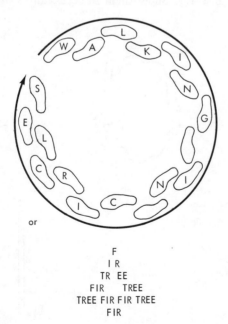

or

```
        F
       I R
     TR  EE
    FIR    TREE
  TREE FIR FIR TREE
       FIR
```

Figure 8-2.

they have created on individual word-cards. These cards can be laid out on large brown paper sheets much in the fashion of advertising layout. Cards can be moved around and tried in various patterns to achieve different spatial relationships; even the letters of a word can be cut apart to try for unique spatial effects. Once a final pattern has been determined, the cards can be pasted or stapled to the brown paper. Watercolor, crayon, felt pen, or India ink can be used to add color to the written poem. The same technique can be employed using a magnet or flannel board. Word cards bearing the words of a poem written by a child or a group of children can be juggled around on the board until the poet decides that he has the space-word relationship he wants.

PREPOETRY EXPERIENCES:
BUILDING SOUND-WORD RELATIONSHIPS

1. *Writing noises into poetry.* Some of the sound effects of poetry can be derived from noises that are not typically expressed in words. Take, for instance, the way Vachel Lindsay uses lion noise in "Daniel Jazz":

> Thus roared the lions:—
> 'We want Daniel, Daniel, Daniel,
> We want Daniel, Daniel, Daniel
> Grrrrrrrrrrrrrrrrrrrrrrrrrrrrrrr
> Grrrrrrrrrrrrrrrrrrrrrrrrrrrrrrrrrr.'[8]

In these lines the poet has himself invented a way of verbally recording a nonverbal phenomenon. Children can experiment in much the same way, working with such phenomena as the sound of—

a dentist's drill	leaves in motion on a tree
a scream	a foot coming down on a leaf
the cry of a bird	the ocean waves
a coin dropping on concrete	a horse's trot
a horn	pneumatic drills
a policeman's whistle	a swing in motion
an arrow flying through the air	radio static

Select one of these noises and have the children listen to the real sound or the sound on record, or have them mimic the noise. Then have them try to write a representation of the noise in letters. This activity works particularly well with small groups of youngsters, each group working with a different sound.

2. *Playing with repetitive words and phrases.* Encourage youngsters to play with some of the repetitive word patterns found in poetry by having

---

8 Vachel Lindsay, "Daniel Jazz," in *Collected Poems* (New York: Macmillan, 1920). Copyright 1920 by The Macmillan Company; copyright 1948 by Elizabeth C. Lindsay; reprinted by permission of The Macmillan Company.

them take one or more words and repeat the word or words over and over, perhaps changing it slightly with each repetition, and then add only four or five other words. For instance, a prepoetry experience could be to play with the word, *red,* repeating it as many times as they want in whatever visual pattern seems right. Then add an image-creating phrase at the end. The result might be—

> red red red
> Red Red Red Red
> RED RED RED RED RED
> BURNING UP THE SKY

Words that work in this context are color words, such as *black, yellow,* and *green,* and words like *fear, stop, fire, wind, up, never,* and *forever.* Try beginning with a word like *drippity, lickity, swishy, diddily, doodolly,* or one that a child invents. Again, children repeat the word in patterns they devise, adding only a *small* number of other words to achieve a sound effect.

> Drippity, drippity, drippity—
> —Plop
> Drippity, drippity, drippity—
> —Plop
> Drippity, drippity, drippity—
> —Plop
> That's the song of a
> DROP

Similarly, give children a phrase: "At the end of a day—," "School means—," "Love means—," "In the spring—," "I like—," or have the children devise their own repetitive introductory phrase. Then suggest that they all write a number of lines that begin with that phrase. If all the children begin with the same introductory phrase, later a poetry-writing team can select several lines and build a poem based on the repetitive element. Using this technique, a sixth-grade group began with "Another day—." Their initial unedited prepoetry lines included:

> Another day to work again for someone else.
> Another day is waking up for school.
> Another day—tomorrow-
> Another day, another bad time
> Another day—a day to come or a day to follow
> Another day, Another hour, with the freshness of a shower

A poetry-writing team, working with the teacher, later organized the lines into a little poem:

Another day—
   a day to come or a day to follow.
Another day—
   to wake again for school.
Another day—
   to work again for someone else.
Another day—
   Tomorrow.

3. *Inventing words.* Following the example of Lewis Carroll, involve youngsters in word-inventing sessions in which youngsters build words that have no meaning but are pronounceable in English. Such a session can be motivated by Sandburg's "Phizzog"—This face you got,/This here phizzog you carry around,"[9]—by Carroll's "Jabberwocky," or by Mother Goose rhymes—"A dillar, a dollar" and "Diddle, diddle, dumpling, my son John." A bulletin board displaying invented words such as *flattercocky, fiddledebob,* and *crumbledeblah* is another way to prompt children to concoct words that sound pleasant to the ear and feel nice on the tongue. Children can build their invented words into repetitive patterns in later sessions.

4. *Playing with exotic-sounding names.* Have children conduct an atlas search for place names that titillate the ear. This activity can be carried on by a group of youngsters who can then put together a bulletin board that bears the exotic-sounding place names. Individually, in groups, or as a class, children then select a word or words from the bulletin board to play with in repetitive visual patterns.

5. *Building assonant and rhyming sequences.* Working with the whole class, start with a word like *wind* and encourage the children to think of verbs starting with *w* that could follow. They may suggest *whistles, waltzes, whines, whips, wrestles, waits,* and *wants,* which, if set down within a visual pattern, almost make a poem:

Wind...whistles and whines
      waits
      wants
      waltzes
      wrestles...Wind

Starting with "The tree," have children look for *t* verbs like *trembled* and *trailed*; starting with "The fly," have them look for *f* verbs; starting with "The car," have them search for *c* verbs. A dictionary and a thesaurus are helpful tools to have available for this activity.

[9] Carl Sandburg, "Phizzog," *Good Morning, America* (New York: Harcourt Brace Jovanovich, 1928).

A similar type of activity can be carried out with rhyming words. Have children build a rhyming sequence on a word like *crash: trash, flash, mash, dash, lash, ash, clash*. Again, written down with some attention to visual elements but without too much concern with meaning, the words are almost a poem.

CRASH!
Dash!
Flash!
Mash!
Trash!
ASH!

Children can build similar sequences on words that rhyme with *thick, go, side, guess, worm, bell, breeze, steam, sleep, cheer,* and *feel.* A rhyming dictionary can be helpful in this context.

6. *Listening to the sounds of words in poems.* Select poems to read to youngsters that derive special effects from sound/word relationships. Below are some examples. Details on anthologies can be found in the resource bibliography, page 218.

"A Lazy Thought" and "Conversation" by Eve Merriam in *Faces and Places: Poems for You,* edited by Lee Bennett Hopkins.

"Hydrants" by Lee Bennett Hopkins in *I Think I Saw a Snail,* edited by Lee Bennett Hopkins.

"Anthill" and "When it Comes to Bugs" in *I Wonder How, I Wonder Why* by Aileen Fisher.

"What Did You Put in Your Pocket?" and "A Sugar Lump is Good to Have in Case Of" in *Something Special* by Beatrice Schenk de Regniers.

"Tambourines" and "Lullaby" by Langston Hughes in *Don't You Turn Back: Poems by Langston Hughes,* edited by Lee Bennett Hopkins.

"The King's Breakfast" and "Disobedience" in *When We Were Very Young* by A. A. Milne.

"A View of Things" by Edwin Morgan in *Man in the Poetic Mood,* edited by Jay Zweigler.

writing poetry of many kinds

There are numerous verse forms in which the imagery, sounds, and visual effects of poetry are expressed: free verse, haiku, cinquain, picture or concrete poetry, rhymed couplets, series of rhymed couplets, and limericks, to name just a few of the genres that are popular in the elementary school. Youngsters can inductively discover the characteristics of a verse form by hearing, seeing, and studying poems written in the particular form. The teacher should experiment with the verse form herself so that some of the examples studied inductively are those she has written. A related technique is to share samples of poems in a verse form written by students in previous years. Youngsters may perceive that poetry writing is something they themselves may enjoy; it is not an activity restricted to professionals.

Of course, children should not be required to replicate precisely the structural characteristics of a type of poetry. Creating a haiku, a limerick, or a couplet can lead youngsters to modify that form into a structure that is uniquely theirs. Perhaps the pinnacle of poetic enjoyment is the invention of a new form in which a child can effectively communicate. Thus a child may invent a form to which he has not previously been introduced, a form like a pyramid, in which the number of syllables per line follows the scheme of 1–2–3–4–5 as in the lines—

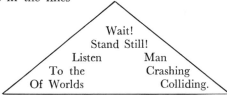

Or children may change a 1–2–3–4–5 pyramid structure introduced to them by their teacher into 1–3–5–7–9 as in these lines:

As teachers, we should not consider a particular form of poetry so perfect or so sacred that a child cannot play with the form itself, modifying it, and creating something different in the process. In this respect, work with the traditional forms of poetic expression in the elementary school should be considered a springboard to carry the mind into original areas rather than merely a replication process.

Let us turn briefly to some of the traditional forms that can serve as springboards for poetic invention.

FREE VERSE

Free or blank verse is unrhymed poetry in which the poet has no restrictions on total length, number of syllables to the line, or rhythmic pattern. The images and the sounds determine the overall product. The poet must sense or feel the point at which to break his lines, the point at which a new stanza should begin, the point at which his image is complete.

To motivate free-verse experiences, encourage children to build images around such topics as love, pain, fear, subways, snow, beach, people, being little, being lost, and being unhappy. Talk about ideas. Brainstorm images with groups of youngsters, recording the impressions given at random. Later, have youngsters individually or in groups build their ideas into verse, experimenting with different arrangements. One group of second-grade youngsters did this and cooperatively produced—

> Spring is a time—
>   for eating ice-cream cones.
> Spring is a time—
>   for riding bikes and jumping rope.
> Spring is a time—
>   for picnics.
> Spring is a time—
>   for happiness.

Joyce Hash, an eleven-year-old, began image-building around the phrase "A mother is a person who—."

A Mother Is—

A mother is a person who says she loves you even though she doesn't act like it.
A mother is a person who calls you in the house just when you're having fun.
A mother is a person who makes you have your room clean everyday.
A mother is a person who will make you wear a coat in June.
A mother is a person who makes you go to bed early even though you tell her that you will get up in the morning.
A mother is a person who washes clothes but makes you iron them.
A mother is a person who is very nice when she makes nice clothes for you.

CONCRETE POETRY

When a poem's image is derived primarily from its visual elements, when it is the way the letters and words of a poem are arranged on a page that communicates the message, the poem is concrete or picture poetry. As Lovonne Mueller notes in an article ("Concrete Poetry, Creative Writing for All Students," *English Journal* 58 [October 1969]), there are several forms picture poetry can take. First, the initial letters of a line can in themselves relate to the image or create the effect. ABC poetry is of this type. After the letter of the alphabet that will be the beginning point his been chosen, each successive line or word must begin with the letter next in alphabetical sequence:

Donuts
  Enter
    Fat   or
      Gaily
        Hopping.

Jumping
  Kangaroos—
    Landing
      Merrily
        Near—
          Open
            Pouches.
              Quickly
                Run
                  Some
                    Tiny
                      Jumping Kangaroos.

Related to ABC poetry is poetry in which the first letters of lines spell out the name of the object, person, or animal under poetic consideration:

Sparkling spot of light
Trailing in the sky
After night is over
Runs away and hides.

Or in—

The tube spews light
Entwining thought in threads—
Like hypnotist—
Entices minds to
Vacant, hollowness.
In desperation
Should not I ask, "Am
I a man or puppet
On a string?"
No, do not ask!

Because it is necessary to find a word beginning with a specific letter, this is rather difficult poetry to write. Its use in the elementary school, therefore, is probably limited to upper grades; based on our own experience writing within the form, we also suggest that such short, specific words as *sun, wind, fog, cat, dog, home, sky, tree, bug, bee,* and *worm* are easier to manipulate than longer words. We also suggest that before beginning to create, children brainstorm words starting with each letter of the title word as in: **S**— *scorching, shining, solar, silver, sweltering;* **U**—*up, under universe, umbrella;* **N**—*noon, 'neath, now, never, night.*

A second, more common type of concrete poetry is that in which the letters themselves are recorded so that the image is shown not only verbally, but pictorially as in the examples on Figure 8–3.

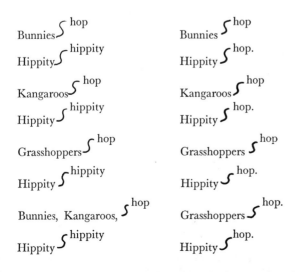

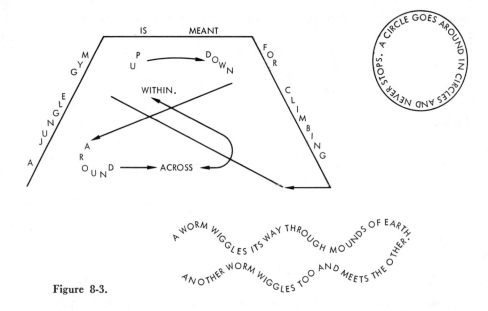

Figure 8-3.

Obviously the medium of concrete poetry does not allow the sophisticated development of imagery possible in free verse because the form is limited by the strictures of visualization. However, because there is a puzzle-like nature to the construction of concrete poetry, the form may appeal to youngsters who usually turn off to poetry based on the more abstract image.

HAIKU, SENRYU, TANKA, CINQUAIN

Shiny blue water
ripples as the boy throws stones
into the still sea.

It is raining now!
Blossoms falling from the trees
fade in the puddles.

JOHN MELCHIONNE, GRADE 6

John's poems are haikus that turn to nature for subject matter, are unrhymed, and adhere to the syllabic scheme 5–7–5. A form of poetry employed for centuries by the Japanese, haiku is a brief interlude of imagery, a glimpse of feeling, that little children can handle with amazing ease and beauty of expression. Haikus can be stimulated by excursions into nature and by parcels of nature brought into classrooms—an opening bud, a gnarled branch, a cactus, a water lily, a hermit crab—by touch, smell, and taste experiences and by abstract art—finger paintings, ink blobs, metal sculpture. Again, ideas can germinate in image-brainstorming sessions. And again, the pattern 5–7–5 does not have exclusive rights on perfection: the child who builds a delicate image adding two or three more syllables or using two or three fewer has manipulated the form to meet the unique requirement of his image. The result is a modification of haiku, or what the Japanese call senryu. Paul did this when he created—

> Dandelion flowers
>   blowing in the breeze...little airplanes
> flying round and round.

Paul Melchionne

The Japanese have carried haiku a step further to embrace larger interludes of imagery that cannot be expressed in the seventeen syllables of haiku. The result is tanka, in which the poet begins with the syllabic scheme of haiku—5–7–5—and adds two more lines—7–7. A poem so constructed has a total of five lines and thirty-one syllables: 5–7–5–7–7. It, too, is unrhymed, and its stress is on the image expressed.

Although the form of poetry called cinquain does not have Oriental origins, youngsters work within the form in much the same way as they create haikus, senryus, and tankas. As with the syllabic forms already considered, cinquains are small interludes of imagery. They are constructed within five lines and typically follow a syllabic scheme of 2–4–6–8–2.

> Candles—
> flickering flames
> that fill the dark with light—
> cast hope where once there lay despair.
> Candles.

> Traffic.
> An endless stream
> Of autos, buses, trucks.
> Stop, start, stop, start, stop, start, stop, start.
> Hours late!

Some writers of cinquains also adhere to the additional stipulations that—

- the first line is composed of only one word,
- the second of two words,
- the third of three words,
- the fourth of four words,
- the fifth of only one word.

RHYMING POETRY

One of the basic building blocks of rhyming poetry is the couplet— at its simplest just two lines of verse each ending with the same sound:

A flower shifting in the breeze
Scatters pollen making me sneeze.

PETE, GRADE 6

Requiring only two rhyming words, the couplet can be an easy introduction to the writing of rhyming-word patterns. With the aid of a rhyming dictionary or lists of rhyming words, children can play with numerous word pairs, building them into couplets.

Once a child can handle the couplet form, he can try writing a series of couplets in sequence as two fifth-grade girls did:

What is Winter?

Winter is snow and ice
  And everything nice—
Skis and skates
  And holiday dates,
Snowball fights
  And very cold nights.
Christmas vacation
  Is a sensation.
THAT'S WHAT WINTER IS.

SUE HUNTER and BABS KILPERT

A step beyond the couplet is the limerick, five lines of verse with a humorous tone and with two sets of rhymes—the first, second and fifth lines rhyming, the third and fourth lines rhyming. Since limericks sometimes start with "There once was——," for children to begin with that phrase can prove as helpful as it was for Bobby, an eleven-year-old boy who wrote:

There once was a stupid cat
Who got hit by a flying bat,
  Soared high in the sky
  She flew like a fly,
And got caught by Officer Fat.

Since a limerick is essentially a rhyming, rhythmic word play, short phrases with a list of accompanying rhyming words can serve as a motivating device for limerick writing:

Base Phrase	Rhyming Words
a plain Jane from Maine	*rain, attain, champagne, complain, Spain, rain, train, drain, cocaine, domain, abstain, hurricane, vain*
some merry mice	*slice, dice, twice, ice, rice, precise, spice, sacrifice, suffice, nice, advice, lice*
a mixed-up chick	*brick, sick, lick, trick, hick, quick, kick, slick, stick, thick*

a Lady of Kent	*bent, gent, scent, circumvent, vent, cement, descent, invent, lent, rent, spent, went*
a man called Jake	*bake, ache, shake, mistake, sweepstake, awake, brake, cake, lake, flake, make*
a musketeer	*fear, insincere, volunteer, severe, steer, beer, cheer, clear, dear, queer, spear*
a bashful bride	*side, chide, pride, broadside, ride, decide, stride, slide, confide, tide*

For children who enjoy working in rhyming patterns, modifications of some of the traditional forms can also prove challenging. The roundel, for instance, has some possibilities because of the simple repetition of words within a refrain. In the following schematic of a roundel, all *a* lines rhyme, all *b* lines rhyme, and the unrhymed refrain is formed from the first word of the poem or some part of the first line and need not make sense:

Line 1:   a
Line 2:   b
Line 3:   a
   Line 4:   refrain
Line 5:   b
Line 6:   a
Line 7:   b
Line 8:   a
Line 9:   b
Line 10: a
   Line 11: refrain

The pattern of the roundel lends itself to the simplification necessary for use by elementary school youngsters. Using an *a–b–a–refrain–b–a refrain* pattern, we can create:

Rivers

a	Rivers rolling downward to the sea
b	No longer clear, no longer clean—
a	Destroyed by waste and dumped debris
refrain	Rolling downward!
b	Rivers that sparkled blue and green
a	No longer fresh, no longer free
refrain	Rolling downward!

The roundel can also be modified to *a–b–refrain–a–b–refrain,* or to *a–b–a–refrain–refrain–a–b–a–refrain–refrain.* The shorter modified roundels are easier to handle and easier to produce than the longer traditional form.

Of course, rhyming in free style with no limitations on syllables, no prescribed rhyming scheme, and no strictures on overall length is easier to conquer than a tighter form. Karin Hennings, a fifth-grade girl, used an unstructured approach when she wrote this poem:

Snow

Snow is light
  and very bright.
Snow is green—
  snow is white.
Snow is the kind
  of thing I like.
  Snow is red.
  Snow is blue.
  Snow is for
  more than two.

taking children into the realm of poetry: our goal

It goes without saying that the majority of youngsters in elementary schools today will not be the great poets of tomorrow. As a matter of fact, it is a rather unique adult who spends leisure or professional time writing poetry. What then is the purpose of taking children into the realm of poetry? We hypothesize that by playing with word-image, word-sound, and word-picture relationships that children become more able to formulate the idea-content that is the essence of all written experience, to handle the English language in patterns valuable even in work with other written materials, and, therefore, to communicate their ideas more effectively. From this point of view, prepoetry writing experiences are a most important element within the elementary language program, for in prepoetry writing children are involved with the building blocks of communication—ideas, words, sounds, visual effects. This involvement is more essential than the production of perfect, fully crystallized poems by all youngsters in a class, which is an objective beyond the teacher's grasp. This involvement may also help children appreciate poetry in all its forms so that they simply come to like it, seeking it out to read on their own. If we can achieve that end, then our time has been well spent.

let children
enter
the realm
of prose

When children create the images of free verse, haiku, cinquain, and rhyming poetry, they are involved with a highly personalized view of events, places, and people; they are playing with feelings to be expressed within word patterns that derive much appeal from visual and aural stimuli. On the other hand, when children make excursions into the realm of prose, they are more involved with producing the inventive idea-content of story and the reflective, conceptual, projective, and logical-expressive content of expository prose.[1] What are the essential elements of the prose forms in which this idea-content is expressed? How can teachers encourage children to enter the realm of prose? Chapter nine focuses on these two questions by turning to story and expository prose forms.

story

In story, the writer's concern is not with the actual; his concern is with the *fabrication* of descriptions, speeches, persons, and/or plots that go

[1] See Chapter 1 for definitions of *reflective, conceptual, projective, expressive, and inventive content.*

beyond actual occurrences. He creates characters who do not precisely resemble any living persons, settings in which action is to occur—settings that may not exist in the real world exactly as he paints them—and sequences of action that may not have happened in that precise way in real life. He has to devise the words and sentences spoken by his characters. In essence, the elements of his medium are invented setting, plot, character, and dialogue.

ENCOUNTERING THE ELEMENTS OF
STORY IN THE WRITTEN WORD

It goes almost without saying that one of the best introductions to setting, plot, character, and dialogue is through the finest of stories written for children. Plot, setting, and dialogue come alive in Beatrice de Regniers's *May I Bring a Friend?* (New York: Atheneum, 1966), as they do in Evaline Ness's *Sam, Bangs, and Moonshine* (New York: Holt, Rinehart & Winston, 1966), in William Steig's *Sylvester and the Magic Pebble* (New York: Clarion, 1969), and in E. L. Konigsburg's *About the B'nai Bagels* (New York: Atheneum, 1967). Characterization is an essential ingredient in Carol Brink's *Caddie Woodlawn* (New York: Macmillan, 1935), in Laura Armer's *Waterless Mountain* (New York: McKay, 1931), and in Scott O'Dell's *Sing Down the Moon* (Boston: Houghton Mifflin, 1970).

Through continued contact with stories, children intuitively come to understand more about the elements of story. During daily storytime in the kindergarten and first grade, youngsters listening to the teacher read such stories as Marjorie Flack's *Angus and the Ducks* (New York: Doubleday, 1939) or Ezra Keats's *Whistle for Willie* (New York: Viking, 1964) follow the actions of storybook characters. In the upper grades, too, portions of books can be read orally to youngsters; children can become acquainted with Homer Price and his now legendary doughnut machine (in Robert McCloskey's *Homer Price* [New York: Viking, 1943]), Long John Silver and the classic "Yo ho ho and a bottle of rum," (in Robert Louis Stevenson's *Treasure Island*), Charlotte as she spins her web (in E. B. White's *Charlotte's Web* [New York: Harper & Row, 1952]), and Mrs. Frisby and her encounter with the rats of NIMH (in Robert C. O'Brien's *Mrs. Frisby and the Rats of NIMH* [New York: Atheneum, 1971]). Individual reading-for-enjoyment can earn similar dividends in intuitive understanding of the nature of story. Take children into the fiction section of the school library to select books to be read on a daily basis in the classroom during periods of independent study.

From everyday encounters with stories, a child may also begin to understand that the realm of story is not exactly like the realm of reality. A kindergarten child will begin to realize that the world painted in Sendak's *Where the Wild Things Are* (New York: Harper & Row, 1963) and other books of fantasy is different from the real world in which he himself exists, that events can happen differently in the world of make-believe, and that people and animals may even act slightly differently in books. By middle elementary school, the child has a high degree of awareness that Pippi Longstocking's experiences (Astrid Lindgren, *Pippi Longstocking* [New York: Viking, 1950]) are not exactly real, that life does not go on quite like that. From encounters with books, children come to know that when they write short stories, they too can depart from reality.

ENCOUNTERING THE ELEMENTS OF STORY IN THE REAL WORLD

Another way of taking children into the world of the imagination is to help them to see opportunities for invention in real life situations. Encourage children to invent action, dialogue, characters based on real people they have observed and real events they have experienced. As children take short walks in the park, along a city street, or through a nature preserve, prime them to look for interesting or unique people and phenomena to work into a story. Suggest cognitive activities:

Action:
Imagine what scrape that boy is going to get into.
Imagine what could happen here at night.
Imagine what happens here in winter.
Imagine what would happen here if this spot were transported to the moon.
Imagine what would happen if those two people bumped into each other.

Dialogue:
Imagine what those two people (observed talking) could be saying.
Imagine what that boy's mother will say to him when he gets home.
Imagine that the birds are actually talking. What are they saying?
Imagine that Mama Monkey is actually talking to Mike, the baby monkey. What are they saying?

Character:
Imagine what kind of a person that man may be.
Imagine what he does, what he enjoys doing, where he lives, how he talks, and how he acts.
Create a name for the person or animal you are observing.

Setting:
Describe this place as it would look at night, in the summer, in the winter.
Describe this place as you imagine it will look next year.
Describe what this place would look like during a storm, on a hot day, filled with hundreds of people, or inhabited only by animals.

Brainstorming groups of youngsters can carry on the activity from an observational site: sitting on a grassy plot by a popular park path, on a bench in the outdoor zoo, or on an old log in a wooded area; standing discreetly by a supermarket entrance or a busy street corner; or even looking out of the classroom window. Observing can be assigned as an individual activity: "During the next week, 'people-watch.' See if you can find a real person who would make a good story character." The children's task is to use the real as stimulus for excursions into the imaginary.

In the same vein, have children keep an idea book (a flip-back spiral notebook of the type used by stenographers or a homemade variety) in which they record ideas for possible future transformation into imaginary descriptions, characters, and plots. These ideas are based on observations but go beyond actual observations. Children jot ideas into their personal idea books whenever a thought strikes, not just during specially designated writing sessions. In addition, they can be given time in the morning when they first come into the classroom to record in brief fashion observations made on the way to school, during the previous afternoon, or at home— observations that could be transformed into the inventive idea of story.

ENCOUNTERING A VARIETY OF STORY FORMS

There is no reason to restrict children's writing of inventive content to what is typically called a short story. Although children can be motivated to write amazingly delightful short stories by the types of activities described in chapter three, children can experiment with other story forms: the picture-story book, the fable, the tall tale, mystery and adventure stories, comic strips, and plays.

Picture-story books.   With children in the upper grades who have listened to and read picture-story books during their early years, one way to motivate excursions into story writing is to encourage the youngsters to write their own picture-story books. This is not at all as immense a task as it appears on initial appraisal.

First, children who have read extensively in picture-story books know this form of literature better than any other. Some children even seem to know instinctively that repetition of key words and phrases can be used to add to the effect of a story, which is a typical technique employed in picture-story books. A sixth-grade boy intentionally built repetition into his story when he wrote "The bunny rabbits laughed at him. The chattering squirrels laughed at him. The wise old owl laughed at him. Worst of all, his brothers and sisters laughed at him."

Second, children can collaborate on book writing: one child does the pictures while another does the written lines, or several children work together as a team. In this way the task is not overwhelming to the individual child.

Third, picture-story books written by youngsters in grades four through six can be taken to the lower grades and read by the authors to younger children. The older youngsters, therefore, have a purpose in writing: their writing is to be shared with others. Fourth, part of the story is told through pictures, lessening the verbal writing task.

To get the activity started, a teacher in the upper elementary grades may decide to show such a film as *The Story of a Book* (Churchill Films, Los Angeles, California) in which Holling C. Holling explains how his book *Pagoo* (Boston: Houghton Mifflin, 1957) gradually came into existence, or *The Lively Art of Picture Books* (Weston Woods, Weston, Connecticut) in which Robert McCloskey, Barbara Cooney, and Maurice Sendak talk about their writing. She may have children reread picture-story books read to them as primary school children, although the children's purpose is different now because they are authors in search of technique. If she is lucky, a teacher may even be able to locate an actual author who will come and speak to her children on how he goes about writing a book.

There are numbers of techniques for assembling children's picture-story books. One is to take a spiral-bound notebook from which almost all of the pages have been torn and mount the pages of the children's story on the front and back sides of the remaining pages. Colored term-paper binders can be used as book covers into which the pages of text and illustrations can be fastened. A child can also construct his own book cover by covering pieces of cardboard with colored paper; the pages of his book are then either clipped or stapled inside the cover.

Fables. If a teacher wants to begin book-writing activity on a smaller scale, all members of a class can become involved in writing a class book or literary magazine to which each youngster may contribute a story with accompanying illustration. Writing fables—short prose pieces building toward a moral—lends itself particularly well to this activity. Motivated by *Aesop's Fables* (*Louis* Untermeyer, ed., New York: Golden Press, 1965) read by the teacher or even by Victor Borge on a film produced as part of the Bank Street Reading Incentive Series (New York: McGraw-Hill Films), children select a moral from a fable and write fables that build toward that moral. Children who prefer can go a step further; motivated by William Wondruska's *Mr. Brown and Mr. Gray* (New York: Holt, Rinehart & Winston, 1968), they can write an original fable. With an accompanying illustration, the fables are compiled into a class book by a team of students. Here is Patty Coombs's fable as it appeared in "Fables by Sixes," a sixth-grade class book:

A Chicken Who Spoke a Foreign Language

Once there was a chicken who could speak a foreign language. The language that he could speak was Spanish. Every morning he went to all his friends'

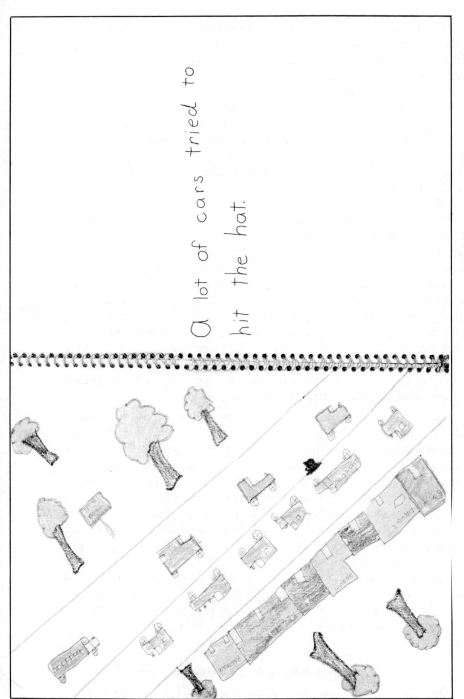

Figure 9-1. *A double page from a picture story book, "The Lost Hat," written and illustrated by Fred Doot, a fourth-grade boy.*

homes to play with them. But they would never play with him because he couldn't speak English.

One day when the chickens were playing, that is all except Puncho, a wolf was hiding in the bushes. Puncho saw him and didn't know how to warn his friends.

Suddenly, Puncho ran right out in front of the wolf to attract his attention. The wolf ran after him and the other chickens were safe.

Later they saw Puncho pass their house. The next morning when Puncho came to their house, the chickens were happy to see him and they played with him all day.

Moral: ACTIONS SPEAK LOUDER THAN WORDS

Tall tales. The writing of tall tales may turn on youngsters who turn off to fables. After meeting Paul Bunyon and Babe the Blue Ox, children can write and illustrate their own books of tall tales on an individual basis, in collaboration, or as a whole class with each child contributing a tale to a class book. Vicky Giambra's story was entitled simply "Worms" in her sixth grade's "Tall Tales of Nature":

Worms

Did you know that a long time ago when Mother Nature was setting up housekeeping, worms played a very important part in helping her?

The Tape Worm would furnish the tape measure so that the Inch Worm could measure the right lengths on their projects. Their projects ran anywhere from making flowers to making honeysuckle vines.

Then the Angle Worm would make sure the angles were correct. After that, the Cut Worm would cut out whatever pattern or design every other worm was making. When that was finished, the Pin Worm would pin on the leaves to the bushes.

At mealtime the Grub Worm would furnish the "grub" for all the worms to eat. While the worms were eating, the Book Worm would read to them about people. When it got dark, the Glow Worms would provide light so the worms could continue their work.

When they had completed their work in one place, they would call on the Skip Worms to furnish transportation along the "Route" Worm to another place where they could do more work and start over on their tasks again.

Mystery or adventure stories. "Let's read a mystery story (adventure story)" may be the beginning of a mystery-writing activity in which children toy with the unknown, the frightening, the weird, or of an adventure story activity in which children invent exciting events. When children are in the mood, having listened to a story read to them in a partially darkened room, the teacher can help youngsters to start by supplying an exciting introductory paragraph:

It was almost dark as Susan/Ken and I started down the lonely country road. Suddenly, she/he grabbed my arm and whispered, "Do you see what I see?"

Comic strips.   A similar type of activity can be motivated by reading popular comic strips. Read *Peanuts, Pogo, Nancy, Henry,* and *Blondie* strips to children. Then encourage them, working either individually or in illustrator-writer teams, to invent characters and create a strip. Since this activity requires the writing of dialogue—words to fill the little balloons above the characters' heads—it focuses children's attention on the contribution of dialogue to story. It is also easy to produce a class publication by stapling the children's strips on large pieces of brown paper in the style of the funnies.

Plays.   Writing plays brings children into direct contact with the elements of story. A group of youngsters working together to write a play that they will eventually perform must decide what characters they will write into their play, what the plot will be, and, of course, what lines each character will speak. In addition, they must consider what kinds of props they will use and what kinds of costumes, if any, they will wear. In dramatizations involving puppets they must paint scenery on the sides and back of the puppet stage to communicate setting, and they must construct puppets whose shape, form, dress, and coloring communicate some dimensions of character. They must use dialogue and movement to carry the plot forward.

Play-writing activity perhaps has a beginning in the creative play

Figure 9-2.   *Children's comic strips.*

activity of young children. For example, as a child plays with plastic dolls representing make-believe characters who dwell in the swamp with Pogo—the owl, the alligator, the turtle—he may pretend that the owl is talking to the alligator and may carry on an imaginary dialogue, or he may load all his plastic animals into his dump truck and pretend that they are going for a ride through the swamp. What the child does with his toys during such creative playtimes carries him into the world of invention. It can be a first step toward the eventual writing of a story.

When a child puts a long green sock puppet—an alligator—on his hand and improvises with it, he is taking another step in the writing of story. Now he is no longer Tommie—he is Albert, the alligator who lives in the swamp with Pogo. He must act and talk the way he thinks the alligator acts and talks, and he must create conversation and action. Another child holds a body puppet in front of himself and also ceases to be himself. He is one of the three bears returning home. He too must create conversation and action.

Older children can go a step further: they can take a character met in a picture-story book or a TV cartoon and compose a playlet, a scene in which the familiar character meets a lonely bear, a friendly hippo, or perhaps a giant whale. Later on, children can use as their major character a strange old man seen in the park, a little bird who could not seem to fly, or the friendly fellow who sells ice cream on the corner by the school. When several children work together on such play-writing projects as these, the result can be rather exciting; the children can both write and perform the play, even recording a performance on audio or video tape.

letter

When we take children into the realm of letter writing, our primary concern is no longer with the inventive content of story; rather, our concern is with realistic ideas growing out of everyday occurrences in the real world. The writer of a letter, drawing on his skills to observe and to report on his observations, may tell about an event that has occurred; retell or summarize something heard or read; question, request, or order; state facts, opinions, feelings, or judgments. An accurate mirroring of real events is particularly essential in all these instances.

Fundamentally, a letter is written conversation that can be conducted either formally or informally. As with oral conversation, tone may be as important as factual content in getting the message across. Since the writer typically communicates in a letter not only the facts, but also his feelings toward the facts, his tone—bantering, light, humorous, matter-of-fact, sincere, serious, demanding, intimate, remote—may communicate his feelings more clearly than his words.

A letter is also written communication directed toward a specific, limited audience—an individual or group of individuals about whom the writer may know something or for whom the writer may hold some kind of feeling. He may like, love, despise, respect, or be indifferent toward the one to whom he writes. His feelings may determine his tone.

Finally, a letter is a traditional form of communication about which numerous social and business conventions exist. Just as there is an accepted method of wielding knife and fork at dinner, so there is an accepted method of placing words on paper. A business letter typically follows this form:

25 Walnut Street
Lancaster, California 93534
May 29, 197–

The American Toy Company
16 Friend Street
Toyville, Colorado 80302

Gentlemen:

Would you send me one mini-racer, catalogue number 5984. I am enclosing a money order for $5.30. If there are other shipping charges, would you tell me, and I will send the additional amount immediately.

Very truly,

Joseph Anderson

Joseph Anderson

A social letter tends to follow this form:

25 Walnut Street
Lancaster, California
May 29, 197–

Dear Bob,

Will you come to my birthday party? It is at 3:00 p.m. on Saturday, June 15, at my house.
I hope you can come.

Your friend,

Marty

Should the traditional conventions associated with social and business correspondence be taught? We think so. In today's world a correspondent is still judged by the way in which a letter written by him is laid out; it may determine whether he gets a job for which he is applying, whether a cause he espouses is given consideration, or whether a request he is making is handled with dispatch. Whether an individual decides to adhere to the accepted fashion is, of course, his own decision. But the teacher who decides that such conventions need not be taught is taking away the individual's right to decide for himself.

TAKING A FUNCTIONAL APPROACH TO
LETTER WRITING

If a letter does not typically project the inventive content of story, and if a letter is essentially written conversation between people, then it follows that letter writing in classrooms should occur in functional situations. When children are conversing in written form, they should be addressing themselves to real people about genuine concerns. To ask a youngster to write a letter applying for a job that may not exist and that he may not want is more an exercise in invention than one in realistic letter writing.

In this respect, letter writing should be an integral aspect of classroom activity rather than a unit-type experience in which youngsters are exposed to letter writing for a three-week period every year. In short, letters in classrooms should be written as they are called for by the ongoing life of the class, the everyday occurrences in which letter writing would naturally be required.

Three facets of the ongoing life in classrooms supply opportunities for letter writing:

- content units in science, social science, language, art, mathematics;
- events in the world outside the classroom that have direct significance for youngsters;
- the general social life in the classroom.

For instance, business letters of request can be written as part of content units and sent to—

- authors, community leaders, or the principal, requesting that the individual come to speak to the class on a topic under study
- companies and agencies, such as the American Petroleum Institute for materials and information related to a unit of study. Sources can be identified in such volumes as *Free and Inexpensive Learning Materials* (Division of Surveys and Field Services, George Peabody College for Teachers, Nashville, Tennessee) and *Sources of Free and Inexpensive Educational Materials* (Field Enterprises, Inc., Education Division, Chicago, Illinois)
- embassies, international organizations, international airlines, or travel agencies, such as Japan Travel Bureau, for material or information about a particular country or region of the world
- authorities in a subject area, requesting information on a topic. If a single authority in an area is contacted, it is perhaps wiser to send only one letter rather than deluging the authority with numbers of letters from different children. Also, write for specific information, not for general information readily accessible in reference books. One biologist with a leading pharma-

ceutical firm recalls one request made of him: "Kindly tell me everything you know about the frog"

- citizens, requesting that they go out and vote, recycle bottles and cans, or not add pollution to the environment by burning leaves. This type of letter can be mimeographed and distributed to members of the community
- airports, industries, and private gardens, requesting permission to visit the sites.

Letters of opinion or protest focusing on events of significance to the children can be written to—

- the school principal, stating a class opinion on a particular school issue
- the local or school newspaper, stating an opinion on a particular social issue, such as pollution of the environment, building a new school, sex education in the curriculum, crime in the streets, or drug abuse
- the Governor, Representatives, Senators, or the President, stating an opinion on a piece of pending legislation or a governmental policy
- local industry, stating an opinion on a specific industrial policy that affects the community
- national and state agencies, such as the U.S. Public Health Service, state fish and game commissions, and local consumer agencies, stating an opinion on a problem handled by the agency.

The general social life of the class can call for the writing of letters of invitation to—

- parents, to attend back-to-school night
- parents, principal, and other classes, to attend a performance, fair, or display being presented by the class;

letters of thank you to—

- another class, for an assembly program or an invitation to attend a performance
- the principal, a parent, or a community leader, for coming to speak to the class
- a person or firm that allowed the class to visit his business, or that supplied the class with materials or books;

friendly letters to—

- a classmate at home sick
- a classmate who has recently moved away
- a classmate away on an extended trip
- a pen pal in another state or country. (Addresses can be obtained from American Junior Red Cross, 17th and D Street, N.W., Washington, D. C.; School Affiliation Service, American Friends Service Committee, 160 North 15th Street, Philadelphia, Pa.; Pen Friends Division, The English-Speaking Union, 16 East 69th Street, New York, N.Y.)

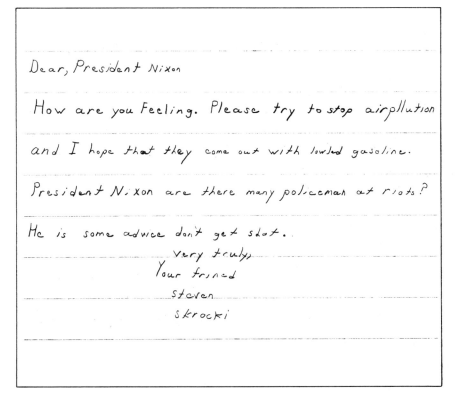

Dear, President Nixon

How are you Feeling. Please try to stop airpllution

and I hope that they come out with lowled gasoline.

President Nixon are there many policeman at riots?

He is some advice don't get shot.
                          Very truly,
                          Your friend
                          Steven
                          Skrocki

Figure 9-3. *A second-grader's first attempt at letter-writing.*

- service men stationed abroad (Community leaders may be able to supply names of local service men to whom letters can be sent.).

TEACHING LETTER-WRITING FORM INDUCTIVELY

Since children need to know how to handle the forms in which social and business letters traditionally have been written, there is some call within the ongoing life of classrooms for teaching the conventions of letter writing. This can be done in lessons that are organized so that children not only are involved with the forms of letter writing, but also are gaining skill in fundamental thinking processes. Lessons constructed within an inductive framework allow this dual orientation.

To teach letter-writing forms inductively, a teacher must have model letters available for children to analyze. For instance, in a lesson on social forms, the teacher asks, "What kind of information is given in all of the letters? Let's make a list." Then, "Where on the paper is each type of information placed?" And eventually, "Let's make a schematic indicating the overall appearance of a letter." The resulting schematic is discovered by the students through their step-by-step analysis of the information contained in the model letters and the placement of that information within the letters. It might look like this:

> street address of writer
> town, state and zip code of writer
> month, day, year of writing

Dear_____,

_____

_____ . _____ . _____

_____ .

_____ . _____

_____ .

> Your friend,
> *signature*

During the revision phase of the writing of actual letters, children can refer to their schematic to check the layout of their letters or to double-check one another's papers against the prescribed form. Through this technique children not only are learning letter-writing conventions; they are learning how to design a schematic and how to use one to construct their own samples. That is an advantage of inductive teaching over a system in which the teacher presents the elements and the schematic to be memorized.

Other similarly organized lessons can be constructed around the forms of business letters, envelopes for business letters, envelopes for social letters, and later variant forms for business and social letters, such as slant versus block forms, forms for use on paper bearing a letterhead, and highly stylized forms for use on extremely formal occasions. In every instance, the teacher can begin with numerous models which the youngsters analyze to determine the essential elements and build schemata, as in Figure 9–4.

Two cautions should be pointed out in reference to an inductive system of instruction. First, make the models upon which discovery is dependent clearly visible to all. One third-grade teacher worked inductively with model envelopes constructed out of large sheets of paper and measuring at least four feet across. She had her models mounted on the magnetized chalkboard with disc magnets. In the upper grades, models can be handwritten or typed on ditto sheets and reproduced so that every youngster gets a copy to study at his desk. Second, remember that the amount of detail included in the models is dependent on the children's cognitive development and increases through the grades. In the first grade, the teacher may write social

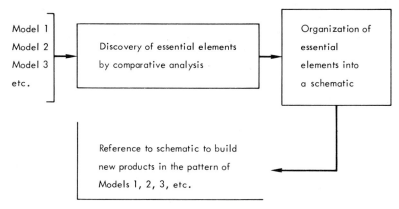

Figure 9-4. *Model of inductive learning scheme.*

letters with her children that adhere in a rather general fashion to this format:

> Dear Mother,
>   We are having a party in school on Tuesday, January 10. It will be in our room at two o'clock. We want you to come.
>   Love, *Chris*

Additional detail appears in successive grades, and youngsters begin to handle the more complicated forms.

reaction

In an age of rising dissent, one of the most legitimate writing activities in which youngsters can be involved is the production of what, for lack of a better term, can be called reaction. A reaction is a point of view that is founded to some extent on an analytical base. Essentially it is an expression of preference, opinion, or judgment: the writer proposes, "I prefer this book to that one because ——;" he states, "The president should —— because——;" he writes, "Applying these criteria, I judge this policy as inadequate for the following reasons: ——." Each of these reactions is similar in that reasons are given to substantiate the point of view. They differ in the amount and level of substantiation that will follow. A judgment presents a highly sophisticated argument in support of a point of view, with reference made to predetermined criteria. A preference simply presents a liking or disliking with only a limited set of supporting reasons. An opinion is a belief about the rightness, goodness, or propriety of a course of action and lies somewhere between a judgment and a preference in the amount of substantiation supplied.

There are subjective elements inherent in every kind of reaction. What one person judges to be superb another may judge to be inferior, and each person may support his judgment with an extended rationale. In *Since Silent Spring,* for example, Frank Graham, Jr. quotes from numerous reviews published in reaction to Rachel Carson's *Silent Spring.* Some reviews were highly favorable, expressing the view that Miss Carson's book was a notable contribution both to science and society. Diametrically opposed were reviews that considered Miss Carson's work unscientific and myopic. Obviously each reviewer was judging the Carson book in terms of his own knowledge of and attitudes toward pesticides and the environment.

Not only are there subjective elements inherent in any kind of reaction, but there also are analytical, factual, and conceptual elements. A comprehensive reaction separates a whole into its component parts, focusing on the individual parts, the relationships among the parts, and the relationships between the parts and other data the reactor introduces into the situation. As he breaks the whole into its parts to show relationships among the parts, the reactor is basically analyzing. As he brings to the fore additional data that may have a bearing on the case at hand, he is identifying and working with facts and concepts.

BUILDING REACTIONS INTO THE SCHOOL PROGRAM

As early as first grade, children can be introduced to the essential elements of reaction by being encouraged to talk about their own reactions towards real events, things, and ideas. The teacher asks questions urging children to express preferences and opinions: "What part of the movie did you like best? Did you like least? Why? Would you like to see that movie again? Why? Why not?" Eventually the teacher can elicit a general reaction by asking, "Did you like it more than you disliked it? Why?" She can record their reaction for them:

> We didn't like the movie. It was scary. When the snake grabbed the frog, we got scared. Sandy said the music scared her.

The format for such a lesson is simple:

- *Involvement* with an event, thing, or idea, such as watching a movie.
- *Talk* about the event, thing, or idea.
- *Formulation* of an opinion about the event, thing, or idea.
- *Recording* of opinion.

As children advance through the grades and begin to express opinions on complex issues, search for supporting documentation becomes part of the reacting scheme. The talk stage may uncover the fact that children do not have the background on which to formulate a logical opinion. "Do we have enough information or evidence on which to base an opinion?" the teacher must query at this point. Individually or in small groups, children are encouraged to search books, magazines, newspapers, and pictures for related information, to contact authorities in the field, and to study other people's opinions on the topic. Reacting for them has become Involvement–Talk–Search–Formulation–Recording.

One way to encounter opinion and judgment in the upper elementary school is to work with a controversial question for which there is more than one answer. Junior high students who have just been introduced to the metric system may struggle with the question "Should the United States convert to the metric system?" Sixth-grade youngsters studying freedom of the press may formulate opinions as to whether the press should publish reports harmful to the country's standing abroad. Youngsters studying poverty problems may decide whether everyone should be assured a basic annual wage.

In work with controversial issues, structure talk and search activities so they occur in small groups. Each group writes an opinion or judgment following the scheme suggested below. This scheme parallels the format of a formal resolution, "Whereas——, whereas——, then——," and prepares youngsters for more sophisticated writing activity.

> Reasons supporting majority opinion or judgment
>   1.
>   2.
> Majority opinion or judgment
> Reasons supporting minority opinion or judgment
>   1.
>   2.
> Minority opinion or judgment

Each group then presents its majority-minority opinion paper for total class consideration. If interest is high, different viewpoints can be informally debated. In this way youngsters begin to see the subjective nature of opinions and judgments as well as the importance of adequate supporting evidence.

SUPPLYING A VARIETY OF STIMULI FOR REACTION

The events, things, or ideas to which children can react are boundless.

> *Fashion trends:*
> Do you like the new longer/shorter skirts? Why? Why not? Do you like short/long haircuts for boys? Do you like straight/curly hair for girls? Why? Why not?

Magazine articles:
Do you react positively or negatively to an article in *Junior Scholastic, Newsweek, Time?* Why? Why not? (A reaction of this type may be written and sent in the form of a letter to the editor of the magazine.)

TV programs and editorials:
How do you react to a certain TV show? To the news reporting on Channel 2? To the editorials given on television? Why? (A letter to the station can be a positive means of taking action)

Books:
Would you recommend this book to a friend to read? Why? Why not? Did you like the main character in the story? Would you want that character for a friend? Why?

Motion pictures:
Would you recommend this movie to a friend? What part of the movie did you like best? What part did you like least? Would you want to see this movie over again? Why? Why not?

Commercials:
Is the commercial for product X based on fact, on suggestion, on biased use of scientific evidence? Would you buy the product as a result of hearing that commercial? Is the commercial a good one? a poor one? Why?

News reports and editorials in newspapers:
Was the reporting of this event honest and accurate? Is the point of view in this editorial well substantiated? In what way? (This type of reaction stating a counter-opinion can form the content of a letter to the editor of the paper.)

Commercial products:
Do you like this kind of cereal? Why? Is brand X better than brand Y? In what way? Does packaging of a product give a false idea about the content? In what way?

Situations:
Is the war in X justifiable? Should the U.S. continue to send aid to country W? Should cigarette smoking be banned in public buildings? Should Community Y or Company Z be allowed to dump its wastes in the Mississippi? Why? Why not?

To introduce older youngsters to the distinctive style of such reactions as movie reviews and editorials, start with actual samples. Where movie reviews are done on television, assign children to listen for the play on words and light humor so characteristic of the literary form. Have children make a collection of editorials for reading during independent study periods so that they will come to know the issues currently being argued. Clip the letters-to-the-editor sections from newspapers and news magazines, posting them on the Look Here! bulletin board. During independent study periods, make browsing through the clippings a possible option. Also make available copies of *The Horn Book, Elementary English,* and the Sunday book supplement of a newspaper such as *The New York Times.* Youngsters in upper grades can read reviews of children's books found in these sources.

report

In a report the writer provides coverage of an event, topic, or article not by inventing character, action, and dialogue, nor by recounting his own opinion of it, but by constructing a factually accurate rendition mirroring an actual event, topic, or article as closely as possible. Of course, the writer's report is not the scene-by-scene rendering that would be recorded on tape and film; neither is it a word-by-word reproduction of all the sources used as reference. The reporter's job is essentially to select the facts and the data that communicate a clear, honest picture. In this respect, reporting has subjective elements: the way in which the writer originally defines the dimensions of the subject, his own conception of what is relevant, and even his own point of view, affect his selection of data.

The writer must also organize his data into a framework. Sometimes the framework is simply a chronological ordering that parallels the event itself; at other times, however, when the writer is dealing with events and topics of greater complexity, the projection of a framework through which to communicate a clear picture is as creative an endeavor as is the invention of plot or character. A biographer may employ flashbacks to engender interest. A scientist may devise schemata, graphs, and tables to present his data succinctly. A Rachel Carson may clothe her facts in an introductory fable. A historian may build suspense into an account of Spain during the Inquisition by holding back facts until a climactic point. A Nobel prize winner may interject stories of infighting among scientists into an otherwise technical account of discovery to appeal to a broader audience. These writers know that facts alone tend to be boring, that the appeal of nonfiction is as dependent on style and organization as is the appeal of fiction.

Numerous skills are involved in writing accurate accounts of real events, articles, and topics. Obviously, all reports are not cut from the same fabric. Some reports tell about events or things directly observed by the reporter, and observational skills are primary. Other reports tell about events or topics in which the writer was not directly involved, so he must rely on his skills to search the topic through reading, listening, and interviewing. Still other reports attempt an analysis of the data uncovered through observation and search; in these cases the writer must be able to identify relationships, to perceive reasons, and to hypothesize skillfully. Because written reports can be so varied, let us focus on specific kinds of reports and consider ways in which teachers can help children build the skills necessary to handle these reporting tasks.

REPORTING ON OBSERVED EVENTS

Supply opportunities for observation by structuring activities that specifically lend themselves to observation and reporting. As suggested in

Chapter 1, arrange observational sites in the classroom—incubating eggs, germinating seeds, growing crystals, feeding fish. Take children on walks during which the primary objective is to "people-watch"—children with notebooks in hand locate people or things to describe as accurately as possible. Encourage children to participate in community activities about which they can report back to the class. Have children read such books as Florence Heide's *Sound of Sunshine, Sound of Rain* (New York: Parents' Magazine Press, 1970) and Ann Grifalconi's *City Rhythms* (Indianapolis, Ind.: Bobbs-Merrill, 1965) that make them aware of the significance of things around them. Many of the observational activities discussed in chapter two are workable in this context.

To aid children in systematic reporting, help them develop a checklist of questions to be considered when reporting on an event. A checklist might include the following items:

> What happened?
> When did it happen?
> Where did it happen?
> Who was involved?
> How did it start?
> How did it end?
> How long did it last?
> Why did it happen?
> What were people's reactions to the happening?

Each child uses the checklist as a guide. He records answers to the items on the checklist that are relevant to the specific happening he is investigating. These answers are the notes on which he bases his written report.

One way of encouraging children to write written reports is to assign the position of class reporter to several children each week. Class reporters take notes and report on classroom happenings: movies seen by the class; an assembly program; accidents occurring in the class; projects; visits by principals, community leaders, or parents to the class; class trips; or a sports event or contest in which the class participated. At the end of the week the reporters write headlines for their class news stories and compile them into the weekly class newspaper, which is posted on the bulletin board. Don't be surprised by the physical size of the product that results from the endeavor; when the children's stories are printed by hand and mounted on paper, the physical size of the project may well be comparable to the overall dimensions of a real newspaper.

Another way to encourage children to write about things they have observed is to develop the recording habit by having them keep a daily journal. Allow time each day, perhaps as part of an individual seatwork period, for children to write in their journals about things that have hap-

pened to them during the previous day. They can describe something that
they saw on the way to school, that happened at home the night before,
that happened in the playground or in the classroom. The teacher, of
course, cannot and need not read all that children write in their journals.
Children select one or two reports to share with the teacher during an
individual conference scheduled every week. Children's writing problems
that are noted during the conference are placed on the individual child's
editing guide, and inductive lessons in how to handle certain English structures are developed by the teacher in response to similar weaknesses in the
writings of several children.

Figure 9-5. *An illustrated page from a second grader's daily journal.*

Scientific investigations carried on in a classroom lend themselves
particularly well to reporting based on observation. Demonstrate a scientific
phenomenon—for example, expansion of colored water in a narrow tube
when heated, combustion of a magnesium strip, the action of a siphon or
a pendulum. Have children watch and record what was done, the results,
and their reactions to what happened, perhaps in mathematical terms which
require counting, timing, and measuring. Below is a workable form for
observational recording (see Figure 9–6). This format parallels the more
complex system of laboratory reporting—procedure, result, discussion—that

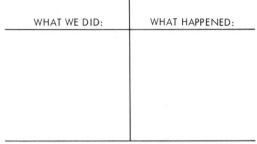

| WHAT WE DID: | WHAT HAPPENED: |

Figure 9-6.   WHAT WE THINK ABOUT WHAT HAPPENED:

students will probably employ as they move through the grades. In this sense it prepares them for more advanced writing activity.

Scientific observations, of course, need not be restricted to teacher demonstrations. Children can become involved in actual investigations in which they compare and contrast leaves from a single tree to find out about variety in nature, study the runoff of water from different land areas, or grow seedlings under varying conditions. Again, children record what they did and what happened, moving on to propose explanatory hypotheses and relationships. If children carry out investigations of this type in groups and each group collects data, the cooperative writing of a class report can be a profitable activity. Groups pool data, producing more valid conclusions.

REPORTING ON A TOPIC

A type of writing assignment found at all educational levels from fourth grade to university is what has, for lack of a better name, been called a research paper—a paper in which the writer, having thoroughly investigated a topic through reading, listening, and interviewing, presents major facts and concepts about the topic and attempts an analysis of it. Although children in the upper elementary school can begin to develop the search and organizational skills necessary for successful completion of this extensive writing task, it is apparent to anyone who has worked with youngsters at this stage of development that many youngsters are really not ready to handle lengthy and numerous sources, and cannot produce a highly sophisticated analysis of data. To ask youngsters to try is to force them to copy.

What can we ask of children at this stage? Beginning in fourth grade, a child can search several sources and compile a very brief report on a topic based on those limited sources. Working within the boundaries of such a realistic assignment, he can gain some of the skills he will need when he eventually attacks a sophisticated research paper at a higher level.

One fundamental skill is the identification or pinpointing of a topic. A child announces that he is going to write a report about horses. The teacher who wants to help the child build skill in identifying a manageable topic will ask, "What do you want to know and report about horses? Are you interested in the evolution of the horse? Do you want to write about what horses do for man? Do you want to investigate the different kinds of horses and what each does?" The child can be encouraged to phrase his topic as a question, for this helps him to zero in on the actual problem. For instance, a child who begins to think about reporting on cacti and who hears "What specifically about cacti are you interested in?" from the teacher may come up with the manageable topic-question "How do cacti survive on the desert?"

As youngsters in upper elementary grades attempt slightly more extended reporting tasks, a teacher by continuing to ask "What specifically about x are you interested in?" can help children identify several organizing questions. For instance, a boy who says he wants to write about astronauts may narrow his topic to three questions: What kinds of problems does an astronaut meet in space? What training is necessary to prepare astronauts to meet these problems? What kind of man makes the best astronaut? Then he can collect data helpful in answering his questions. If, on the other hand, the boy begins to write without first zeroing in on his topic, he has no criterion by which to judge the significance of facts and concepts encountered in the search process. He has no logical way of determining what to include. As a result, his report may become a potpourri of assorted facts and concepts culled from a variety of sources.

At this level a teacher can also introduce youngsters to interesting ways of presenting factual, conceptual content. Children reporting on a historical event can write their reports in the form of—

- a TV program: "You Are There!,"
- a radio or TV newscast as it might have been recorded at that time in history with modern technology,
- a newspaper story of that day, or
- a series of flashbacks recalled by a participant in the event.

Children writing about a country as part of geographical study can organize their reports into—

- a travel folder that gives details about the country,
- an itinerary for a tour,
- an article for the travel section of a newspaper or for a travel magazine, or
- a description of travel through part of the country in the style of *National Geographic*.

Children reporting on the life of a well-known individual can write—

- a TV script for "This Is Your Life,"
- an obituary,

- a biography that moves chronologically backward,
- a biography told by a well-known contemporary—for example, Martha Washington talks about George, or
- an interview with the person.

Here is an example of what can result when a seventh grader looks at biography from such a perspective:

This is the month of August in the year 1826. My name is James Monroe. My friend, John Quincy Adams, and I were having a discussion on politics the other day; the main topic of our conversation being the late Thomas Jefferson, former President of our United States. I quote.

"But why do you think Jefferson was such a great man?" Asked John. I answered indignantly, "Why, didn't he write the Declaration of Independence? He made a fine governor of Virgina. In 1791 he proposed the decimal system of currency which we now use. He advocated religious tolerance, and while he was in France as our Minister, didn't he grieve to learn of the ratification of the Constitution with no mention of religious freedom or personal rights in it? When Washington retired he ran for President against your father and lost, but became Vice President. He was a candidate again in 1800. He ran against Pinckney. He won that time and was reelected in 1804 and didn't he do many fine things for our country?"

"Yes, he did do many things but what was the advantage of each?"

"Well," I answered, "the Declaration of Independence expressed the feelings of all those American colonies against England, and everyone who read it saw the necessity for breaking the political tie with Great Britain."

Mr. Adams was persistent. "What, did he do about no mention of religion and personal rights in the Constitution?"

"Why, he advocated adding the Bill of Rights or the first ten amendments which guarantee us not only freedom of religion but also freedom of speech and of the press."

"What fine things did he do when he was President?"

"In 1802 the port of New Orleans was closed to American shipping by the Spanish governor. Thus, three-eights of our territory had no outlet. The farmers were very much upset so they appealed to Jefferson for help. There was a rumor that New Orleans and all the Louisiana Territory had secretly been given to Napoleon by Spain. Jefferson sent Livingston and myself to buy New Orleans and West Florida from this empire-hungry dictator. We were startled when he offered us all the Louisiana territory. The price agreed upon was 60,000,000 francs but was lowered to $15,000,000, in American money. Napoleon didn't like this price but accepted our offer because he needed money badly. Thus, our territory was greatly increased and so our trade was helped.

"After this Jefferson sent Lewis and Clark to explore the Louisiana Purchase. They left St. Louis on May 14, 1804, with forty-five picked and trained men, with Meriwether Lewis and Captain William Clark in command. They reached the mouth of the Columbia river in November, 1805. The journey was four thousand miles and only one man died. They returned to St. Louis in the month of September in the year 1806. This expedition later gave us claim to Oregon.

"There was great excitement in 1807 when the British man-of-war, *Leopard,* fired a broadside into the American frigate, *Chesapeake,* killing or wounding twenty-one men. The *Leopard* did this because the Captain of the *Chesapeake*, Baron, denied that he had British deserters aboard. The *Chesapeake*, her guns still unmounted, was forced to surrender. The British then seized four deserters, three of whom were Americans. Jefferson was compelled to act. He ordered all British vessels out of American waters, demanded a British apology and called Congress to an early session.

"Jefferson started the Democrat-Republican political party. Later on in life, after he retired from the Presidency he founded the University of Virginia. Now do you agree with me?" I asked.

"Yes, I do," John answered slowly. "Jefferson was truly a fine American and he helped the United States more than I ever realized before. This country suffered the loss of a great statesman when he passed away last month on the fiftieth anniversary of the signing of the Declaration of Independence."

JUDITH EGAN BRUCKNER

Still another report-related skill children in grades four, five, and six can encounter is how to indicate sources of facts and ideas. Although complete footnoting and bibliography will come in junior high school, children in the fourth grade can begin by noting the names of the authors and the books from which they drew materials, by underlining the names of the books, and by grouping all sources (perhaps two or three) alphabetically at the end of the report. At the next level, dates can be added to citations. By the sixth grade, children can be shown how to footnote a direct quotation from a source. Footnotes do not have to be detailed: author, book title, and page suffice for beginning reporters. To help children recall the form of footnotes and bibliography, draw up a style sheet of examples for them to keep as a ready reference in their writing folders.

A corollary activity relates to library use. Children can be introduced to the card catalog, the Dewey Decimal or Library of Congress system, and indexes. Lessons of this type can be fun when a teacher employs large-sized mock-ups of index listings; of book bindings showing classification number, author, and title; and of author, subject, and title cards. For example, children holding mock-ups of book bindings line up in the order in which the books would be found on the shelf. Armed with information from an enlarged subject card, a child attempts to locate the desired book from the lineup of book bindings held by other youngsters.

Now is also the time and place to teach the search-related skills through which children look for ideas to be expressed in written form. Teach children to summarize, to identify quotable quotes, and to search a variety of sources. (See Chapter 3 for specific suggestions.)

REACTION REPORTS

Some pieces of prose include both a factual, analytical handling of data and the writer's opinion or judgment related to the topic. The book or movie analysis in which the writer describes key aspects of a book, analyzes rather objectively, and then expresses his own liking or disliking is a case in point.

A reaction report to a TV program is a positive way of introducing children to this form of written expression, for it teaches them to react to what they see on television, not to be passive receivers. It also makes the time spent viewing TV more productive. Supply youngsters with a viewing guide for reaction reports such as —

Name of program:
Type of program:
Channel: Time:
Main Characters:

Name	Role Played

Example of typical incident:

Opinion (Recommendations):

For programs in a series or programs that may be repeated, reaction reports can be posted on the bulletin board for reference by other youngsters who may want to see if a program is recommended for viewing. If several children write reaction reports on the same series, a composite report can be compiled by a team. The composite can be sent to other classes as part of a TV recommendation guide. A similar activity can be carried on with cinema, stage, and book offerings. Emphasis is on sharing information and recommendations with others.

content and craft—an overview

To teach writing is to teach children to work with ideas—to produce the idea-content that is the essence of any form of communication. To teach writing is also to teach children ways of organizing their ideas, of building word and sentence patterns, and of revising what they have written. But, as indicated in the discussions of poetry, story, letter, reaction, and report, in actual classroom situations activities related to the idea-content of writing merge with activities related to the craft of writing. Both elements are closely interwoven in an overall writing program in which children, playing intellectually with lines, sentences, stanzas, and paragraphs, build words into the stuff of poetry and of prose.

epilogue

We are such stuff
As dreams are made on, and our little life
Is rounded with a sleep.

Shakespeare, The Tempest

The teaching of written expression in the elementary school has often been conducted within a framework of isolated lessons: the teacher has motivated a specific writing lesson and the children have written during the remaining half-hour; the teacher has corrected the written work followed by the children copying papers with the corrections indicated by the teacher. Instead, conceive of teaching written expression as a continuous program in the manner suggested in this book. The advantages are obvious.

First, children in a continuous writing program are involved in writing experiences as part of the everyday ongoing activities of the classroom. They write as they encounter science and social-science content; they write in reaction to life in the world of reality and the world of fancy; they write when the social needs of the class mandate; they write to share their ideas with others. During independent study times they dictate into tape recorders, they work on papers from their file folders editing materials written on a previous day, they jot ideas into idea books, they record in their journals, they finish poems begun on the way to school, and they work in groups to compile a gag book, a class newsletter, or a book of fables. Organizing continuous writing is not as difficult as it first appears. Such purposeful writing activities can simply be added to the options listed for what has in the past been called seatwork, taking the place of mechanical fill-in-the-blank exercises. Children working independently select from suggested options the ones most meaningful to them while the teacher works with other youngsters individually and in small groups.

Second, a continuous writing program takes direction from the overall activities within a class. Youngsters write not only stories, letters, and poems; but many kinds of reports and reactions grow out of encounters with social-science and science content and with experiences in the real world. In this way, a balanced writing program is maintained.

Third, a continuous program approach is an integrated language arts approach. The teacher supplies speaking experiences not just to help children gain skill in speaking, but to encourage expression of ideas as part of the writing program; conversely, writing experiences may be a prelude to speaking activity. Likewise, the teacher supplies a rich experience with literature not just to develop enjoyment of books, but to encourage inventive ideas and intuitive understanding about the way words go together on the printed page. She supplies first-hand experiences that serve as a base for all language activities—reading, listening, speaking, and writing. Isolated lessons have little to offer in such an approach.

Fourth, a program approach in which youngsters are writing continuously, developing corollary writing skills when needed, and revising their own work in terms of the weaknesses noted on an editing guide does not emphasize external teacher evaluation. The notion of evaluation has intentionally been omitted from this book, for too often evaluation has been interpreted in practice as a process of marking a piece of work as A, B, C, D, or F, and as a process of correcting errors carried on solely by the teacher. Both these interpretations limit the scope of a child's writing experience because although he produces ideas and records them, he is not involved in review and revision, which are essential aspects of the writing process. In a continuous program approach, on the other hand, self-analysis and revision, combined with related skill development via inductive instruction, take the place of external evaluation by the teacher. Teacher conferences and individualization of writing experiences are the keystones of such an approach.

Fifth, a continuous writing program is one allowing encounters with the idea-content of writing to merge into encounters with the craft of writing. As part of their ongoing classroom activity, children are encouraged to think about innumerable things—to reflect, conceptualize, project, feel, and invent; and they play with words, sentences, lines, paragraphs as they attempt to communicate their ideas to others. When writing is carried on as a continuous classroom activity, work with ideas and work with verbal structures to express ideas become woven into a total writing program.

last thoughts

In conclusion, let us look again at the question that has been the focus of this book: What is it that we do when we teach children to write? Clearly, the answer is not simple; clearly, it is not singular. We are helping children—

> To see a world in a grain of sand
> And a Heaven in a wild flower
> [to] Hold Infinity in the palm of your hand
> And Eternity in an hour.[1]

We are showing—

> the children to green fields, and make their world
> Run azure on gold sands, and let their tongues
> Run naked into books, the white and green leaves open
> History theirs whose language is the sun.[2]

We are introducing children to the "exalted ideas of fancy" and "a suitable vesture of phrase,"[3] to "winged words"[4] and "words that weep and tears that speak,"[5] to "large, divine, and comfortable words,"[6] to "words of truth and soberness."[7] We are helping children to know that—

> There is no Frigate like a Book
> To take us lands away
>   Nor any Courses like a Page
> Of prancing Poetry[8]

We are showing that the writer is—

> Nature's real king, to whom the power was given
> To make an inkdrop scent the world for ever.[9]

Should not this be "such stuff as" both dreams and school "are made on"?

1 William Blake, "Auguries of Innocence."
2 Stephen Spender, "An Elementary Classroom in a Slum," in *Selected Poems* (New York: Random House, 1964). Copyright 1934, 1942, 1946, 1947, 1949, 1955, 1961, 1964 by Stephen Spender; copyright 1958 by Encounter Ltd.
3 Aristophanes, *The Frogs.*
4 Homer, *The Iliad.*
5 Abraham Crowley, *The Prophet.*
6 Alfred Lord Tennyson, *The Coming of Arthur,* line 267.
7 *The Bible,* Acts XXVI: 25.
8 Emily Dickinson, *The Poems of Emily Dickinson,* ed. Martha Dickinson Bianchi and Alfred Hampon (Boston: Little, Brown, 1930).
9 William Henry Davies, "Shakespeare," *Collected Poems of W.H. Davies,* 1943.

resource
bibliography

MUSICAL COMPOSITIONS ON RECORDS
TO MOTIVATE WRITING ACTIVITY.

Children can react to the recordings, put into words the sounds they hear, or use the record sounds as a setting for the development of plot.

van Beethoven, Ludwig. *Wellington's Victory*—actual cannon and musket sounds and the joyous sounds of victory; use the Mercury Records recording by the London Symphony that has an explanation of the firing of musket and cannon.

Copland, Aaron. "Prairie Night" and "Celebration" from *Billy the Kid*—the contrasting sounds of the quiet loneliness of the desert and the raucous joy of celebration.

Denny, Martin. Interpretation (on Liberty Records) of—
"Quiet Village"—sounds of jungle animals;
"Return to Paradise"—sounds of jungle drums, wind chimes, and cymbals;
"Hong Kong Blues"—sounds of the Orient;
"Lotus Land"—melodious sounds of the South Pacific;
"Similau"—sounds of war whoops and jungle.

Dukas, Paul. *The Sorcerer's Apprentice*—the magical sounds of bewitched brooms.

Griffes, Charles Tomlinson. *The White Peacock*—a musical interpretation of the movements of a graceful peacock.

Moussorgsky, Modeste. *Pictures at an Exhibition,* orchestrated by Maurice Ravel; specifically *Ballet of Unhatched Chicks*—sounds of chicks hatching, and *Gnomus*—sounds of the gnome cracking nuts between his teeth.

————. *A Night on Bald Mountain*—sounds of witches and goblins (good stimulus for Halloween writing).

Rimsky-Korsakov, Nicholas. *Flight of the Bumble Bee*—sounds of furious buzzing.

Schubert, Franz. *The Bee*—less frantic sounds of buzzing (why not have children decide which rendition, Schubert or Rimsky-Korsakov, is the more realistic interpretation).

Tchaikovsky, Peter. *The Nutcracker Suite*—the sounds of dream replete with soldiers, princes, and fairies.

REPRODUCTIONS OF GREAT ART TO MOTIVATE WRITING ACTIVITY.

Children can express opinions and preferences about the pictures, can simply describe the pictures, or use them to suggest plots for short stories.

Great Pictures Children Will Enjoy: The Instructor Picture Series. Dansville, N.Y.: F. A. Owen.
   Portfolios of the greats in the art world.

Instructor Modern Art Series. Dansville, N.Y.: F. A. Owen.
   Large-sized reproductions of such modern artists as Joan Miro, Marc Chagall, Pablo Picasso, and Henri Matisse.

FILMS TO MOTIVATE WRITING ACTIVITY.

"Autumn" (10 min., color). Thorne Films.
   Sights and sounds of fall: maples, twigs, greens, and golds; a stimulus for poetry writing experiences and the writing of realistic description; for grades K–8.

"Blinkity Blank" (6 min., color). International Film Bureau, Inc.
   Pictures created with knives, needles, and razor blades so that abstract images appear in the dark and gradually become real, such as love birds; for grades K–8. (Some other similar McLaren films that help to stimulate imagery are "Fiddle De Dee," "Begone Dull Care," and "A Chairy Tale.")

"The Day Is Two Feet Long" (8 min., color). Weston Woods.
   An audio-visual haiku experience; a stimulus for the writing of haiku; for intermediate grades.

"Dimensions" (12 min., color). The National Film Board of Canada (680 Fifth Ave., N.Y., N.Y. 10019).
   An animated film without words in which simple actions achieve surprising results; helps children look at objects from different viewpoints; for primary, intermediate, and junior high school grades.

"Family of N'gumba" (11 min., color). Sterling Educational Films
N'gumba's story told by puppets; any introduction to the writing of folk tales; for primary grades.

"Hailstones and Halibut Bones," Part 1 (6 min., color). Sterling Educational Films.
A Celeste Holm narration of the Mary O'Neil poems with accompanying animation; a stimulus for writing impressions of the colors; for primary grades.

"The Hunter and the Forest: A Story Without Words" (8 min., black and white). Encyclopedia Britannica.
The presence of a hunter in the forest; a medium that can motivate the translation of a visual story into words; for intermediate grades.

"Icarus and Daedalus" (6 min., color). Sterling Educational Films.
Animated version of the Icarus story; a good introduction to the writing of myths; for primary grades.

"Images from Nature" (7 min., color). Thorne Films.
Sounds and sights of the seasons (no narration); a poetry-writing stimulus; for intermediate grades.

"Junkyard" (10 min., color). Bailey Film Association.
The shapes, colors, and moods of a junkyard (no narration); may provide a setting in which children can create plot; for intermediate grades.

"Leaf" (7 min., color). Pyramid Film Distributors.
The flight of an autumn leaf in the air and waters of Yosemite; a stimulus for the writing of haiku; for grades K–8.

"The Little Mariner" (20 min., color). Encyclopedia Britannica.
A small boy and an enchanted sailboat in a California harbor (no narration); can stimulate plot invention; for primary grades.

"Once Upon a Time There Was a Dot" (8 min.). Zagreb: Contemporary Films.
Transformation of a dot into a myriad of different forms and shapes; can be an aid in helping children think about visual effects; for grades K–6.

"Rainshower" (15 min., color). Churchill Films.
Sights, sounds, beauty, and rhythm of rain; can stimulate production of descriptive adjectives and prepoetry experiences; for primary and intermediate grades.

"Textures of the Great Lakes" (6 min., color). Thorne Films.
An artistic picture of the textures of water, beach, wood, and dune; a stimulus for talking about elements of description; for grades 6–8.

"A Visit to a Valley" (9 min., color). Encyclopedia Britannica.
A look at a valley through the eyes of a squirrel; children can go on to view the world through the eyes of other animals; for primary grades.

POETRY COLLECTIONS TO MOTIVATE WRITING ACTIVITY.

Atwood, Ann. *Haiku: The Mood of Earth.* New York: Charles Scribner's, 1971.
Haiku illustrated with striking, full-color photographs.

Bianchi, Martha Dickinson, and Hampson, Alfred Leete, eds. *Poems by Emily Dickinson.* Boston: Little, Brown, 1957.
All of the Dickinson poems written between 1890 and 1935.

Ciardi, John. *I Met a Man.* Boston: Houghton Mifflin, 1961.
Poems with humorous twists and sounds pleasing to the ear; example: "I Met a Man with Three Eyes," "Guess," and "I Met a Man That Showed Me a trick."

———. *The Monster Den.* Philadelphia: Lippincott, 1963.
Poems in which Ciardi uses italics, capitals, and parentheses in unique ways.

Coatsworth, Elizabeth. *The Sparrow Bush.* New York: Norton, 1966.
Poems expressing feelings about the world of nature: "Storm at Night," "The Lilac Spires," "The Fish."

Cole, William, ed. *I Went to the Animal Farm.* Cleveland: World Publishing, 1958.
Animal poems for young children.

de Regniers, Beatrice Schenk. *Something Special.* New York: Harcourt Brace Jovanovich, 1958.
Poems that build "delicious" sounds and images.

Doob, Leonard, ed. *A Crocodile Has Me by the Leg.* New York: Walker, 1966.
African poems dealing with everyday life and feelings.

Fisher, Aileen. *I Wonder How, I Wonder Why.* New York: Abelard-Schuman, 1962.
Nature poems that tickle the ear.

Frost, Robert. *You Come Too.* New York: Holt, Rinehart & Winston, 1959.
Favorite poems for young readers.

Hopkins, Lee Bennett, ed. *I Think I Saw a Snail.* New York: Crown Publishers, 1969.
Poems for the seasons.

———. *Me! A Book of Poems.* New York: Seabury Press, 1970.
A collection of poems that relate to the child as a person.

———, and **Arenstein, Misha,** eds. *Faces and Places: Poems for You.* New York: Scholastic Book Services, 1971.
Poems that are great for modern, active young people.

Hughes, Langston. *Don't You Turn Back: Poems by Langston Hughes,* ed. Lee Bennett Hopkins. New York: Knopf, 1969.
A selection of Hughes's poems having special appeal for children.

Jacobs, Leland. *Just Around the Corner.* New York: Holt, Rinehart & Winston, 1964.
Poems that take one "just around the corner" to spring, summer, fall, and winter.

Merriam, Eve. *It Doesn't Always Have to Rhyme.* New York: Atheneum, 1965.
Poems that build on the non-rhyming sound effects of words.

Milne, A. A. *When We Were Very Young.* New York: Dutton, 1961.
Poems that have been children's favorites for years, such as "The King's Breakfast," "At the Zoo," "Happiness."

Nash, Ogden. *Girls Are Silly.* New York: Franklin Watts, 1961.
Poems about girls from the boy's point of view.

O'Neil, Mary. *Hailstones and Halibut Bones.* Garden City, N.Y.: Doubleday, 1961.
Poems that build delightful images on colors: "What Is Purple?" "What Is Black?" "What Is Gold?"

Sandburg, Carl. *Wind Song.* New York: Harcourt Brace Jovanovich, 1953.
Poems selected by Sandburg because of their special appeal to children.

Selections from Brian Wildsmith's Mother Goose. New York: Scholastic Book Services, 1964.
A collection of Mother Goose favorites illustrated in full color by Wildsmith.

Stevenson, Robert Louis. *Child's Garden of Verses.* New York: Franklin Watts, 1966.
Old favorites that blend flowing rhythm with lilting rhyme.

Weygant, Sister Naomi. *It's Spring.* Philadelphia, Pa.: Westminster Press, 1969.
An experience with nature through poetry and full-color photographs.

Williams, Oscar, ed. *Immortal Poems of the English Language.* New York: Pocket Books, 1952.
Poems that are truly immortal.

Zweigler, Jay, ed. *Man in the Poetic Mood.* Evanston, Ill.: McDougal, Littel, 1971.
An anthology that contains numerous poems that derive their appeal from visual effects.

Zolotow, Charlotte. *All That Sunlight.* New York: Harper & Row, 1967.
Poems that build playful images for children.

MULTIMEDIA, INDIVIDUALIZED LEARNING PROGRAMS

Use the following materials to develop thinking, organizational, and search skills:

Bracken, Dorothy; Hays, Jimmye; and **Bridges, Clara.** *Listening Skills Program, Grades 1–6.* Chicago: Science Research Associates.
A series of tapes, tape cassettes, or record discs focusing on such skills as following directions, developing sentence patterns, listening for cause and effect, distinguishing fact from opinion.

How To Use the Dictionary and How To Use the Library. Tulsa, Okla.: Educational Progress Laboratory.
A series of tapes or tape cassettes to build basic reference skills.

Raths, Louis; Wassermann, Jack; and **Wassermann, Selma.** *Thinking Skills Development Program.* Westchester, Ill.: Benefic Press.
Activities for children to encounter thinking processes: observing, looking for assumptions, collecting and organizing data, comparing, classifying, hypothesizing, coding, problem solving, and summarizing; for upper elementary grades.

Spelling Progress Laboratory Spelltapes. Tulsa, Okla.: Educational Progress Laboratory.
A series of tapes developed on eight skill levels in which words are studied in pattern groups so that students perceive structural relationships.

Springle, Herbert. *Inquisitive Games, Discovering How To Learn.* Chicago: Science Research Associates, 1969.
Activities through which young children begin to solve cognitive problems; make decisions; gather, organize, apply, and communicate information and ideas; for early childhood.

Teaching Resources Corporation. *Attribute Games.* (100 Boyleston Street, Boston, Mass. 02116).

A set of attribute blocks to develop skill in sequencing, sorting, and handling class relationships. The "Giant Set" (No. 36–110) contains 60 plastic blocks.

————. *Sorting and Sets.*

Six decks of cards that can be sorted in several different ways to develop skill in making comparisons and in perceiving relationships.

part II: general sources of motivational materials

(Most sources provide catalogs of complete listings upon request.)

Caedmon Records Inc.
505 Eighth Avenue
New York, New York 10018

Kinds of materials available:

1. Recordings of poetry
   - TC 1124   *Carl Sandburg's Poems for Children*
   - TC 1156   *Discovering Rhythm and Rhyme in Poetry*
   - TC 1227   *Miracles: Poems Written by Children*
   - TC 1078   *Nonsense Verse*
   - TC 1015   *Ogden Nash* (author's reading)
   - TC 1060   *Robert Frost* (author's reading)
2. Recordings of stories
   - TC 1256   *The Twelve Labors of Hercules*
   - TC 1100   Kipling's *Jungle Books: How Fear Came*
   - TC 1221   Aesop's *Fables*
   - TC 1113   *Madeline*
   - TC 1073   Anderson's *Fairy Tales*
   - TC 1038   *Just So Stories*

Miller-Brody Productions
342 Madison Avenue
New York, New York 10017

Kinds of materials available:

1. Newbery Award Records (cassettes): narration of Newbery stories by distinguished actors and actresses
   - 3010   *From the Mixed-Up Files of Mrs. Basil E. Frankweiler*
   - 3011   *Caddie Woodlawn*
   - 3018   *Sounder*
   - 3016   *The Door in the Wall*
2. Newbery Award Sound Filmstrips: filmstrip-record sets
   - NFS3001   *The Wheel on the School*
   - NFS3004   *The Cat Who Went to Heaven*
   - NFS3008   *Amos Fortune, Free Man*

3. Listening Library Talking Books: 12-inch records of stories
   MB1612 *Grimm's Fairy Tales*
   MB1622 *Arabian Nights*
4. *Pearl Primus' Africa:* three long-playing records in which Miss Primus presents folktales, legends, and proverbs of Africa within a framework of song and music
5. *Pick a Peck o' Poems:* six sound filmstrips and records presenting poems by such poets as Zolotow, Aldis, Hughes

   Weston Woods
   Weston, Connecticut 06880

Kinds of materials available:

1. Records: poets reading their own poetry
   WW703 David McCord reads his "Snowman," "Cocoon," "Frog in a Bag," and others.
   Harry Behn reads his "Toy Horse," "Spring Rain," "The Gnome," and others
   WW704 Karla Kuskin reads her "Snow," "Lewis Has a Trumpet," "The Balloon," and others
   Aileen Fisher reads her "Ladybug," "Bird Talk," "December," and others
2. Animated color films: films of children's books
   Drummer Hoff
   The Snowy Day
   The Happy Owls
3. Iconographic films: films of picture-story books in which action is simulated by movement of the camera across the pages of the book
   Time of Wonder
   The Cow Who Fell in the Canal
   The Red Carpet
   The Story About Ping
4. Live-action films
   "The Doughnuts" from *Homer Price* by Robert McCloskey
   The Sorcerer's Apprentice
   The Day Is Two Feet Long
5. Sound filmstrips: record (or cassettes) and filmstrips of well-known children's favorites, usually distributed in sets of four
   Set 27 *A Letter to Amy; Ola; Tikki, Tikki, Tembo; The Holy Night*
   Set 25 *Umbrella; Just Me; Peter's Chair; Drummer Hoff*
6. Spanish language materials: motion pictures, sound filmstrips, and records similar to the English language materials produced by Weston Woods

   McGraw-Hill
   330 West Forty-second Street
   New York, New York 10036

Kinds of materials available:

1. Bank Street Reading Incentive Series: color films in which well-known stage and screen personalities read selections from children's literature
   Gilberto and the Wind, narrated by Harry Belafonte

Aesop's Fables, narrated by Victor Borge
Rich Cat, Poor Cat, narrated by Bill Cosby

2. Animal and Plant Life Study Prints: large full-color study prints on natural themes; material to encourage both descriptive and inventive writing

Series A *Introducing Animals* (60 prints, primary grades)
Series B *Animal and Plant Communities* (60 prints, intermediate grades)
Series C *The Variety of Living Things* (60 prints, upper elementary grades)

Educational Progress Corporation
8538 East Forty-first Street
Tulsa, Oklahoma 74145

Kinds of materials available:

1. Paper Play Series: four Japanese folktale books composed of pop-up pages and movable parts that serve as scenes for the story, and tapes or cassettes of the stories for primary grades
2. Play for Reading: a box of materials to be used to encourage oral reading of plays; a means of helping children develop oral interpretation skills for middle grades
3. Sound filmstrips: stories from other lands

9–9261 *The Girl Who Loved Danger* (Congo)
9–9262 *Hamdaani* (Zanzibar)
9–9263 *The Greedy Man and The Stranger* (Senegal)
9–9264 *The Unbending King* and *The Man with Two Wives*

Teaching Resource Films (Educational Enrichment Materials)
83 East Avenue
Norwalk, Connecticut 06851

Kinds of materials available:

1. Sound filmstrips of favorite stories for children

Set 1 *Life Story* by Virginia Lee Burton
Set 2 *Favorite Folk Tales* illustrated by Ed Emberley
Set 3 *Mousekin* by Edna Miller

2. Records

Volume 6 *Children of Other Lands* by Lisl Weil
Volume 9 *Aesop's Fables*
Volume 10 *Laugh with Us*
Volume 11 *Folktales of Different Lands*

3. Sound filmstrips of folksongs by Tom Glazer

Singalong: "On Top of Spaghetti," "Blue-tailed Fly"
Participation: "This Old Man," "Frog Went-a-Courtin' "
Ballads: "I Know an Old Lady," "The Fox"

4. Tape cassettes

World Folksong Tour (Africa, Southeast Asia, the Orient, Europe, America) by Addis and Crofut (all grades)
Oscar Brand's American Folksong Archives (Colonial Days, Westward Movement, Bad Men Ballads) (all grades)

5. Sound filmstrips in the School Times Series

The Curious George Series: Curious George, Curious George Gets a Medal, Curious George Takes a Job

6. Filmstrips in the School Times Series: filmstrip versions of wordless books "with picture stories that very young children can 'write'"
    Frog, Where Are You? by Mercer Mayer
    Out, Out, Out! by Martha Alexander
7. Picture-book filmstrips with captions
    Blackboard Bear and *We Never Get To Do Anything* by Martha Alexander

Hudson Photographic Industries, Inc.
Educational Products Division
Irvington-on-Hudson, N.Y. 10533

Kinds of materials available:

1. "U" Film, "the write-on filmstrip": materials for creating filmstrips; children can draw a story on the 35mm filmstrips included in the kit
2. Filmstrips: silent filmstrips that can be used to stimulate children's talk activity, writing of descriptions, or writing of captions to accompany the strips
    1001 *Let's Talk About*—Things We Know, Bridge and Boats, Signs We See, and Fun in the City (primary)
    1002 *More To Talk About*—Shapes We See in the City, Colors We See in the City, Buildings We See in the City, Neighbors We See in the City (primary)
    1011 *Simple Concepts II*—What's Hard? What's Soft? What's Rough? What's Smooth? (primary)
3. Sound filmstrips: filmstrips with record or cassette; record can be purchased in which narration is in both Spanish and English
    3001 *City Rhythms* by Ann Grifalconi

Charles E. Merrill Publishing Co.
1300 Alum Creek Drive
Columbus, Ohio 43216

Kinds of materials available:

Spoken Arts Cassette Libraries: stories and poems done on tape
    0957 Mini-Library 4—*Tales from Across the Ocean:* 6 cassettes
    0955 Mini-Library 2—*Children's Stories and Rhymes:* 6 cassettes
    0958 Mini-Library 5—*The Listening Book:* 6 cassettes
    0900 Library for Young Listeners: 50 cassette tapes that contain fairy tales, excerpts from Shakespeare, fables and stories, poetry, Lewis Carroll favorites, Kipling favorites, and speeches

Franklin Watts, Inc.
845 Third Avenue
New York, New York 10022

Kinds of materials available:

Picture series: large black and white or color photographs to stimulate discussion and writing; examples—
    Man on the Move: 16 visual teaching pictures and teacher's manual by Dr. Deborah Elkins, Professor of Education, Queens College, N.Y.
    A Trip Through a School: 16 visual teaching pictures and teacher's manual by Lee Bennett Hopkins.

Brian Wildsmith's Animal Portfolio: 8 full-color prints of animals.
Grabianski's Portfolio: 12 prints from the illustrations of Janusz Grabianski's books.

Scholastic Magazines, Inc.
904 Sylvan Avenue
Englewood Cliffs, New Jersey 07632

Kinds of materials available:

Posters: large, colorful posters to stimulate talking and writing
   Visual Unit, *The Forms of Poetry:* large-sized posters that give examples
      of free verse, concrete poetry, and other forms
   Art Poster Portfolio: full-color reproductions of the work of artists such
      as Miro, Picasso, and Massey
   Figurative Language: ten humorous drawings illustrating figures of
      speech
Record Book Sets: recordings of children's stories such as *Curious George Rides
   a Bike, Caps for Sale,* and *The Emperor's New Clothes*
Children's Books: paperbacks of many of the classics in children's literature.
Special Items like *The Laugh Book* by Ruth Gross, 1970, a paperback that plays
   with words in picture, poem, and prose

Developmental Learning Materials
3505 North Ashland Avenue
Chicago, Illinois 60657

Kinds of materials available:

Picture series: large black and white or color photographs to stimulate writing on
   realistic topics
   The Many Faces of Youth: pictures on up-to-date topics that would
      appeal to young people in grades 5–8
   The Many Faces of Childhood: pictures of current interest that would
      appeal to youngsters in grades 2–4

Ginn and Company
6900 East 30th Street
Indianapolis, Indiana 46218

Kinds of materials available:

Story Starters: a set of cards, each of which gives a first paragraph from which
   children can write stories, and a set of pictures to stimulate descriptive and
   inventive writing. Teachers can keep the packet on an available shelf and
   children can select card or picture to write about during seatwork periods.

part III: books to develop children's interest in language

Alexander, Arthur. *The Magic of Words.* Englewood Cliffs, N.J.: Prentice-Hall,
   1962.
   All about picture-writing, origins of symbols and code messages, animal
   sounds, and signs.

Amon, Aline. *Talking Hands.* Garden City, N.Y.: Doubleday, 1968.
> An introduction to the language of gesture as nonverbal communication.

Applegate, Mauree. *The First Book of Language,* illus. Helen Borten. New York: Franklin Watts, 1962.
> A description of the parts of speech, sentences, punctuation, and paragraphing "rules" in story form.

Brown, Ivor. *Mind Your Language.* Chester Springs, Pa.: Dufour Editions, 1964.
> A consideration of usage, slang, dialect, words, and invention for children in the upper elementary and junior high grades.

Clifford, Eth. *A Bear Before Breakfast,* illus. Kelly Oechski. New York: Putnam, 1962.
> A concept picture-story book that develops an understanding of colloquialisms through two storybook characters, Jack and Jean, who take literally the figures of speech used by their elders.

Epstein, Sam and **Epstein, Beryl.** *The First Book of Words.* New York: Franklin Watts, 1954.
> A simple history of the English language for boys and girls in the intermediate grades.

Ernst, Margaret S. *More about Words.* New York: Knopf, 1951.
> A type of random dictionary for upper elementary grade students who relish words. Emphasis is on word origins and change.

Feelings, Muriel. *Moja Means One: Swahili Counting Book.* (New York: Dial, 1971).
> A counting book that introduces children to the way numbers are written in Swahili.

Ferguson, Charles W. *The Abecedarian Book.* Boston: Little, Brown, 1964.
> The background and meanings of such tongue-tickling, big words as *abecedarian, pusillanimous,* and *xenophobia.*

Funk, Charles Earle. *A Hog on Ice and Other Curious Expressions.* New York: Harper & Row, 1948.
> The origin and development of the pungent and colorful phrases we all use: "to put the cart before the horse," "to feather one's nest," "to pull the wool over one's eyes," "to keep one's fingers crossed," "to put a spoke in one's wheel."

Greet, W. Cabell; Jenkins, William A.; and **Schiller, Andrew.** *In Other Words: A Beginning Thesaurus.* Glenville, Ill.: Scott, Foresman, 1968.
> A thesaurus that introduces young children to related sets of words—things: *bunch, clump, cluster, bale bundle;* animals: *pack, swarm, school, litter, flock, herd.*

———. *In Other Words: A Junior Thesaurus.* Glenville, Ill.: Scott, Foresman, 1969.
> A thesaurus for intermediate-grade students.

Helfman, Elizabeth S. *Signs and Symbols Around the World.* New York: Lothrop, Lee & Shepard, 1967.
> The signs and symbols related to such fields as music, art, science, language, religion, and mathematics.

Laird, Helene, and **Laird, Charlton.** *The Tree of Language.* New York: World Publishing, 1957.
> The development and history of the English language with special

emphasis on word stories; appropriate for children in the upper elementary and junior high school grades.

Lambert, Eloise. *Our Language: The Story of the Words We Use.* New York: Lothrop, Lee & Shepard, 1955.
A history of English spoken in America written for children in upper elementary grades, with concepts developed through specific words.

Miner, Irene. *The True Book of Communication,* illus. K. Evans and I. Miner. Chicago: Children's Press, 1960.
The history of communication from the cave man to today for use with children in the intermediate grades.

Nurberg, Maxwell. *Wonders in Words.* Englewood Cliffs, N.J.: Prentice-Hall, 1968.
The mystery and wonder of words, stories in words, words right off the map, flowery language, names, animals in words, and superstition and prejudice embedded in words, for middle school children.

Parish, Peggy. *Amelia Bedelia,* illus. Fritz Siebel. New York: Harper & Row, 1963.
A unique and humorous story book that develops an understanding of the nature of American English for children in primary grades. Amelia Bedelia, a family maid, follows exactly the instructions that are left for her. Among other things, she literally "draws the drapes," "dresses the turkey," and "dusts the furniture."

Pei, Mario. *What's in a Word?* New York: Hawthorne, 1968.
Language origins, language problems, and a glimpse of language for the future; for junior high youngsters.

Severn, William. *People Words.* New York: Ives Washburn, 1966.
The background and meanings of words and expressions in our language for children in the middle school; an anthology-type volume.

Sparke, William. *The Making of Linguistics.* New York: Abelard-Schuman, 1969.
An introduction to the question What is Linguistics? for junior high and high school students.

Waller, Leslie. *Our American Language,* illus. Aurelius Battaglia. New York: Holt, Rinehart & Winston, 1960.
The development and history of the English language as spoken in the United States for boys and girls in primary grades.

White, Mary Sue. *Word Twins,* illus. Stan Palczok. Nashville, Tenn.: Abingdon Press, 1961.
An introduction to homonyms for children in the primary grades.

part IV: teacher references on language concepts

Alexander, Henry. *The Story of Our Language.* Rev. ed. Garden City, N.Y.: Doubleday, 1940.
A history of the English language.

Anderson, Paul S. *Linguistics in the Elementary School Classroom.* New York: Macmillan, 1971.
A collection of articles describing some linguistic theories and practices.

Bellack, Arno A., et al., *The Language of the Classroom.* New York: Teachers College Press, 1966.
An investigation of verbal communication in the classroom.

Bernstein, Theodore. *Miss Thistlebottom's Hobgoblins.* New York: Farrar, Straus & Giroux, 1971.
> A demolition of outmoded rules of English usage.

Brengelman, Fred. *The English Language, An Introduction for Teachers.* Englewood Cliffs, N.J.: Prentice-Hall, 1970.
> An introduction to the study of language and grammar, sounds and letters, words and language variation; indispensable reading for any teacher who wants to understand how linguistics can be integrated into the English program.

Chomsky, Noam. *Syntactic Structures.* The Hague, Netherlands: Mouton, 1957
> A sophisticated analysis of transformational grammar.

Durkin, Dolores. *Phonics and the Teaching of Reading.* 2d ed. New York: Teachers College Press, 1968.
> A comprehensive book on phonics that contains an excellent section on linguistics.

Eisenhardt, Catheryn. *Applying Linguistics in the Teaching of Reading and the Language Arts.* Columbus, Ohio: Charles E. Merrill, 1972.
> Practical coaching suggestions.

Friend, Joseph. *An Introduction to English Linguistics.* New York: World, 1967.
> An analysis of the structure of English words; the morphology of verbs, adverbs, pronouns; sentence patterns; dialects. Chapter six on expansions and transformations of basic sentence patterns is most helpful.

Fries, Charles C. *Linguistics and Reading.* New York: Holt, Rinehart & Winston, 1963.
> An approach to the teaching of spelling and reading. This well-known linguist describes the backgrounds of modern English spelling by analyzing changes as they occur in relation to specific periods in the history and development of language.

Grant, Barbara M., and **Hennings, Dorothy Grant.** *The Teacher Moves: An Analysis of Non-verbal Activity.* New York: Teachers College Press, 1971.
> An analysis of nonverbal classroom activity.

Hall, Edward. *The Silent Language.* Greenwich, Conn.: Fawcett, 1967.
> A study of nonverbal communication.

Hall, Robert A. *Linguistics and Your Language.* New York: Doubleday, 1960.
> An introduction to the notion that right and wrong are not concepts applicable to a discussion of usage; it goes on to consider "How Language Is Built," "Language in the World," and "What We Can Do about Language."

Hanna, Paul; Hodges, Richard; and **Hanna, Jean.** *Spelling: Structures and Strategies.* Boston: Houghton Mifflin, 1971.
> A sophisticated analysis of linguistic concepts applicable to the teaching of spelling.

Lamb, Pose. *Linguistics in Proper Perspective.* Columbus, Ohio: Charles E. Merrill, 1967.
> Applications of linguistics to the fields of language arts, reading, spelling, grammar, and usage.

Lefevre, Carl. *Linguistics, English, and the Language Arts.* Boston: Allyn & Bacon, 1970.
> Recommended reading for anyone wishing an in-depth understanding of

linguistic concepts useful in the elementary school; specific teaching suggestions galore.

Malmstrom, Jean, and **Ashley, Annabel.** *Dialects, U.S.A.* Champaign, Ill.: National Council of Teachers of English, 1963.
An analysis of dialectal differences and their causes, linguistic geography in the U.S.A., forces underlying dialectal distribution in the U.S.A., the main dialectal areas of the U.S.A., and the influence of foreign language settlements.

Marckwardt, Albert H. *American English.* New York: Oxford University Press, 1958.
An analysis of the growth and development of the English language in America as language relates to culture.

Pyles, Thomas. *Words and Ways of American English.* New York: Random House, 1952.
An interpretation of the English language as spoken and written by Americans that deals primarily with the word stock of American English—coinages, adaptations, survival adoptions from foreign tongues.

Reed, Carroll E. *Dialects of American English.* New York: World Publishing, 1967.
A comprehensive analysis of dialectal regions of the United States.

part V: teacher references on nonstandard English

Baratz, Joan C. "Linguistic and Cultural Factors in Teaching Reading to Ghetto Children," *Elementary English* 46 (February 1969): 199–203.
An article suggesting that beginning reading be in the child's own language and only later should children be moved into standard English; implies that beginning writing should similarly be based on the language of the child.

Corbin, Richard, and **Crosby, Muriel,** co-chairmen. *Language Programs for the Disadvantaged: The Report of the NCTE Task Force on Teaching English to the Disadvantaged.* Champaign, Ill.: National Council of Teachers of English, 1965.
A volume containing excellent material on language of the disadvantaged by such authorities as Walter Loban, Lee A. Pederson, and Samuel A. Kirk.

Fasold, Ralph W., and **Shuy, Roger W.** *Teaching Standard English in the Inner City.* Washington, D.C.: Center for Applied Linguistics, 1970.
Essays advocating functional bidialectism for the inner-city child who comes to school speaking a nonstandard English dialect; contains articles by Shuy, Stewart, Baratz, and others.

Gladney, Mildred R., and **Leaverton, Lloyd.** "A Model for Teaching Standard English to Non-standard English Speakers," *Elementary English* 45 (October 1968): 758–63.
A brief article that presents the concepts of school talk and everyday talk.

Hoffman, Melvin J. "The Traditional Language Arts Teaching Method When Used with Disadvantaged Afro-American Children." *Elementary English* 47 (May 1970): 678–83.

An article suggesting that structural linguistics has much to offer to language programs for youngsters who speak in a different dialect.

Hopkins, Lee Bennett. *Let Them Be Themselves.* New York: Citation Press, 1969.

An interesting volume containing language arts enrichment ideas for use with disadvantaged children in the elementary school.

Labov, William. *The Study of Nonstandard English.* Champaign, Ill.: National Council of Teachers of English, 1970.

An examination of the predominant dialect of the black urban ghetto and the related research.

Robinet, Ralph F. "An Interdisciplinary Approach to Oral Language and Conceptual Development: A Progress Report." *Elementary English* 48 (April 1971): 202–8.

A description of oral English programs geared to Spanish-speaking youngsters.

Smith, Louis M., and **Geoffrey, William.** *The Complexities of An Urban Classroom: An Analysis toward a General Theory of Teaching.* Holt, Rinehart & Winston, 1968.

An intensive analysis of a single classroom situation in the ghetto.

Stewart, William, ed. *Nonstandard Speech and the Teaching of English.* Language Information Series 2. Washington, D.C.: Center for Applied Linguistics, 1964.

An examination of the implications of nonstandard speech patterns on the teaching of English in schools.

Strickland, Dorothy S. "Black Is Beautiful vs. White Is Right." *Elementary English* 49 (February 1972): 220–23.

A discussion of the implications of two divergent approaches to teach English to nonstandard-English-speaking youngsters.

Venezky, Richard L. "Nonstandard Language and Reading," *Elementary English* 47, (March 1970): 334–45.

An article presenting alternatives for teaching speakers of nonstandard dialects to speak and read the standard dialect; contains an extensive bibliography.

index